Winter · Business and the Environment

Georg Winter

Business and the Environment

A handbook of industrial ecology with 22 checklists for practical use and a concrete example of the Integrated System of Environmentalist Business Management (the Winter Model)

In collaboration with H. J. Ewers, M. Gege,
C. M. Andreas, N. Blackburn, F. Blom, C. Gelderloos,
R. Hackstein, F. J. Heeg, J. Hensmann, V. Hoffmann, W.G. Jocher,
H. Jung, C. Maas, H. Meffert, P. C. Mohr, L. Wicke;
also ERL, INFORM and Joost & Preuss

Foreword by Stanley Clinton Davis, Member of the Commission of the European Communities

McGraw–Hill Book Company GmbH
Hamburg · New York · St. Louis · San Francisco · Auckland · Bogotá
Guatemala · Lisbon · London · Madrid · Mexico · Milan · Montreal
New Delhi · Panama · Paris · San Juan · São Paulo · Singapore
Sydney · Tokyo · Toronto

This book was initiated as a contribution to European Environment Year 1987/88 by the Commission of the European Communities as part of its activities in the field of environmental information, opinion-forming and education.

Title of the original version: **Das umweltbewußte Unternehmen**

CIP-Titelaufnahme der Deutschen Bibliothek

Winter, Georg:
Business and the environment: a handbook of industrial ecology with 22 checklists for practic. use and an example of the integrated system of concrete environmental business management (the Winter model)/Georg Winter. Assisted by H.J. Ewers ... Foreword by Stanley Clinton Davis. – Hamburg; New York [u.a.]: McGraw-Hill, 1988
Einheitssacht.: Das umweltbewusste Unternehmen <engl.>
ISBN 3-89028-223-7

Cover and typesetting by GDS, Grafik Design Studio GmbH, Hamburg.
Printed and bound by Mladinska Knijga, Ljubljana

Printed in Yugoslavia
ISBN 3-89028-223-7

Contents

C. A list of arguments for environmentalist business management

D. Checklists for environmentalist business management
Page 65

E. The significance for Europe of environmentalist business management
Page 185

F. International organisations dealing with environmental management

Page 191

Foreword

The environmentalist approach to business management – a model for European business

1985 marked a fresh start for environmental policy in Europe. It saw the signing by the Heads of State and Government of the Member States of the European Community of the "Single European Act", a document which, apart from calling for the completion of the European internal market by 1992, also makes mention for the first time of environment policy as a fully-fledged policy sector.

A second indication of the fast-growing importance of environment policy in Europe is European Environment Year 1987, to which end a symbol was designed showing a cog wheel and a flower. A more critical artist would probably have given us an image of the flower being crushed by the cog wheel, but the official emblem shows the cog wheel meshing harmoniously with the flower petals.

It symbolises one of the major themes of Environment Year, i.e. the striving for harmony between our technical civilisation and our natural environment. This aim cannot be achieved quickly and effectively enough with the use of legal instruments alone. It is up to companies throughout the European Community to go beyond what the law requires and do everything in their power to overcome the dichotomy of economic considerations on the one hand and ecological demands on the other.

By publishing this book in several European languages, the Commission of the European Communities hopes to provide companies with information on how management policies can be environment- and profit-oriented at one and the same time. The guidelines have been shown to work in practice, and have been set out in the form of checklists. As a result, the European business community now has a comprehensive and practical handbook on the environmentalist approach to business management, something which will be of interest not only to company directors, but to all members of the business community.

The book is based on the tried and tested "Integrated System of Environmentalist Business Management" (the Winter Model), which covers all the main aspects of management (corporate objectives, worker motivation and training, materials management, production technology, waste disposal, building, international relations, etc.) and is geared to a planned and gradual implementation process in companies.

The environmentalist approach to management can increase company profits, e.g. by saving water, energy and expensive raw materials or by offering new environment-based business opportunities. At the same time, though, it serves all members of the community by helping to protect our health and our natural environment (air, water, soil, flora and fauna).

The question we should be asking ourselves is whether the cog wheel and flower symbols are to remain irreconcilable opposites. The whole point of the 1987 European Environment Year is to show how reconciliation can be achieved. I very much hope that the book will be widely circulated and, above all, put to practical use.

Stanley Clinton Davis
Member of the Commission of the European Communities

Preface

The damage done to the environment in the Federal Republic of Germany is put at an annual DM 103 500 million (cf. A.I.). In the European Community as a whole, the annual rate of damage is at least equivalent to the gross national product of a country the size of Belgium – quite apart from the kind of damage which is at least as serious, but which cannot be expressed in money terms.

Industry is – along with the energy sector, transport, agriculture and private households – one of the prime causes of this damage, which is why industry is a prime target for attempts to improve the environmental situation.

Of course, it is true that industry supplies people with essential goods, and cannot do so without causing some damage to the environment, nor can it be denied that industry has been remarkably successful in improving the trade-off between value added and the adverse environmental effects.

But the Seveso, Bhopal, Chernobyl and Basle disasters have dramatically highlighted the fact that environmentally aware business management has become one of the key issues in the world today. And it must be remembered that the effects of these spectacular but isolated incidents are small compared with the summation of damage being caused all the time by a large number of smaller polluters – all of them complying individually with the legal norms. These "everyday" incidents are the real problem, and the damage could be reduced substantially if environmentalist management (going beyond what the letter of the law requires) were to become part and parcel of everyday business practice.

Consequently, the Commission of the European Communities is appealing to the higher management echelons in industry in the 1987 Year of the Environment to gear business management increasingly to environmental considerations. This book is the Community's first major publishing venture in this central subject of environmentalist concern and the market economy.

The book is addressed first and foremost to businessmen and managers, but has a lot of important things to say to public-sector administrators and politicians specialising in economic, social and environmental issues, and indeed to anyone working in business or for business. Its recommendations are also addressed to private households and to anyone who feels some measure of responsibility for the future of Europe, and who is prepared to do whatever he or she can (in politics, at work or at home) to protect the environment.

Most of the recommendations in the book have been tried out in practice, and most are relevant to all sectors of the economy and to firms of any size in any country. Among the multitude of questions answered in the book, the following are perhaps fairly representative:

- What environmental protection measures can be instituted quickly and without any major capital investment with a view to reducing costs and increasing profits?
- What measures can be taken to enable the company and its management to guard against the increasingly stringent environmental liability to which they are subject?
- How can the company react promptly to the risks and opportunities resulting from the accelerating demand for environmentally acceptable alternative products?
- Has a system been tried out in practice for introducing environmental considerations into all corporate sectors without jeopardising profits?

Part A discusses the need for an environmental approach to business management. The environmental damage in Europe is quantified, and European companies urged – in their own interests as well as those of the environment – to take an active part in tackling the problem.

The practical aspects of the environmentalist approach are dealt with in Part B, taking as an example the "Integrated System of Environmentalist Business Management" (the Winter Model), detailing the activities of the Bundesdeutscher Arbeitskreis für Umweltbewußtes Management, BAUM (German Environmentalist Management Society) and calling for international cooperation.

Part C, with its "List of Arguments for Environmentalist Business Management", juxtaposes for the first time the main objections to the environmentalist management Model with the main arguments in favour.

The 22 checklists in Part D set out in practical terms how the businessman can do the right thing by the environment at the same time as maintaining or even increasing his company's profits. Measures which can normally be introduced fairly quickly and without undue difficulty with a view to avoiding or cutting costs are marked with an *.

Part E is devoted to the importance of the environmentalist approach to business management for Europe.

Finally, Part F contains an overview of international governmental organisations and international industry-based non-governmental organisations dealing with environmentalist business management.

I would like to thank the European Community for having commissioned me – through the agency of Mr Claude Pleinevaux and Dr Gunther Schneider – to write a book for the 1987 Environment Year on the environmentalist approach to business management on the basis of practical experience with the Winter Model.

I should also like to thank all the authors who helped to produce the checklist part (D); their names are listed at the end of the book. My special thanks are due to Professor Hans-Jürgen Ewers of the Technical University of Berlin for his final coordinating revision of the checklists. I am also grateful to Professor Lutz Wicke, Scientific Director at the Federal Environmental Agency in Berlin for his section on the enormous losses occasioned in Europe by damage to the environment (Part A.I.).

I gratefully acknowledge all the important information I received from the environment committees of the Deutscher Industrie-und Handelstag, DIHT (German Chamber of Commerce and Industry), the Verband Deutscher Maschinen- und Anlagenbau, VDMA (German Mechanical and Plant Engineering Association), the Studien- und Fördergesellschaft der Schleswig-Holsteinischen Wirtschaft (Schleswig-Holstein Business Study and Promotion Association), the Hamburg Chamber of Trade, the Industry Committee of the Lübeck Chamber of Trade and Industry, the Arbeitsgemeinschaft für Umweltfragen, AGU (Working Party for Environmental Questions) and the Ecology Committee of the Bundesverband Junger Unternehmer, BJU (Association of Young German Businessmen). The last-mentioned Ecology Committee worked in 1985 under the direction of Mr C. M. Andreas –

and largely on the basis of the measures applied at Ernst Winter & Sohn – on a "checklist for more environmental protection in the company", which should be mentioned here.

I should like to join my brother and co-shareholder, Mr Ernst Michael Winter, in thanking the company's environment manager, Dr Maximilian Gege, for his collaboration in the development and in-house application of the Integrated System of Environmentalist Business Management, incorporating the pilot projects. Thanks also to the Technical Director, Dr Hans-Robert Meyer, the Research and Development Director, Mr Dietrich Borse, the Materials Management Director, Dr Axel Büttner, the Personnel Director, Mr Klaus Lieding, the Works Doctor, Prof. Herbert Lewerenz, the members of the environment committees, the members of the maintenance departments, the safety experts, the apprentice supervisors, the people in charge of the suggestions scheme and all the other people involved in in-house environmental protection – especially the members of the personnel department and of the works council. A number of the checklist authors also acted as advisers to the company and deserve my thanks for their cooperation, which yielded important material for inclusion in the checklists.

These days, any businessman concerned to secure the profitability and long-term viability of his company is bound to give thinking space to the question of environment-oriented business management. Over and above the purely business considerations, though, the environmentalist approach must also be seen as a question of lifestyle and job satisfaction. Enhanced job satisfaction grows out of the knowledge that one's work is no longer being done to the same extent at the cost of environment, personal health and that of one's own children and generations to come.

Espousing the environmentalist approach means becoming involved in a historic project to save and regenerate our natural environment. It is an attitude to work which goes beyond the mere profit motive and can awaken powerful latent creative powers in people. In this respect, it is at the same time a sound basis for successful business management.

Georg Winter Hamburg, 17 January 1987

Note on the English edition

Until recently the manager determined to run his entire company both profitably and with an eye to the environment was daunted by numerous complex and almost insoluble problems. Although a wealth of experience with individual problems was available and interesting isolated solutions – mostly in the field of environmental technology or marketing – had been found, international business lacked an overall ecological/economic concept already successfully tested in practice, covering all sectors of a company and including concrete recommendations for action in the individual areas. This gap was closed by the development and publication of the Integrated System of Environmentalist Business Management.

In view of strong international interest the McGraw-Hill Publishing Company decided to bring out this English version of the book "Das umweltbewußte Unternehmen", now in its second edition in Germany. Its publication in French, Spanish and Italian is to follow shortly.

The general information in Parts A to C of the book and the 22 checklists in Part D which contain recommendations for successful and nonetheless environmentally acceptable management in the various sectors of a company can be used almost without exception irrespective of the corporate location. When necessary, in particular in the case of the checklist on finance, information has been differentiated according to countries.

The checklists were compiled by recognised experts with great care and on the basis of solid experience. However, practical application of the recommendations – for example technical measures – and any consequences to which such measures may give rise are exclusively at the responsibility of the user and shall not involve liability on the part of the authors, the collaborators, the editor or the publisher.

A selection of relevant databases, publications and organisations is to be found in Appendix I. The material has been systematised according to the 20 sectoral checklists (D III 1–20). The

British sources were compiled by ERL (Environmental Resources Limited, London), the American ones by INFORM (New York) and the German sources mostly by the authors of the individual checklists (see list of authors in Appendix II). The international sources were "picked out" from all the available resource lists.

At this point I wish to express my thanks to all the individuals and organisations who helped to collect this important information.

I am also indebted to Mr Nigel Blackburn, a director at the International Chamber of Commerce, and his assistant Miss Caroline Gelderloos, who compiled the overview of international governmental organisations and industry-based non-governmental organisations dealing with environmental management for Part F of this edition.

It is my hope that the book will make it easier for companies in the various countries to reconcile successful business with environmental protection and thus contribute to conserving our vital natural resources.

Finally let me relate a small occurrence from company life that renewed our courage in the face of the hard business of day to day environmentalist management. A man so far unknown to us who had heard on the radio of our firm's environmentalist business activities asked us by letter to assist him and his friends in investing a considerable sum of money: "Just as you are no longer willing to run your company contrary to the interests of nature and common sense, we are only prepared to invest our capital where a company's compatibility with the environment is its first concern... Left-wing or right, poor or rich, conservative or progressive, none of this is of the slightest interest to me. Survival for my children and grand-children is all that counts... I became blind at the end of the last War."

Must we grow blind before we learn to see?

Georg Winter Hamburg, June 1988

A. The need for environmentalist business management

Year in, year out, environmental damage causes financial losses on a stupendous scale in Europe, along with the destruction of irreplaceable resources whose value cannot be expressed in money terms (I.). This is the challenge which industry is facing: to restore the environment with the same panache with which the European economy was rebuilt after the Second World War (II.). This challenge can only be met on the basis of an environmentalist approach to business management, which for a variety of reasons is also in the firms' own immediate interest (III.).

I. The financial losses in Europe resulting from environmental destruction

Although the phenomenon of forest die-back in Germany has become glaringly obvious even to the layman; although housing estates have been found to be built on abandoned industrial landfill tips; although the pollution of rivers has reached such a pitch that there is practically no life left in them, there are still too few people who are prepared to take action to get the situation improved. Most people prefer to take the easy way out and get on with their normal business (often polluting the environment themselves in the process) as soon as the banner headlines are committed to the wastepaper basket. In the light of this apathy, scientists have tried to express the degree of damage being done to the environment by the day-to-day produce-and-consume process in the kind of language which most people understand – that of money. A quantified "ecological balance sheet" drawn up for the Federal Republic of Germany (cf. Lutz Wicke, "Die ökologischen Milliarden", Munich 1986, p. 123) looks like this:

Damage category	Cost (in thousand million DM per year)
Atmospheric pollution	approx. 48.0*
– health damage	over 2.3 – 5.8
– material damage	over 2.3
– damage to crops in the open	over 1.0
– woodland and forest damage	over 5.5 – 8.8
Water pollution	well in excess of 17.6
– damage to rivers and lakes	over 14.3
– damage to North Sea & Baltic Sea	well over 0.3
– damage to groundwater	over 3.0
Soil damage	well in excess of 5.2
– Chernobyl and "Chernobyl prevention costs"	over 2.4
– disposal of "inherited pollution"	over 1.7
– habitat and species conservation costs	over 1.0
– token entry: miscellaneous soil contamination	well in excess of 0.1
Noise	in excess of 32.7
– loss of residential value	over 29.3
– loss of productivity	over 3.0
– noise-induced welfare payments (including invalidity pensions)	over 0.4
Total damage	well in excess of 103.500

* These DM 48 thousand million are obviously not the sum of the individual items in the atmospheric pollution category. The figure is in fact the result of a representative household survey conducted in Berlin to ascertain willingness to pay for purer air, and grossed up to the FRG population. This willingness to pay can be seen as a measure of "loss of enjoyment caused by air pollution". It goes well beyond the directly ascertainable costs, including such intangible factors as "impaired well-being".

This balance sheet ignores a number of factors, either because they do not lend themselves to quantification, or because we lack the ecological know-how to attempt such an exercise.

Among the factors which have been omitted as being non-quantifiable are such general, pollution-induced effects on the quality of life as waste tips, smell nuisance, dust and noise pollution and planning blight, illness and fear of falling ill, and grief at the premature loss of a loved one. Nor has any attention been devoted to the importance which people attach to the very fact that certain areas of land are left untouched or certain plant and animal species are conserved, or that an inhabitable environment is bequeathed to subsequent generations.

Examples of the damage which are simply not quantifiable (because we do not know enough about ecological principles) are:

- loss of natural habitats and of animal and plant species,
- non-compliance with overall environmental impact thresholds,
- the long-term effects of noxious substances released into the environment.

This means that the overall figure of DM 103 500 million cited in the ecological balance sheet (something like 6 per cent of GNP in West Germany in 1984) represents a minimum figure, and that the actual amount of damage is much higher. This is borne out by the fact that practically all the items in the balance sheet were quantified on the principle "if in doubt, underestimate rather than overestimate".

Let us now take a look at what these figures mean in European terms.

First, a question of principle: None of the other Community Member States can so far boast an ecological balance sheet such as that produced by Wicke for the FRG. The well-publicised announcement by the OECD environment ministers in 1979 to the effect that annual environmental damage in the OECD Member States represented between 3 and 5 per cent of gross national product was no more than a rough-and-ready estimate which has never been backed up by a full analysis.

Wherever damage caused by air and/or water pollution has been quantified (e.g. in the USA, France and the Netherlands), the totals have come to much less than 3 per cent of GNP (cf. OECD, International Conference on the Environment and Economics, Paris 1984, Volume II, p. 73). This does not necessarily mean, though, that actual damage (or even just the minimum estimated figure) is much less serious in the other Community Member States than in the FRG. For one thing, the GNP shares calculated as environmental damage in the above-mentioned foreign studies are lower simply because no attempt has been made so far to include all items systematically in a quantified balance sheet.

Of course, the German figures cannot be applied without further ado to other countries. The FRG is characterised by above-average population and industry density. Whether this means that the other countries' share of GNP is that much lower than in the

FRG is open to doubt. The fact is that it was precisely these factors which caused German companies to concentrate on tackling the problem of hazardous emissions at an earlier stage than their counterparts in most of the other EEC countries.

Whether the minimum level of annual ecological damage in the EEC is 4, 5 or 6 per cent, the fact remains that it is an alarming figure. Even at 4 per cent it represents roughly the GNP of a country the size of Belgium. Quite apart from the ecological and moral considerations, there are sound economic reasons why damage on this scale can simply no longer be tolerated.

II. A challenge for Europe's business community

After the wholesale destruction wrought by the Second World War, the business community throughout Europe rightly saw its historic task as one of economic recovery – a task which it brought to a successful conclusion. The hard-hit peoples of Europe put their economic potential to good effect and created not only a sound economic base for themselves, but also a material standard of living which is more than presentable in global terms.

Today we are once again the victims of a major destruction process, this time affecting our environment. The pollution of the air we breathe and the contamination of our soil and water may be less conspicuous than ruined cities and whole areas of land laid to waste, but their long-term effects are on much the same scale. Today, Europe's business community is once again facing a historic challenge.

Today's challenge lies in conserving an acceptable standard of living for all people throughout Europe at the same time as conserving or restoring the viability of the natural environment – and hence the very basis of human life. Europe's environmental technology industry is among the world's best, and can, if properly stimulated, make a major contribution to accomplishing this task.

Just as the reconstruction of our ruined economies after the Second World War was made possible largely by the free market economy, so today we need the dynamic forces of free market competition to help us restore our ruined environment.

What we are so far lacking are politicians capable of altering the framework conditions of our free market economy such that economic success can only be maximised by maximising the environmental acceptability of products and services. Environmentally acceptable business activity must be made economically profitable to enable the dynamic forces of free competition to work to the advantage of the restoration of the environment. There is plenty of job creation potential in the process.

In the Federal Republic of Germany, companies are beginning to see the reconstruction of the environment as a task for the future. According to a poll conducted by the Association of Young German Businessmen in the summer of 1984, involving 842 businessmen from 36 sectors of the economy, 76.7 per cent would welcome incorporation of the concept of environmental protection into the constitution. Some 75 per cent intend in future to adopt a more environmentalist approach to production, while 60 per cent are prepared to make economic sacrifices in the interests of the environment. Similarly, in other countries of Europe, many companies are coming to realise that protecting the environment is one of the imperatives of our age.

III. The response: Environmentalist business management

The European economy can only accomplish its new task of making a major contribution to the reconstruction of the ravaged environment if individual companies are prepared to go along with the environmentalist concept.

1. Reasons for environmentalist business management

There are six major reasons why any businessman or business manager with a sense of responsibility (and with his own interests at heart) should apply the concept of environmentalist business management in his firm:

- Without environmentalist-minded companies there can be no environmentalist-minded economy – and without an environmentalist-minded economy the human race cannot expect to survive for a life that is worth living.
- Without environmentalist-minded companies there can be no public consensus with the business community – and without a public consensus with the business community there can be no free market economy.

- Without environmentalist business management there will be a loss of fast-growth market openings and a risk of the company being held liable for environmental damage for enormous sums of money, thus jeopardising the future of the company and of all the jobs dependent on it.
- Without environmentalist business management, boards of directors, management executives, heads of department and other members of staff are more likely to risk liability for environmental damage, with the consequent jeopardisation of jobs and careers.
- Without environmentalist business management, substantial potential for reducing costs will go by the board.
- Without environmentalist business management, businessmen will be in conflict with their own consciences – and without self-respect, there can be no real sense of identification with one's job.

2. The philosophy of environmentalist business management

The concept of environmentalist business management can enrich and strengthen the corporate philosophy, and help to attain the classic corporate aims (provided they are not in conflict with the environment).

The essential principles on which the long-term success of a properly and responsibly run company rests are quality, creativity, humanity, profitability, continuity and loyalty. All six are easier to comply with if the management takes an environmentalist view of things:

- **Quality and the environment**
  A product can only be said to be high-quality if it is produced in a way which is not inimical to the environment and can be used and disposed of without causing damage to the environment.
- **Creativity and the environment**
  The creativity of the company's workforce can be encouraged by working conditions which take account of human biological needs, e.g. low noise levels at the workplace, healthy air temperature and humidity levels, ergonomically designed office furniture and vitamin-rich canteen food.
- **Humanity and the environment**
  The general working atmosphere can be made more "humane" by gearing the corporate aims, strategies and activities not only

to the economic criteria, but also to a sense of responsibility vis-à-vis all forms of life.

- **Profitability and the environment**
  Company profitability can be improved by adopting cost-reducing environmental protection measures covering such things as raw materials and energy- and water-saving programmes, and by exploiting market openings for environmentally sound products.
- **Continuity and the environment**
  In the interests of continuity, it is becoming more and more important to make sure that the company is not adversely affected by liability risks under the increasingly stringent environmental legislation and by the market risks resulting from the reduced level of demand for environmentally damaging products.
- **Loyalty and the environment**
  In the final analysis, the managers and staff of a company can only be loyal to the laws and aims of the state if the sentiment is a genuinely felt one, and that in turn is only possible as long as the country has not sacrificed its intrinsic value to the forces of environmental destruction.

3. The starting point for environmentalist business management

If a businessman has taken the plunge and decided to take environmentalism seriously, there is no reason why the company should hinder him in any way. Indeed, the company's connections and potential can act as a genuine tool for the achievement of environmentalist aims.

Without abandoning the aim of making a reasonable profit, a company can still act as a spearhead in the drive for environmental protection. By committing itself as an "environmentalist organisation", it can complement the work of other like-minded organisations; after all, it can boast unusually favourable starting conditions:

- The company has access to particularly potent – often international – information channels.
- It can exert a direct influence on chambers of commerce and industry and professional organisations.
- A company which has espoused the environmentalist approach

cannot be branded as an other-wordly set-up if it is patently successful.

- The company, as a non-party organisation, is not subject to the frictional losses of political conflict.
- The effectiveness of a management team trained and experienced in setting itself targets and seeing that they are achieved can be extended to the environmental context.
- The workforce is in effect a "representative in-house cross-section of the population", which is ideally suited to environmentalist pilot projects (e.g. environmental counselling for households).
- There is such a thing as a "company bonus", meaning that an otherwise sceptical member of the staff is likely to be more open to environmentalist matters if the initiative comes from the company.
- Staff creativity can be mobilised for the environmentalist cause (e.g. through the staff suggestions scheme).
- Planning practical pilot projects (e.g. an environmental information, suggestion and invention exchange) can be facilitated by an in-house ecology/economy dialogue.
- An industrial company often has access to a wide range of specialists who can bring their knowledge to bear on environmentalist pilot projects.

B. Practical aspects of environmentalist business management

A number of companies are "into" environmentalist management techniques. The European Community has identified the "Integrated System of Environmentalist Business Management", developed by a European company with its headquarters in Hamburg and Norderstedt (Schleswig-Holstein) as an exemplary scheme (I.). In the Federal Republic of Germany, several companies have got together to form the "Bundesdeutscher Arbeitskreis für umweltbewußtes Management", BAUM (German Environmentalist Management Society) (II.), which is interested in international cooperation with similarly minded companies (III.).

I. An example of environmentalist business management (the Winter Model)

On the occasion of the 125th anniversary of the foundation of Ernst Winter & Sohn, manufacturers of diamond tools, in 1972, the company officially declared environmental protection as one of its corporate aims. All members of staff were given copies of E. Snyder's book "Please stop killing me", which deals with the ecological situation of the earth. The environmentalist concept has since become part of the firm's tradition, with the continued support of joint owners Ernst Michael Winter and Dr Georg Winter.

Over recent years the company has developed the Integrated System of Environmentalist Business Management (known as the Winter Model), which incorporates all sectors of the company, ranging from apprentice training to adult training and re-training, from programme policy to research and development, from materials management to production and recycling and from new plant construction to the equipping and selection of company vehicles.

Even at Winter & Sohn there is still a lot to be done. However strict the precautions, human error or technical malfunctions are still bound to occur, and even where the legal requirements are being more than met, there is still room for improvement. In other words, there is no cause for back-slapping and self-congratulation. The will to improve must be maintained, and suggestions from other companies which have made technical, organisational or other forms of progress in the field are always welcome.

The environmentalist activities at Winter & Sohn are part and parcel of the company's aims. What this boils down to is that, while paying all due attention to staff satisfaction and the natural environment, the firm must produce high-quality products and services to achieve a result which will justify the inputs and place the company and the jobs it provides on a sound footing.

Improving environmental protection and conserving jobs do not need to be a contradiction in terms. For instance, the company managed to launch a number of much-discussed environmental protection pilot projects, while at the same time expanding business and creating a substantial number of new jobs (now totalling 1500).

The company's commitment to the environmentalist cause is not designed to boost sales. Clearly, a buyer of diamond tools in the metalworking, electrical, stone, glass, plastics, engineering, precision engineering, optics or automobile industry is going to be more concerned about getting value for money than with the environmentalist image of the manufacturer, however beneficial such an image might be in certain branches of the consumer goods industry.

Nor can the company reasonably be called a typical manufacturer of "environmental protection technology". Firms working in that field are bound to be interested in promoting ecological principles if only to boost sales. Winter & Sohn, however, are strongly motivated by the realisation that companies, being prime consumers of natural resources, must have an above-average sense of responsibility for conserving those resources.

On 6 July 1985, Ernst Winter & Sohn (GmbH & Co) became the first holders of the environment prize awarded by the Association of Young German Businessmen, while the Schleswig-Holstein Business Study and Promotion Association voted the company "Environmentalist Company 1986" for its work on the environmentalist approach to management. At the ceremony held in Norderstedt on 12 December 1986, the President of the German Employers' Association, Dr Klaus Murmann, referred to the

Winter Model and pointed out the pioneer role of Ernst Winter & Sohn at both regional and national level.

We have selected a few examples of the company's in-house and outside environmentalist activities. Numerous detailed recommendations (a large proportion of which were derived from practical experience at Winter & Sohn) are set out in the checklists in Part D.

1. Environmentalist staff training

Each member of staff is a "cell" in the living corporate organism, and as such, no ecology-minded firm can operate effectively unless its workers are well versed in the environmentalist outlook.

For this reason, Winter & Sohn organise environmentalist seminars and excursions for their trainees. Talks are given to workers on environmental issues, and brochures produced by the Federal German Environment Agency and the Ministry of Health are distributed. The in-house newspaper has a section on the environment, and competitions are organised on themes centering on nature.

Much more remains to be done, however. For instance, a mobile shop selling organically grown goods was allowed to take up a pitch regularly in front of the factory gates, but this proved – for the time being at least – to be a failure. The range of goods, the prices and the general conditions were felt to need improving, and there was a need to inform workers on alternative foodstuffs.

On the strength of its environmentalist and conventional courses, the company was selected in December 1986 to take part in a pilot project on environmental issues in occupational training, a subject which is felt nationally to be of importance for the future.

2. Environmental counselling in employees' households

Something like 30 to 40 per cent of all environmental problems have their roots in private households. Here too, the firm can take a hand. Starting on 1 April 1985, an 18-month pilot project was conducted, whereby the company paid for five environmental counsellors to visit and offer their advice in employees' and other private households in Hamburg and Norderstedt.

These counsellors advise people how to reduce water consumption, make better use of electricity, take the strain off the waste disposal system by pre-sorting, use fewer chemical products in the garden and replace consumer articles by officially approved alternative products.

The project was financed partly by an endowment of DM 160 000 by Winter & Sohn and partly by the Federal Labour Agency's job creation scheme. The fact that Winter & Sohn produce no household consumer articles obviated any suspicion that the firm might be trying to boost its own sales, using the counselling scheme as a front.

The project was placed in the hands of the Hamburg and Schleswig-Holstein sections of the Bund für Umwelt und Naturschutz Deutschland e.V., BUND (German Environment and Nature Protection Federation). The rapid spread of the idea in the Federal Republic of Germany and beyond is largely thanks to the Aktionsgemeinschaft Umwelt, Gesundheit, Ernährung e.V., AUGE (Environment, Health and Nutrition Action Group) and the Basle-based PROGNOS AG. (For more detailed information on environmental counselling for households and local authorities, see Gege/Jung/Pick/Winter, Das Öko-Sparbuch für Haushalt und Familie, Munich 1986, p. 190 et seq.)

The idea of environmental counselling for households and local authorities was the brainchild of Dr Maximilian Gege, a member of the Ecology Committee of the Association of Young German Businessmen. In an honorary capacity, he took charge of the pilot project and is now responsible for promoting, introducing and developing the concept via AUGE, an organisation he set up himself.

There are now something like 260 counsellors in the Federal Republic of Germany employed by local authorities and other organisations to give advice to the authorities themselves and to private households. Now that the Federal Labour Agency has agreed to make job creation scheme funds available to subsidise counsellors' salaries, there has been a dramatic increase in the number of local authorities prepared to create posts in the field.

This trend is likely to speed up as soon as AUGE's and PROGNOS AG's current research programme has furnished proof that environmental counsellors' salaries and ancillary costs are more than balanced out by the savings possible through the purchase of low-pollution alternative products and water, energy and waste disposal savings.

The Commission of the European Communities has commissioned AUGE to extend the environmental counselling model project to the United Kingdom, France and Spain. With effect from the end of 1986, 15 posts were created in Spain under an EEC programme for an initial period of two years, with a further 12 posts in France and 10 in the United Kingdom.

Austria and Switzerland have likewise created counsellor posts on the lines of the AUGE model, and there seems every likelihood that the next few years will see a rapid increase in the number of such jobs in many countries, to the benefit of the people of those countries and to the ultimate benefit of the environment.

AUGE runs 6- and 12-month seminars with a standardised curriculum, leading to an examination and qualification as an environmental counsellor. The organisation also has a computer-assisted energy- and water-saving advice programme.

3. Environment managers, committees and suggestions schemes

In-house environmentalist work needs a powerful set of institutions. At Winter & Sohn, an environment manager is responsible for coordinating the in-house environmentalist activities, his duties going way beyond those of the "environment officer" as required by law for certain companies. He has departmental management status, and is in constant touch with the two managing directors, while at the same time working closely with the works council. His job is "environmental management" at a professional level.

The "Inter-disciplinary Environment Committee", comprising representatives of the various parts of the company, decides on the environmental action plan, plays an active role in the various parts of the company, and meets periodically to take stock of what has and what has not been achieved. The inter-disciplinary committee is chaired by the company's environment manager, and works in close conjunction with the "Environment Committee – technology" chaired by the technical director.

A company is a living organism, which means that, in environmental terms as in every other field, there is always plenty of room for improvement. Reality will always deviate to some extent from the ideal.

The staff suggestions scheme is used to elicit suggestions from the entire workforce. Suggestions resulting in energy or water savings or which serve the cause of environmental protection in some other way are rewarded more generously than other suggestions (30 per cent instead of 20 per cent of the value of the annual saving over two years). One particularly noteworthy suggestion occasioned investment to the tune of DM 24 000, and yielded an annual saving in energy costs of DM 60 000.

4. Environmentalist product and process development

Developing environmentally acceptable products is already seen to be in the company's commercial interest. Winter & Sohn, for instance, produce diamond circular saw blades for stone cutting, the perceived noise level of which is only half that of conventional diamond blades. Many saw works near to residential areas are dependent on such blades if they want to stay where they are.

Thanks to research and development work, it is possible to do without asbestos in all types of diamond wheel without any loss of performance.

Whereas until very recently environmental acceptability was a barely noticed by-product, it is now an important selling point, and will in the near future be a sine qua non if the product is to be sold at all.

Winter & Sohn are also working hard on developing environmentally acceptable manufacturing processes. For instance, new conveying equipment for powdered plastics has been installed which virtually eliminates the dust hazard. This just goes to show that measures designed to protect the environment can serve to enhance product quality and reduce production costs. For an initial investment of DM 250 000 and generating annual savings to the tune of DM 60 000, the equipment will pay for itself within the space of some four years.

Converting three works from oil-firing to lower-emission natural gas and installing energy-saving thermostats and fluorescent tubes has produced an annual quantifiable saving of some DM 278 000. At this rate, the investment will have paid for itself after a mere 2½ years – another instance of how environmental measures can work to the company's commercial interests.

5. State-of-the-art waste disposal

An environment-minded company will always keep in touch with the state of the art as regards waste disposal technology, with a view to doing more than the legal requirements demand wherever possible. Allowing over-generous transitional provisions on the conservation of old plant in new, more stringent legislation makes little sense unless there are adequate facilities for conserving nature – the basis of life itself and logically of industry too.

Winter & Sohn are determined to go beyond what the letter of the German environmental protection law demands. For instance, there are two highly automated and effective treatment plants for neutralising and de-toxifying waste waters from electroplating processes.

In many parts of the plant, dust filters and waste gas scrubbers were installed long before they were prescribed by law.

Subsidiaries in countries with less stringent environmental legislation are gradually brought up to the parent company's standards. To take an example, a waste water treatment plant for a plant in the Mediterranean area was designed to current German standards.

Every effort is made to recycle as much as possible. The heavy metal oxides resulting from the neutralisation of waste water from electroplating are processed, yielding cobalt and nickel, which together account for 10 to 12 per cent of the dry sludge. The annual savings on tipping and credits for the recovered cobalt alone amount to some DM 50 000, to which can be added the DM 8 000 saved from re-using the caustic soda from the electroplating process in the treatment plant.

The more savings can be made, the more money will be available for longer-term "altruistic" measures.

6. Environmentalist raw materials procurement

By making full and fair use of what is known as "demand power", an industrial company can exert influence on its suppliers to switch to environmentally more acceptable products.

Winter & Sohn commissioned a scientific institute to take a systematic look at its materials management policy and decide what economically advantageous (or at least justifiable) changes could be made to minimize the load on the environment.

Changes have already been made to a number of procurement

items such as paper, office supplies, paints and lacquers, cleansing agents, coolants for metalworking applications, building materials and vehicles. Seen as a proportion of total purchases, though, the results achieved in the substitution drive still fall well short of the ideal.

As advocated by the Bundesdeutscher Arbeitskreis für umweltbewußtes Management, BAUM (German Environmentalist Management Society), Winter & Sohn work together with other firms to boost demand for low-pollution alternative products with a view to inducing the supply side to respond faster to the "new market" (see also B. II.).

7. Environmentally benign industrial premises

Industrial premises designed with consideration to environmental or ecological factors represent a social service of prime importance, being the kind of service which is not for immediate consumption, but which has a long-term effect on the well-being of company employees. A high-quality environment is also a stimulus to good work.

The factory built recently by Winter & Sohn in Norderstedt, housing Europe's largest diamond grinding wheel production plant, was designed by an industrial architect and a second architect specialising in "environment-friendly" building and design techniques. Ecological criteria were incorporated systematically as regards overall design, structural considerations, technical equipment, lighting and material selection. During building itself, a firm specialising in cybernetic techniques (the "KOPF-System") was brought in to keep actual building costs well below planned costs.

One of the aims of the Winter pilot project was to show the manufacturers of building materials and technical equipment what they should be concentrating on in the future. More development work is needed, for instance, on woollen carpeting designed to cope with castor-mounted office chairs, on competitively-priced and functional electric cable with non-halogen sheathing, and on ventilation units which can be installed on grassed roofs and can be relied on to filter out pollen.

While there are already instances in Germany of houses and office buildings designed with the use of environmentally benign techniques, this was the first industrial building designed to these principles. The main findings from the pilot project were submitted to the Council of Europe in Strasbourg to enable them to look into the question of whether environmentally benign techniques could be used in designing the new Court of Human Rights. This would be a unique opportunity to demonstrate to the public at large the "human right" to a healthy environment.

The prime aim of the Winter pilot project from the word go was to encourage other companies to specify "environment friendly" design and materials for new buildings. The greater the demand for such services and materials, the better and more competitive they will become, thus forcing conventional contractors to take a closer look at ecological alternatives. Manipulating demand is a legitimate tool in the free market economy for forcing change on the supply side. The quickest way to "ecologise" the construction industry is to boost demand for ecologically acceptable products and services.

8. Environmental considerations in plant location policy

If thought is being given to relocation or setting up a new works, the management should take the opportunity to create good environmental conditions for itself and its workforce. By deciding against locations which are already heavily polluted, a company is in effect indicating to the local authorities that, unless they pursue a coherent policy of environmental renewal, there is little chance of them attracting or holding on to businesses.

When Winter & Sohn, for example, were looking round for a suitable location for a subsidiary in the USA, one interesting site which would otherwise have been perfectly suitable was ruled out because of the high level of atmospheric pollution caused by local industries.

9. Environmentalist work in professional associations

A medium-sized company has only limited potential for exerting influence on the aims and strategies of chambers of commerce and business associations. Nonetheless, Winter & Sohn attempt to use their membership in a variety of environment committees under the auspices of business associations and chambers of commerce to bring business interests into harmony with the exigencies of environmental protection, supporting whoever is prepared to espouse the following aims (which, incidentally and gratifyingly, seem to be meeting with more and more interest and approval):

- The association (or chamber) should be both representative of its members' interests and (internally) the guardian of certain standards of environmental behaviour.
- Protection and restoration of the natural environment should be declared one of the association's official aims and be given high priority in strategic and day-to-day decision-making.
- The association should seek to modify general business conditions (e.g. tax law) so as to strengthen firms' commercial interest in environmentalist management.
- General trade associations should not be allowed to act on behalf of more specialist associations on matters involving the environment – either publicly or in parliamentary lobbying terms – if the result would be contrary to the interests of large sectors of industry, such as companies in the environmental technology field.
- Something should be done to counter the current underrepresentation of environmental technology firms in the internal decision-making machinery.
- More attention should be given to concrete problem-solving rather than to vague statements of intent.
- Special support should be given to the kind of pilot projects which are likely to have a widespread impact in the business community.

10. Using the company's contacts to assist local citizens' initiatives

Companies often have contacts which can be used to give local citizens' initiatives more muscle. For instance, Winter & Sohn conducted an international survey on the state-of-the-art in flue gas cleaning technology in power stations on behalf of a concerted (politically neutral) drive on the part of local citizens' initiatives for less atmospheric pollution in Hamburg. The original plan had been to build a coal-fired power station equipped with an obsolescent flue gas desulphurisation facility next to the company's head office.

The results of the hearing were submitted to the political heads of the "Land" governments, and Baden-Württemberg's Minister-President Späth introduced legislation in the Bundesrat (second chamber) designed to tighten up the relevant legislation, quoting from the survey's findings. As a result, the city of Hamburg now insists on coal-fired power stations complying with limit values below the official limits in the existing legislation (e.g. only half the legal maximum for SO_2). This in turn had the effect of giving a sign nationally that the higher values contained in the legislation had lost their political legitimacy once and for all.

The pilot project brought out new findings as regards the relationship between industrial companies and local citizens' initiatives, the most important of these being that there need be no major conflict of interests. Given the same interests, there is no reason why an industrial company and a local citizens' initiative should not be capable of being allies in the same cause. Thanks to worldwide information channels and professional methods on the one hand, and local contacts and popular solidarity on the other, it is possible to achieve a "synergetic" effect, whereby the overall effect is greater than the sum of the inputs. As a result, the company gains in grass-roots contacts, and the local group gains more specialist back-up (the "convergence" effect).

If a company is prepared to cooperate with a local group to resist the anti-environment behaviour of another firm (assuming that the other firm's management has not responded to appeals through the normal channels), the company itself becomes a kind of "corporate citizen", and sheds the mantle of anonymity which tends to alienate it from ordinary individuals. At the same time, the company is adopting an entirely new role – in some ways similar to the production of antibodies in an organism under attack from outside – something akin in fact to a "self-regulatory business attitude".

11. Financial support for environmentalist organisations

The activities described above can only go some of the way towards meeting a company's obligations vis-à-vis the environment. Another aspect is the provision of financial support for a variety of environmentalist organisations.

The organisations receiving aid from Winter & Sohn include the Conservation Park Association, the German Federation for the Protection of Birds and the Eekholt Wildlife Park, whose animal enclosures, nature trails and classrooms are particularly suitable for staff environmental training.

The company is also planning to finance the appointment of

a management consultant for a particularly worthy environmental protection association, with a view to giving instruction to the association's management team in modern management methods and ways of enhancing effectiveness by the introduction of rational forms of organisation. It is essential for industrial managers and environmentalists to learn from one another.

12. Environmental information and invention exchange system

The very positive public response to Winter & Sohn's environmental activities produced a number of contacts with environmental protection innovators, which in turn introduced the company to the problems which inventors encounter in marketing their new products and services. The company thereupon decided to try to help inventors to find a way out of their isolated situation.

Under the Winter Model, which provides for company resources and contacts to be used for environmental protection, the company issued a general invitation to an "environmental invention exchange" on 26 February 1985, where innovators would have a chance to present their ideas briefly and then discuss them with representatives of public authorities, chambers of trade, industrialists, scientists and the press.

Another idea behind the event was to look for ways of stepping up the pace of innovation in the environment sector. According to inventors, some of the main barriers to innovation, hindering the rapid introduction of ideas and inventions in the field of environmental protection, include the established companies' cartel-like protection of markets against environmentalist innovations, as well as a multitude of restrictive standardisation, safety and administrative provisions which have not kept pace with technical developments.

The invention exchange was well received, finding favour for instance among the European Community's environment experts. It is to be hoped that this and other forms of innovation promotion in the environmental sphere will be taken up and developed by other private and public-sector bodies.

Summing up, we can say that the ecological movement will bring about an unprecedentedly drastic and rapid change in traditional markets. Many firms are not entirely happy with the situation, although there is nothing they can do to slow the pace. The more flexible firms, though, have adapted to the trend towards environmentally sounder goods and services and made it part and parcel of their corporate planning.

Businessmen with a sense of responsibility, and who are concerned about the future of the planet as well as of their company, have a moral duty to do everything possible to speed up the move towards more concern for the environment. One of the most effective ways of doing so is to alter the demand situation with a view to twisting the arm of the supply side. It makes no odds whether the spadework is done by a switch to environmentally benign building principles, by a non-profit organisation employing environmental counsellors for private households, by organising "invention exchanges" or by working towards such aims as an environmentally sound materials procurement policy.

II. BAUM – The German Environmentalist Management Society

More and more companies are realising the need for an environmentalist approach to business management for the conservation of a humane environment, if not for the future of their own firms. For instance, a number of well-known industrial companies have got together to form the German Environmentalist Management Society (with the evocative acronym BAUM – German for "tree") (address on p. 210).

The idea of such an organisation goes back to a suggestion put forward by Winter & Sohn in 1984, the aim being to continue work on the Integrated System of Environmentalist Business Management through an ongoing exchange of information, and to encourage the practical introduction of environmental protection measures in member firms, while at the same time giving wide circulation to the ideas worked out in the course of the project.

What BAUM is seeking to achieve is to get the environmentalist approach adopted in all branches of management covered by the checklists in Part D of this book, i.e. management motivation, corporate aims and strategies, marketing, in-house environmental protection arrangements, staff motivation and training, working conditions, canteen food, environmental counselling for employees' households, energy and water-saving, product development, materials management, production technology, disposal and recycling, company vehicles, building, finance, the law, insurance and international business relations and public relations work.

BAUM has decided to concentrate initially on the question of low-pollution materials management, with a view to persuading companies to take as their procurement criteria not just the conventional ones of quality, service, price and delivery time, but to bear in mind the question of environmental acceptability too. The idea is that, in future, purchasers should ask their suppliers at regular intervals whether their goods are produced in an ecologically acceptable way, whether they adversely affect the environment (assuming the instructions are followed), and what environmental repercussions their disposal may have.

As soon as industry is faced with a massive demand for ecologically acceptable products, it will automatically speed up the switch in its production programme. In this way, BAUM hopes to encourage a rapid switchover in industrial production to meet environmental requirements, but using the tools of the free market economy.

BAUM also intends to get involved gradually in the other management areas, the timing and scale of activities depending on the rate of membership recruitment and the personnel and material resources. The detailed aims are as follows:

1. Strengthening the businessman's sense of responsibility

BAUM sees itself not just as a business pressure group, but also as a community of interests with the joint aim of strengthening businessmen's sense of responsibility vis-à-vis the environment, this being (in BAUM's view) not so much a matter of image-building as a human concern, with clear demands on members' business behaviour.

2. Passing on environmentalist business know-how

BAUM provides firms with practical know-how showing them how to combine success in business with protection of the environment in all company departments. This can take many forms, such as producing this book, providing information on counselling services or organising seminars for business executives. As far as materials management is concerned, possible aims include wider use of the information for buyers coming from the Federal

Environmental Agency, organising environmental seminars for buyers, distributing a practical handbook for an ecological materials management policy, and drawing up a list of raw materials according to environmental acceptability (with alternative proposals), along with a list of alternative products offering a price advantage over conventional products.

3. Organising exchanges of information from firm to firm

BAUM intends to organise exchanges of information between its member companies in the form of regional or problem-specific "environmental quality circles" under the leadership of experienced people from science and business and covering the full range of business functions. The idea is that BAUM member firms should pass on to other firms know-how for which they have no immediate commercial use and which there is no point in withholding for reasons of competition.*

4. Coordinating pilot and research projects

BAUM encourages its members to engage in – and ensure media coverage of – pilot projects in all aspects of environmentalist management to achieve a signal effect on the business community as a whole. It also sets out to act as a kind of linchpin between science and the everyday world to bring together member firms and suitable private and public scientific institutions in a coherent series of research projects in the most important practical fields of environmentalist management.

5. Extending suppliers' environmental liability

While respecting the principles of fair-play and cooperation, BAUM urges its member firms to impose more stringent conditions on their suppliers by extending the obligation on them to disclose details of materials supplied, by making them jointly responsible for the environmental impact of products and by

* In May and June 1988 eight working groups were initiated in cooperation with the Rationalisierungskuratorium der Deutschen Wirtschaft (RKW) in Hamburg. The subjects were: environmentalist purchasing, energy management, environmental liability and how to reduce liability risks, weakness analysis and crisis planning, ecological value analysis, objectives and methods of corporate environmental strategies, environmental protection and public relations, state subsidies (e.g. grants to cover interest, financing, tax concessions, etc.) for environmental measures.

demanding a waste disposal guarantee. Clearly, member firms are liable to the same rigorous conditions if they are themselves in a supplier situation.

6. Making use of insider and group advantages

BAUM gives its member firms the opportunity to obtain low-pollution materials, environmental engineering goods and environmental counselling services at preferential rates. This is often the first step towards overcoming the psychological barrier along the road to environment-oriented alternative solutions.

7. Developing a career profile in "business ecology"

It is BAUM's medium- and long-term aim to help create a new career profile in "business ecology", the aim being to install such professionals as environmental advisers with senior management status or to train candidates to act as self-employed management consultants in the introduction and development of environmentalist management techniques. The curriculum would cover business and ecology studies, process engineering, materials science and, last but not least, management psychology, and would encourage creative thinking over a broad spectrum. This might involve a flexible kind of university course, based on existing courses, but enabling students to add certain specific elements to their conventional studies.

8. Complementing the work of other institutions

BAUM is non-profit-making, independent and politically neutral, and sees itself neither at present nor in the future as being in competition with other business organisations. On the contrary, BAUM places great importance on cooperating with chambers of commerce and industry and with business associations whose aims can thus be complemented in a clearly defined sphere. The aim is also to intensify cooperation with the Federal Environmental Agency (contacts exist since November 1984), the Technical University of Berlin's Economics Institute, the German Materials Management and Procurement Association (BME) and the Rationalisation Curatorium of the German Economy (RKW).*

* The members of BAUM include both small to medium size companies and well-known major companies such as AEG, Commerzbank, Desowag, Deutsche Bank, Elida Gibbs (Unilever), Hewlett-Packard, IBM, NOVA-Versicherungen, Otto-Versand, Philips, Tetra Pak and Zweckform.

Further information on the aims, activities and services provided by BAUM can be obtained from the Bundesdeutscher Arbeitskreis für umweltbewußtes Management e.V., Christian-Förster-Str. 19, D-2000 Hamburg 20, Tel. 040/407 721 or 040/491 18 14.

III. BAUM, ARBRE, TREE – A call for international cooperation

The call for environmentalist business management is coming through clearer and clearer in all the countries of Europe. Future-oriented companies everywhere will adjust as quickly as possible to the resultant risks and opportunities. BAUM invites such companies to cooperate in an international effort.

The German organisation – the Bundesdeutscher Arbeitskreis für umweltbewußtes Management – has chosen the acronym BAUM (German for "tree") to reflect the sense of responsibility it feels vis-à-vis the natural environment. It would be encouraging to see environment-oriented companies in other countries set up similar organisations, with the French organisation (just a suggestion!) bearing a name like ARBRE – Association pour le Respect de la Bioécologie dans les Réalisations des Entreprises – and in English-speaking countries TREE – Team for the Reform of the Economy on Ecological/Environmentalist Principles.

The Commission of the European Communities could assume an important catalyst function here in creating and organising channels of cooperation between the various national associations for environmentalist management.

C. List of arguments for environmentalist business management

The following list of arguments is an entirely new departure. For the first time, it sets out in tabular form arguments for and against the introduction of the Integrated System of Environmentalist Business Management (the Winter Model).

The Model has been well received in the press, on radio and on television. Judging by the discussions at events organised by chambers of industry and commerce, business associations and economic science faculties, the attitude of specialists (theoretical and practical alike) is generally favourable.

It is important, though, to take criticism seriously, especially as it can often be a starting point for improvements. Taking a conscientious look at the pros and cons, it is evident that not all reservations can be dismissed just like that; the fact remains, though, that the positive aspects are in the majority.

The list of arguments sets out to achieve three things:

1. It is intended to help the businessman to decide whether to introduce the Integrated System in whole or in part in his company or in his particular sector.
2. It is intended to give additional help to those responsible for introducing the Model into a company on how to avoid the kind of procedural or psychological mistakes which could jeopardise the chances of success.
3. It is intended as an additional argument for anyone who is determined to work for the more widespread application of the Model, be it on an economic, cultural, religious or political level.

The list of arguments provides answers to the question of what the Model means in terms of:

- The businessman himself and his view of his work (I.)
- The management team's chances of success (II.)
- Cooperation with the workforce (III.)
- The various management sectors (IV.)
- Public relations work including activities in professional organisations (V.)

The list is set out in the form of a pro/contra balance sheet comprising forty pairs of contradictory arguments. Beginning in each case with the objection, it sets out to help protagonists of the Model to avoid the mistake of overwhelming people with arguments from the outset, and instead to take note of the objections, think them through, defuse them and go onto the offensive with the arguments in favour.

Over and above the ability to listen to the other side's arguments, advocates of the Model must always be receptive to other arguments and be prepared to modify their own opinions in the light of what the other side has to say. After all, the Model is not permanent and unchanging for all time, but has to be constantly tested against new practical and scientific developments and be flexible enough to adapt to the situations in a wide variety of companies.

The word "businessman" is taken to mean both independent and salaried entrepreneurs and managers.

I. The importance of the Model for the businessman himself and his view of his work

Contra

1. *Succumbing to a passing trend*

All this talk about the threat to humanity from destruction of the environment is just as much a trend phenomenon as the anti-authoritarian education wave in the 1960s, which died a natural death. It is not reasonable to disrupt normal business activities for a passing trend.

Pro

Coming to terms with the future

Along with the unemployment problem, the question of the environment is of the utmost importance and will continue to gain ground as damage to the environment becomes increasingly evident. For a family-run business the environmentalist approach to management is nowadays a matter of ensuring that there is someone for the owner to hand the firm on to. After all, the next generation is likely to be more conscious of its environment, and in many cases may not be prepared to persevere with a firm which does too much damage to the environment.

Contra

2. *The arrogance of the do-gooder*

An environment-conscious company cannot save the world on its own – especially as it is not only industry which creates environmental pollution, but also power

Pro

Making a start "at home" on improving the environment

If all firms were to reduce their energy, water and raw materials consumption by just a few per cent – and it takes a few companies to make a start – a substantial number of air-polluting stations, transport, agriculture and private households.

power stations could be done away with, a lot of woodland and wetlands could be conserved and many important resources saved. The environment is too valuable for even the smallest contribution from just a single company to be superfluous.

3. *Beyond the letter of the law*

Environmentalist management means that the businessman is always doing more for the environment than the law requires, e.g. using less water, energy and noxious chemicals, creating and disposing of less waste and releasing fewer hazardous substances into the environment. Complying with the law ought to be enough, given that the legislature receives advice from experts to ensure that a ban is placed on any behaviour which is really inimical to the environment.

Rescuing the market economy

It often happens that the legislative or administrative authorities cannot place a ban on environmentally damaging products and practices (or only too late or partially) because the economic basis is essentially a liberal one, the appeal system is highly developed and plenty of compromises are enforced by the industry lobby. An economic system which does not match free-market generosity with environmentalist self-restraint is in danger of gambling away the free market economy in the political sense.

4. *Frustrating a genuine move to improve the environment (The "radical" argument)*

"The free market economy system makes it impossible to effect a genuine and thoroughgoing process of environmental recovery. It therefore follows that a businessman who is prepared to exploit the system

Ecologising the market economy

Experience has shown that a centrally planned economy and other economic systems provide even less protection for the environment than does the social market economy, which can at least be developed in the direction of an ecological/social without any environmentalist scruples and thus hastens the system's political bankruptcy is in the final analysis acting much more "environmentalistically" than his counterpart, who, with the best intentions, reduces pollution and thus delays the collapse of the system by camouflaging its intrinsic hostility to the environment."

market economy by having all companies subscribe to the Integrated System of Environmentalist Management and by ensuring that the legislature makes the threshold values for dangerous substances more and more stringent and changes the economic outline conditions such that only environmentalist business practice is profitable.

5. *Self-ruination by cost escalation*

Generally speaking, companies only spend as much on protecting the environment as is necessary to comply with the law. Any company indulging in the luxury of going beyond mere compliance with the law is in danger of ruining its competitiveness.

Cutting costs and gaining a competitive advantage

There are many measures – such as water, energy and raw materials saving – which serve both the cause of environmental protection and corporate cost cutting (and the acquisition of a competitive advantage). The contention that effective protection of the environment will always involve higher costs can be seen to be a prejudice: the fact is that environmental protection can be pursued more effectively with a lot of know-how and little money than with a lot of money and little know-how.

6. *Jeopardising directors' positions*

If, by voluntarily adopting environmental measures, the board of directors of a company reduces the level of corporate profit, it will

Securing a management career

Any manager (e.g. of an energy-generating company) who sets out to maximise profits without concern for the highly sensitive public reaction to environ-inevitably set the alarm bells ringing in the supervisory council and among the shareholders, with the attendant risk that its contract of employment may not be extended. Salaried managers therefore have much less room for environmental manœuvre than businessmen who are not only managers but also owners of the company.

mental issues, and who refuses to apply the available environmental protection technology, is provoking a public reaction and business turmoil. As a result he is jeopardising his position much more than a manager who cultivates the social context by voluntary environmental protection and a sense of proportion, to the ultimate good of the company. There have already been cases of shareholders refusing to grant discharge to the board of directors because of their failure to act in an environmentally responsible manner.

7. *Wearing the executive down*

Competitive pressure, taxes, pay conflicts, structural change, red tape, information *en masse* and – the final straw – public criticism of private enterprise already place enough strain on the battered nerves and faculties of the businessman or manager. A corporate commitment to environmental protection going beyond compliance with the legal requirements is quite simply not on.

Rediscovering a sense of pleasure in work

Many businessmen are plagued by their own consciences, by their families and by society in general with the claim that, by polluting soil, air and water, and by an immoderate use of finite raw materials, they are destroying the very basis of life for their own children and generations to come. The environmentalist approach to management gives them the chance to regain peace of mind, family harmony and social respect, to be able to identify 100 per cent with their own careers and to gain strength for new tasks from a renewed sense of pleasure in work.

II. The importance of the Model for the management team's chances of success

Contra	*Pro*
8. *Making conflicts of interests inevitable*	*Ensuring ongoing company profitability*
If the profit motive is joined by the aim of maximising environmental conservation, the result is that the company is divided in its aims, leading in turn to much expenditure of time and effort.	There is no such thing as a conflict of interests; both co-exist side by side. Just as the environmentalist approach to management is a non-starter without adequate profit potential, company profitability cannot be ensured in the long run without an environmentally-minded management policy.
9. *Diverting the attention of key management executives*	*Giving the company a sound base*
A commitment to the environmentalist movement diverts key manpower in sales, technology, materials management, research and development, personnel and finance from their normal activities, and might be reflected in lower company profits.	Decisions are demanded nowadays from all key executives on environmental policy producing crucial risks and opportunities for the company. While many companies go to the wall as a result of environmental liability claims or tumbling sales, others are managing to expand on the basis of an environment-oriented programme policy.
10. *Institutionalising internal disputes*	*Lightening the departmental heads' work and risk-load*
It is the job of the environ-	By fulfilling his informational,

ment manager to implement the environmentalist approach across the board – from technology through sales and procurement to personnel and finance. The upshot could very well be a running battle between him and the departmental heads.

counselling and monitoring duties vis-à-vis the departmental heads, the environment manager is not interfering in their management functions. Indeed, he is relieving them of a major burden in guarding against what might be tricky problems of environmental liability.

11. *Provoking budgetary conflicts*

Conflicts between the environment manager and the departmental heads are virtually inevitable on the company's annual cost budget. In fact, the direct competition between environmental protection and the classic commercial expenditure items could escalate into an all-out battle of attrition and a tense and uncomfortable atmosphere.

Optimising inputs

Heads of the classic corporate departments are now rapidly realising that the environmental factor is increasingly becoming an essential component of their particular sector, and there is an increasing readiness to reflect environmental considerations adequately in their departmental budgets.

III. The importance of the Model for staff cooperation

Contra

12. *Paralysing cost-awareness*

Voluntary investment in protecting the environment is still seen largely as

Pro

Overcoming the conspicuous consumption mentality

If staff are trained to realise that voluntary investment in environmental protection serves a luxury. The problem is that, if the company is seen to be indulging in luxuries, many workers fail to see why they should be expected to help in cost-saving, the result of this perception perhaps being a creeping paralysis of cost-consciousness.

the aim of saving finite and important raw materials, it should have a beneficial effect on the widespread conspicuous consumption mentality. This may prompt them in turn to be more careful with how they use energy, water and raw materials and avoid any unnecessary expenditure so as to leave more in the kitty for investing in environmental protection.

13. *Uncontrolled escalation of worker aspirations*

If staff are "spoiled" with biological wall-paints and PVC-free floorings, there is a danger that they may start demanding more and more benefits, and where will it all end? With the official-issue hammock for creative thinking? Give them an inch and they'll take a mile!

Encouraging quality-consciousness

There can be no question of "spoiling" workers and boosting their aspirations so long as the environmental protection measures taken at the work-place are designed merely to balance out the serious deficits hitherto. A high-quality immediate working environment stimulates quality-consciousness and reduces the reject quota.

14. *Cultivating a "cripple mentality"*

Too much voluntary measuring of threshold limit values for noxious substances and unnecessarily sensationalist information on health hazards tend to create an excessive concern with one's own health, not to say a hypochondriac "cripple mentality", which

Fostering health and confidence

Medical science has recently come to realise how many illnesses have environmental factors as their root cause. A systematic reduction in contact with noxious substances at the place of work (even going beyond the legal requirements) and an objective and scientifically well-founded information tends to make "princess and the pea" wimps out of "real men". The result is likely to be a longer sicklist.

campaign will have a lasting effect on workers' health, trust and enthusiasm.

15. *Encouraging social conflicts*

Any money which is made available for voluntary environmental protection measures will clearly not be available elsewhere, e.g. for staff bonuses. Once employees get the impression that environmental improvement is taking place at the cost of their Christmas bonuses, idealism will go by the board and industrial disputes will ensue.

Solidarity and collective sacrifices for a good cause

Clearly, the time is not yet ripe for voluntary environmental protection measures on a scale which would have a substantial effect on the usual bonuses paid by the firm. However, as environmental damage increases, people will gradually come to realise that the very basis of life on earth can only be preserved by both workers and owners making financial sacrifices.

16. *Politicising the working atmosphere*

The conflict between economic and ecological considerations has already split parliaments and society down the middle. What point is there in management introducing this conflict into the firm and allowing different factions to form, thus splitting the workforce and jeopardising the harmonious working atmosphere?

Immunisation against ideologies

If staff can be shown that environmental problems can be tackled better by practical activities than by ideological prejudices and rallying cries, they will build up an immunity at work and on the streets to polemics and agitation. Co-operation between management and workers in the interests of the environment has an integrating effect which extends into other spheres of life.

17. *Staff losses*

Cost-boosting environmentalist measures might lead to more and more polarisation at all levels of the hierarchy and spread concern and dissension among members of staff. The upshot might be that good workers would leave the firm.

Getting a lead in a competitive market

By backing it to a man, the management team can ensure that the environmentalist ideal is accepted at all levels of the hierarchy without any major problems, thus strengthening the workers' links to their place of work. A company which has acquired a reputation for its commitment to the environment will find it easier to recruit enthusiastic apprentices, skilled workers with a sense of initiative and future-oriented executives.

18. *The ecological imperative as a form of authoritarianism*

In the final analysis, the environmentalist style of management is simply a relapse into the old authoritarian style of management, with just a change of content. In effect, management is forcing its workers to look at the world through ecological spectacles.

Motivation by conviction

To try to impose the environmentalist ideal in an authoritarian fashion would run counter to the humanitarian nature of the ideal itself and founder on the resistance or reluctance of many "front-line" workers. In a nutshell, the environmentalist approach to management comprises a quarter self-analysis and example-setting on the part of management, a quarter ongoing staff training and retraining, a quarter psychology and motivation skill and only one quarter purely ecological activities.

19. *Dulling people's environmental sensitivity*

Management-organised environmental perfectionism is likely to provoke a reaction, while harping on the need to protect the environment is liable to dull people's own sense of environmental sensitivity. An irritating environmentalist zeal damages the cause more than it helps it.

Encouraging people to take the plunge

Workers who are well trained in environmental matters will develop a sense of commitment to the ideal. When they have reached that stage, they will perceive the range of in-house environmental activities not as a chore, but as a chance to develop their own inner commitment to the cause.

IV. The importance of the Model for the various management sectors

Contra / *Pro*

20. *Overestimating the potential of the environment market*

In the general enthusiasm for matters concerning environmental protection, the sales department is likely to overestimate the demand for environmentally acceptable goods, which could in turn result in a mistaken programme policy.

Discovering the potential of the environment market

The market potential can be gauged by trial runs and demand boosted by consumer information. The market is in a period of flux, with the result that alternative firms and other newcomers which have not yet become too blinkered have particularly attractive market opportunities.

21. *Making the market uneasy*

If the traditional market-leader for a particular product suddenly comes

Consolidating the firm's market share

While it may be true that the market-leader's sales have not increased, the introduction of out with an "ecological" alternative product, a certain proportion of his customers will move over to the new product, which will not increase his sales so much as shift part of them to the new product. The firm then has on the one hand the new clients it has gained with its new product, and on the other, its established clients who are now unsure as to what to make of the old product.

the alternative product will have strengthened his strategic position quite substantially. By having both the traditional and the ecological product in his programme, the market-leader can adopt a flexible approach to the growing trend to environment-conscious purchaser behaviour and consolidate his market share in the face of competitors offering "ecological" products.

22. *Rushing into market launch*

There is a temptation with the environmentalist approach for management to rush into the market launch phase and awaken "sleeping dogs" unnecessarily. It is quite enough to have fully developed ecological alternative products on one side, ready for market launch as and when the situation requires.

Securing the pioneer bonus

The strategy of keeping an ecological alternative product on one side is courting disaster, as such products can normally not be kept secret, the result being that the informed public may become seriously disaffected and may simply refuse to buy the company's marketed products. On the other hand, a company which can legitimately claim to have been the first to solve an environmental problem with its new product will benefit from its pioneer image on the market.

23. *Overstraining the sales pitch*

An industrial client faced with environmental problems himself is unlikely to welcome a committed

Enriching the sales pitch

Given a sensible atmosphere, a client can usually be persuaded that the supplier's environmentalist commitment works environmentalist as a supplier, quite apart from the nagging suspicion he is bound to have that his supplier's voluntary environmental protection measures are overpricing his products.

to the client's advantage too by enhancing the public image of industry as a whole and in particular by improving the product supplied (e.g. by reducing the product's environmental impact and ensuing costs). Another potent argument is that many environmentalist measures (such as a saving of materials or energy) have actually lowered production costs and contributed to the moderate selling price.

24. *Frightening the client*

Unless a client's buyer brings up the subject of the environment himself, it should be avoided at all costs if the buyer is not to be frightened off. Otherwise, he will start asking questions about waste disposal, demand a copy of the material safety data sheet, call for the release of production secrets, obtain alternative bids and, finally, insist on a price reduction.

Creating an atmosphere of confidence with the client

A company whose product is ecologically better than those of its competitors can play this trump card to maximum effect by providing the buyer with information and sowing doubts designed to put the pressure on the competition. Readiness and ability on the part of a supplier to reply competently and truthfully to any questions concerning the ecological implications of his products will boost the client's confidence and will have a beneficial effect on his purchasing decisions.

25. *Misappropriation of research and development funds*

The limited resources available for research and development must be used

Forward-looking research and development

In the light of the growing ecological requirements attached to products, buyers of those for improving the functional quality of the firm's products. In a cut-throat competitive world, a functional deficiency in a product cannot be balanced out by ecological benefits.

products will increasingly come to regard ecological improvements as functional improvements, quite apart from the fact that research and development in the environmental field is eligible for aid under a variety of international, national and regional programmes.

26. *Demotivating technology*

Technology, which is required to bear the brunt of the production process, is degraded because of inevitable environmental burdens to the point of being the company's whipping boy, with all the attendant loss of motivation and innovativeness among technical staff.

Remotivating technology

There is nothing to stop management calling a general works meeting and praising the technical staff for their hard work and achievements in the conventional fields, and at the same time impressing on them that they are the most indispensable element in the firm's attempts to solve its environmental problems. The technical people can thus be motivated to think creatively about ways of tackling their conventional and environmental tasks.

27. *Jeopardising investment in rationalisation*

Rationalisation investment goes by the board because the funds are needed for voluntary environmental protection investment, with a potential adverse effect on the company's competitiveness.

Optimising rationalisation investment

Money invested in energy, water and raw materials saving is at the same time being used for environmental protection and rationalisation. The steeper the rise in energy, water and raw materials prices, the greater the rationalisation effect and the greater the competitive advantage.

28. *Over-dimensioning investment in the environment*

Renewal and expansion investment is rendered unnecessarily costly by overdoing the emission-reduction and recycling bit, with the result that it takes too long for a capital investment to pay for itself.

Preventing wasted investment

If corporate planners fail to take into account from the outset what are likely to be more stringent legal thresholds for emissions of noxious substances, and if the state of the environmental art is not thoroughly researched (on an international basis), subsequent legislation may require re-equipping on a scale which is felt to be unreasonable, with the result that the project is abandoned and the investment is wasted. A forward-looking policy on the environment is the best means of obtaining and maintaining production authorisation, particularly as the legislative authorities are likely in future to allow less and less time for replacing obsolete environmental installations.

29. *Overstretching the materials management department*

The company's materials department will be overstretched if it is asked to keep an eye on the environmental impact issue in addition to the conventional purchasing criteria such as quality, price, delivery deadline and service. Where there are too many jobs to be done on the side,

Securing profitability

The main task of the materials department is to make the most profitable purchasing decisions possible for the company, bearing in mind all factors. However, as environmentally detrimental goods may occasion follow-up utilisation and disposal costs out of all proportion to the price advantage over environmentally more acceptable alternatives, the main job is bound to suffer.

assessing the environmental impact is a legitimate part of the economic equation and thus becomes one of the department's main concerns.

30. *Overstepping the contract award guidelines*

If the purchasing agent of a public-sector undertaking finds that it is still more economical to buy goods despite the attendant waste disposal and in-house damage-prevention costs (e.g. respirators for use with solvent-rich lacquers), he is not justified in applying environmental protection criteria over and above the economic costs. By doing so, he would be running counter to the economy and savings requirements set out in the national public contracts regulations.

Making maximum use of the contract award guidelines

A major breakthrough regarding the contract award regulations was achieved in Germany on 1 January 1985, betokening a move towards environment-oriented purchasing policy in the economy as a whole. The relevant article states that, bearing in mind the budgetary principle of economy and saving, the required performance should be subject only to those criteria which are essential to the task in hand, which may include the environmental protection element.

31. *Time-wasting caused by environmental impact assessment studies*

The purchasing agent is of course free to carry out research into the environmental impact of the goods on offer. Unfortunately, he will not then have sufficient time to compare goods on the basis of performance and price and conduct successful price negotiations.

Avoiding waste disposal problems

A few hours spent on research (perhaps involving an external adviser) may prevent a subsequent expenditure of unreasonable time and money on waste disposal. This is a bitter pill which has had to be swallowed by a number of purchasing agents who have had to take responsibility for the waste disposal of materials they have bought, and have been unable to pass the problem on to other operating sectors (e.g. the technical department).

32. *Arrogating the legislature's duties*

It is the legislature or publicly-funded regulating authority alone which has the right to decide which goods should be allowed and which not. A procurement agent must be able to rely on the fact that goods not banned under law are not inimical to the environment.

Increasing the procurement agent's responsibility

It does not necessarily follow that everything which is for the time being allowed under the laws and regulations (which take much time and effort to amend or modify) is good for the environment (see also point 3). To assess a product's environmental acceptability, the procurement agent must focus his attention on the state of the art in materials technology and business ecology, for which he can gain valuable assistance from such specialist publications as the list of products with the German "blue angel" environmental seal of approval and other specialist sources.

33. *Impairing the firm's credit-worthiness*

A company which is heavily environment-oriented can strike fear into the hearts of the (mostly conservative) banks and other money lenders, who will tend to see the economic imperatives taking a backseat to idealistic aims. As a result, it might

Creating an atmosphere of confidence with bankers

Banks and other money lenders have come to realise how firms can go to the wall as a result of environmental liability and sales risks, while stockdealers are quick to note the rise in value of firms operating successfully in the environmental field. It is therefore likely to help be more difficult to get loan funding.

to create an atmosphere of confidence with the money lenders if a company pursues a coherent policy of opportunity-risk management in the environmental sphere.

V. The importance of the Model in terms of public relations

Contra	*Pro*
34. *Projecting a one-sided image*	*Acquiring new customers*
Experience has shown that, when the media give coverage to an environment-oriented company, all other aspects of the company take very much of a backseat. A company's quality image can be put into the shade by its newly created environmentalist image, which may be a disadvantage if its major customers attach more importance to quality than to their supplier's commitment to the environmentalist cause.	Even if the media reports on the company's environmentalist policy do not promote sales in their own right, they can usually be used as a leader for highly effective additional information which can be placed free of charge in the reports part of newspapers or in radio and television programmes to reach a wide range of the population. It goes without saying that the advertising effect of such PR work is going to be much greater for consumer articles than for capital goods.
35. *Damaging the work ethic*	*Setting up contacts at high levels*
As a result of continuous exposure to the media, executives may be tempted to think more in terms of how the company can get its name into the press than of what is important for the	A thoroughly consolidated company will work hard and take the opportunity to reap the PR effects of its above-average commitment to the environment. The firm will thus become more widely known,

company. The upshot may be alienation from the hard everyday working world, which remains the sole guarantor for lasting commercial success.

which will make it easier for its management to make and exploit important contacts with the leading lights in public administration, science and the professional organisations.

36. *The risk of an image reversal*

A firm which takes a public stance as a pioneering environmentalist organisation and which may (deliberately or not) expose less committed companies to public criticism is likely to be judged by those companies and by the media in the future by the most rigorous standards. The smallest environmental misdemeanour might thus be inflated into a major scandal, with the result that the company's positive environmentalist image might turn to the contrary.

Giving a signal and encouraging imitators

The best means of preventing subsequent public carping is a genuine and credible modesty, whereby the company makes it clear that it is not itself immune to making mistakes and is ready and willing to learn from the environmentalist experience of other companies. On the other hand, the company should not hide its light too much under a bushel, but should act as a focal point for other companies to follow its example.

37. *Undermining business solidarity*

A businessman who imposes rigorous environmental standards in his company and thus provokes the legislature into tightening up the legal provisions is undermining his business colleagues' livelihoods, given that they may be operating on a

Solidarity with all forms of life

Given that, under the present economic conditions, the cost-burden on many companies (e.g. taxes) is so great that no money can be found for investment in ultra-modern environmental technology, entrepreneurial solidarity dictates that the State be called upon publicly to reduce costs to shoestring and simply cannot afford the additional investment. The net result is to do violence to entrepreneurial solidarity.

companies. On the other hand, the sense of solidarity man is required to show towards all other forms of life dictates that everyone (including businessmen) should do everything in his or her power to preserve the natural environment.

38. *Membership of a professional association as a neutralising factor*

If a businessman decides to blaze new trails in environmental protection, he will inevitably have to belong to business associations' environmental committees in order to obtain inside information. This will effectively ensure that his hands are tied, because the dictates of the association will prevent him from steering an independent course.

Rejuvenating official association policy

Association discipline is not absolute nor does it muzzle the individual; each member is free to obey the dictates of his own conscience. There has also been an increasing tendency recently for business associations to make room in their official policies for the ideas and experience brought in by markedly environmentalist members.

39. *Exploitation for party propaganda*

An environmentalist businessman is powerless to stop party politicians of all persuasions using him as a demonstration object for propaganda purposes. At one end of the spectrum, he may be seen as just one white sheep among all the black ones who pollute the environment or as a highly sophisticated reactionary,

Getting down to brass tacks in the environment debate

If a businessman concentrates totally on practical ways of taking the pressure off the environment without allowing himself to be used as a political object by any party, experience has shown that his attitude will be respected by all sides. Politicians of all hues are then quietly but effectively reminded that they should seek to overcome political differences in the intewhile for others he may be dubbed – just as inaccurately – "living proof that environmental protection can be made to work in our economic system without tightening up the legal provisions".

rests of solving the outstanding environmental problems.

40. *Wasting energy*

The public is already so much exposed to anti-industry prejudice that PR work on the part of businessmen in the environmental field is pointless. Any public commitment on the part of businessmen to the environmental cause will immediately be seen as a diversionary manœuvre or as a calculated PR exercise.

Unleashing latent energies

PR work is bound to fail wherever words take precedence over deeds, images over truth and self-seeking over strength of character. PR work will be crowned with success and work for good wherever protection of the environment is seen not as a political, advertising or other gimmick, but first and foremost as a practical manifestation of belief in life itself.

D. Checklists for environmentalist business management

Before takeoff, a pilot runs through a checklist of the vital functions of his aeroplane. The checklist is one of the best methods of getting quickly to the essential points and missing nothing of importance. A businessman preparing for the launch of the Integrated System of Environmentalist Business Management in his company would likewise be well advised to run through a series of checklists. The ones in this book have been produced for businessmen by experts in business and science. Their recommendations are a valuable aid in the decision-making process.

A number of examples are given to flesh out the economic, ecological, technical and psychological realities of running a business. Lengthy explanations are not given, but Appendix I does contain details of relevant databases, publications and organisations. Only a few of the points in the checklists refer exclusively to the relatively rigorous German environmental legislation. Almost all the recommendations can and should be implemented in all the Community Member States, particularly as there is a good chance of the threshold values, standards and monitoring provisions being made rapidly more rigorous in all the Member States under the pressure of public opinion. The checklists are also of great practical value to companies in the USA, Japan and all other countries worldwide, especially those that are technically advanced.

Actually, an economic undertaking is such a complex and sensitive entity that it is probably more akin to a living organism than to an aeroplane. It is up to the businessman then to direct his attention to an integral system of inter-related checklists. Cross-references are included to make this task easier.

Apart from the obvious technical constraints, it is up to him to decide on what scale and according to what schedule he wants to apply the Integrated System in his company. He might be content with seeking to improve his earning capacity in the short term by espousing the cost-reducing environmental protection measures marked with an asterisk in the checklists. Moreover he can derive benefit from using a checklist here or there in isolation; an environment-oriented weak-point analysis of his company would be a useful guide. Finally, he can gear his entire undertaking to the environmental risks and opportunities which are bound to proliferate in the medium and long term by gradually placing his environmental activities on a broader base, working from one checklist to the next.

The checklists may be of use to politicians, too, in yielding suggestions for legislative innovations. Chambers of commerce and industry and professional and business associations can use many of the checklists to draw up codes of practice for their members. If correctly observed (and any violations dealt with appropriately), these codes can do a lot to help the environment and enhance the public image of the association and its members. It might, for instance, be possible to work out a special "environment code for businessmen" along the lines of the British Institute of Management's (far more general) Code of Conduct. First steps in this direction include the German "Code of Conduct for exporting hazardous chemicals" of 11 March 1986 (see the "international business relations" checklist).

The instructions contained in the checklists are not intended to be used rigidly. Where circumstances, experience and intuition require, it may be advisable to adopt a different approach.

Many of the checklists – in fact, the ones which are of particular practical importance – touch on the question of psychology. More especially, the checklists dealing with priority rating, management motivation and staff motivation and training deal with human beings, in other words, individuals with their own highly distinct personalities. It is because of this deep-seated respect for individuality and human dignity that the system can never be applied mechanically "according to instructions". These checklists must not be misinterpreted as a kind of "psychological toolbox". They are simply intended as an aid for management acting with a sense of human responsibility.

Readers are advised to peruse the "overview" (I.) and "priory rating" (II.) checklists before moving on to the sectoral lists (III.).

I. Overview checklist

This checklist answers the question as to which areas of management are covered by the Integrated System of Environmentalist Business Management, and introduces a step-by-step approach to the checklists drawn up for individual sectors.

The numbering sequence is not binding in terms of the practical introduction of the system, nor does it set out the various points in order of importance. Likewise, no priority judgement is involved in the various categories to which the points are allocated (e.g. person-related or technology-related points). The idea is simply to make the system easier to follow.

The Integrated System can be introduced into a company regardless of its organisational set-up. For instance, it is immaterial whether research and development and materials management are separate departments or are subordinated to a technical department; whether waste disposal comes under technical services or materials management; whether the company's transport section is a sub-unit of the technical, materials management or administration department; and whether foreign subsidiaries are managed under the individual departments of the company or as a separate department for foreign subsidiaries.

1. If necessary, acquaint the management team with environment-oriented perception, thought and action processes. (See "management motivation" checklist.)
2. Make protection of the natural environment one of the corporate aims and strategies. (See "corporate aims and strategies" checklist.)
3. Exploit the opportunities and eliminate the risks from environment-induced market trends. (See "marketing" checklist.)
4. Create in-house environmental protection institutions and appoint appropriate members of the staff to manage them. (See "in-house environmental protection arrangements" checklist.)
5. Foster a balanced approach to environment and quality-consciousness by staff motivation and training. (See "staff motivation and training" checklist.)
6. Create humane working conditions in factories, offices and at other workplaces. (See "working conditions" checklist.)

7. Provide good (including organically produced) food in company canteens. (See "canteen food" checklist.)
8. Promote environment-conscious behaviour and health of workers by environmental counselling in their private households. (See "environmental counselling in employees' households".)
9. Achieve a spectacular reduction in costs and help the environment by energy- and water-saving. (See "economising on energy and water" checklist.)
10. Develop ecological products at the behest of, or to mobilise, the marketing department. (See "product development" checklist.)
11. Add the "environmental impact" element to the materials management department's conventional purchasing criteria. (See "materials management" checklist.)
12. Reduce pollution and waste disposal costs by modern production technology. (See "production technology" checklist.)
13. Reduce pollution and material costs by recycling and ensure that waste is properly disposed of. (See "disposal and recycling" checklist.)
14. Select and equip company vehicles with a view to environmental considerations. (See "company vehicles" checklist.)
15. Construct and maintain office and factory premises by reference to environmentally benign principles. (See "building" checklist.)
16. Ensure a healthy financing situation, not least as a precondition for non-profit environmental protection measures. (See "finance" checklist.)
17. Ensure that environmental protection legislation and official instructions are complied with. (See "law" checklist.)
18. Systematically detect and insure against unavoidable and incalculable risks arising from environmental liability on the part of the company or its management. (See "insurance" checklist.)
19. Extend environmentalist management principles to exports, imports and foreign subsidiaries. (See "international business relations" checklist.)
20. Ensure undistorted publicity for company environmental efforts and pilot projects, with a view to attracting imitators. (See "PR work" checklist.)

II. Priority rating checklist

This checklist is designed to help businessmen intending to go in for environmentalist management to lay down priorities and decide on timing.

Systematic environmentalist management is not something that can be introduced from one day to the next. It needs several years of planning, good timing and stamina. Clearly, it is important to start at the optimum point, decide on the optimum sequence of operations and decide on – and stick to – a realistic schedule. The elements to be borne in mind are of a business, ecological, technical, personnel, organisational and psychological nature.

Given the wide range of company types, the "priority rating" checklist cannot give universal guidance for all individual cases or conflicts of aims. Nor can it relieve the businessman of his responsibility for using his know-how, tact, experience and intuition to reach the right decision in each case. What it can do, however, is to postulate typical importance rankings which, if adhered to, will increase the likelihood of the right decision being reached. The more the checklist is used in practice by businessmen, and the more businessmen become acquainted with its yardsticks, the less danger there will be of the wrong decisions being made in the hectic business atmosphere when under fire from all sides.

Respect business priorities

1. Adopt whatever environmental protection measures are required by law. (See "law" and "management motivation" checklists.)
2. Adopt environmental protection measures which will be of benefit to the company. (See all the points marked with an asterisk in the various checklists – especially the "management motivation" list.)
3. Adopt environmental protection measures which will have a neutral effect on the company. (See "management motivation" checklist.)
4. Only then – and only if the conditions are right – adopt environmental protection measures which will be a burden on the company. (See "management motivation" checklist.)

Respect ecological and technical priorities

5. Avert acute health hazards.
   Take thorough safety precautions, e.g. precautionary measurements to ensure concentrations of noxious substances at the workplace are below the TLV (threshold limit value), rather than place at risk a worker's life and health ("the most valuable environmental resource of all") and bear all the grave repercussions for the reputation and financial situation of the company. (See "working conditions" checklist.)
6. Save energy, water and raw materials.
   Cut down on energy, water and raw materials consumption as far as possible (e.g. by more sophisticated regulating technology, mechanical cleaning processes and design improvements), rather than having to meet the environmental and financial consequences of over-use. (See "economising on energy and water", "product development", "production technology", "materials management" and "disposal and recycling" checklists.)
7. Use "ecological" materials.
   Use as manufacturing inputs, raw materials, ancillary inputs and consumables only such as can be manufactured, used and disposed of without any major detriment to the environment (e.g. clay bricks), rather than having to bear the practical or moral responsibility of the requisite environmental protection measures in production, use and disposal being adopted. (See "materials management" checklist.)
8. Prevent environmentally detrimental substances developing.
   Prevent the creation of residual, conversion and noxious substances by switching to "integrated techniques" (e.g. fluidised solids technology) rather than having to resort to "end of the pipe" techniques (e.g. gas scrubbers and dedusters). (See "production technology" and "disposal and recycling" checklists.)
9. Reuse heat and environmentally detrimental materials.
   Recycle and reuse heat and residual, conversion and noxious substances in the production process, rather than trying to dispose of them with minimum harm to the environment. ("Production technology" and "disposal and recycling" checklists.)
10. Suppress environmentally detrimental substances and noise at source.

Suppress residual, conversion or noxious substances and noise at source (by using such emission abatement techniques as enclosing noisy machinery), rather than trying to deal with them once their effect becomes apparent (by such immission defence techniques as noise barriers). (See "production technology" checklist.)

11. Reduce environmentally detrimental substances to a "manageable" state.
    Reduce residual, conversion and noxious substances to a dimension or degree of purity (e.g. by avoiding mixing noxious "cocktails") such that their noxious potential is minimised, rather than having to resort to comparatively expensive conversion or separation processes. (See "production technology" and "disposal and recycling" checklists.)
12. Render individual means of protection unnecessary.
    Eliminate the effects of noise, heat and noxious substances by technical means only (e.g. noise barriers, fans, extractors), rather than imposing additional protective behaviour on those exposed (e.g. ear protectors, respirators or protective clothing, which experience has shown are often neglected). (See "working conditions" checklist.)

Respect personnel and organisational priorities

13. Start with the "right" members of staff.
    Make a start on environmental protection measures in sectors, departments and workplaces already manned by like-minded staff, instead of having to preach the gospel first. (See "management motivation" and "staff motivation and training" checklists.)
14. Recruit the "right" people.
    As well as examining job applicants' academic and technical qualifications, take a look at their attitude to the environment and their knowledge and abilities in environmental matters, rather than having to spend time, money and effort on persuading and training staff later. (See "staff motivation and training" checklist.)
15. Delegate responsibilities to the "right" member of staff.
    Appoint as environment manager someone equally well qualified in ecology, economics and psychology, rather than having

to set up a permanent "running repairs service" to make up for imbalances and shortcomings. (See "in-house environmental protection arrangements" checklist.)

16. Create the "right" organisational units.
 In large companies, take the idea of "profit centres" as a model for setting up autonomous, self-regulating "ecology centres", rather then having to iron out the disadvantages of a centralised and cumbersome environmental protection bureaucracy at some later stage. (See "management motivation" and "in-house environmental protection arrangements" checklists.)
17. Offer the "right" training courses.
 As part of the programme of conventional and environmentalist apprentice and adult training, encourage initiative and self-regulation, rather than having to issue dozens of instructions and make provision for monitoring work later on. (See "staff motivation and training" checklist.)

Respect psychological priorities

18. Give priority to the more personal environmental protection measures.
 Go for the more immediate and personal environmental protection measures first, e.g. by using limited maintenance funds to see that the inside walls at workplaces are painted with biological paint, rather than starting with the outside walls.
19. Give priority to habit-forming environmental protection measures.
 Start with habit-forming environment protection measures, and then move on to measures which do not depend directly on workers and thus have a less obvious "pedagogical" effect, e.g. if it is not possible to do everything at once, start by replacing conventional toilet paper with recycled paper, fit out waste-paper baskets with waste separators and equip vehicles with start-stop devices, and only then go on to grow ivy up the factory walls.
20. Give priority to environmental protection measures with a wide-spectrum or tone-setting effect.
 Adopt environmental protection measures with a wide-spectrum or tone-setting effect rather than those with an unspectacular or limited-application form, e.g. start by equipping the directors' cars with catalytic converters and writing

directors' letters on recycling paper, rather than starting with one of the specialist departments.

21. Give priority to environmental protection measures with other eye-catching effects.
Start by adopting measures which have a pronounced surprise effect, are refreshingly original, appeal to the heart ("save the duck family") or tend to promote solidarity, rather than starting with unspectacular routine measures.
22. Give priority to environmental protection measures with "instantaneous" economic success.
With a view to eliciting an immediate positive response, start with environmental protection measures which will produce an "instantaneous" effect, and then move on to those which are more likely to pay for themselves over the long term and are thus less suitable as a "motivating starter", e.g. start with the simple energy-saving measures before making major energy investments with a protracted pay-off period. (See the points marked with an asterisk, especially the "economising on energy and water" checklist.)
23. Introduce environmental protection measures according to their consensus potential.
Start with environmental protection measures which are required by law and such that are of economic benefit (e.g. dust filters and thermostats), as these are normally uncontroversial. Only then move on to economically neutral measures (e.g. publish environmentalist information on the staff notice board), as there might be psychological resistance here. Not before this should measures be attempted that are (at least in the short term) economically disadvantageous (e.g. environmental seminars for trainees), given that such measures will only be generally accepted if key management staff are given sufficient time to develop a genuine environmental awareness. (See "management motivation" checklist.)
24. Leave controversial environmental protection measures until later, and then ensure that a consensus is possible.
For instance, do not try to counter the passive smoking hazard by imposing a general smoking ban; instead, allow some time to elapse and then seek a consensus, on the grounds that otherwise smokers may be provoked into closing ranks and forming a kind of in-house anti-environmentalist movement. However, the compromise must not be achieved at the cost of non-

smokers' health. Management has a simpler task in countries or states where smoking in offices is prevented by law or jurisdiction. Another example: do not attempt to introduce on a general basis a low-meat or organic diet in the works canteen; instead, allow some time to elapse, then ensure that alternative meals are available. People's eating habits are often perceived as a quasi-religious matter, and the company should not allow itself to get involved in any such conflict.

III. Sectoral checklists

These checklists give concrete form to what the environmentalist management approach means for twenty major corporate departments. They set out clear recommendations as to how each department should be organised in an environmentalist manner.

If what the businessman is most concerned about is short-term success, he should first of all work through the "economising on energy and water" checklist and take a look at all the points in other checklists marked with an asterisk. These recommend measures which are helpful to the environment and to the company as well in that they reduce costs and boost profits. Many of the measures can be introduced with immediate effect and with no significant capital outlay. In other words, even a relatively superficial reading of the checklists can bring the company a cash advantage.

If, however, a businessman is interested in the medium- and long-term viability and profitability of his company, he will realise that – with the escalating environmental problems and their effect on public opinion, markets and legal requirements, and their undoubted importance as the most significant of all future trends – environmental issues should be seriously considered at the planning stage, in which case he should study all the checklists himself or at least have them studied by his departmental heads.

Appendix I contains a selection of the relevant databases, publications and organisations. The material has been systematised according to the following 20 sectoral checklists. The databases, publications and organisations are in turn subdivided into International, British, American and German (the latter including Austrian and Swiss sources). The "International" section contains sources associated with international organisations or dealing with the subject from an international viewpoint.

The French edition of the book, as yet at the preparatory stage, will also contain French sources. Each subsequent version (beginning with Spanish and Italian) will give the specific sources for the country concerned and additionally include all sources listed in all previous editions.

The source lists provide only samples of relevant databases, publications and organisations. They are not comprehensive and do not imply endorsement by the authors, the participants, the editor or the publisher.

The differing length of the source lists does not imply that a larger volume of material is available overall on the subject of one list than on that of another. Nor should the number of sources stated under each country be taken as an indication of the total amount of information available in that country.

As the manner in which sources are quoted differs slightly from one country to another, no attempt has been made to achieve 100 per cent uniformity. Moreover, differences in the depth of information given on individual sources have been accepted for the sake of practical benefits.

Taken together the checklists constitute a large fund of valuable, practical and up-to-date information which will help companies in numerous countries to combine successful business with the responsibility for a healthy environment.

Checklist No. 1: Management motivation

The environmentalist principle of business management can only be introduced with the assent of the management team. Any members of the team who are not yet convinced of the need for such measures must first of all be worked on.

In a public limited company, this kind of motivation work has to be addressed to the board of directors and the shareholders' meeting too, applying the same psychological recommendations as for management motivation described below.

Analyse your own motives and credibility

1. Ask yourself: "Do I have enough respect and understanding for my colleagues, and do I treat them with at least the sense of responsibility I apply to my natural environment (flora and fauna)?"
2. Ask yourself: "Am I really concerned about the environment or is what I am doing intended to give myself a better image or boost my ego?"
3. Ask yourself (in all honesty): "Am I already acting in exemplary environmentalist fashion or do my deeds detract from the credibility of what I say?"

Empathise with the feelings and thought-processes of the person you are talking to

4. Seek to justify the company's environmental management policy vis-à-vis departmental heads by taking examples from their own departments, e.g.:
   - vis-à-vis the head of personnel: in terms of human relations
   - vis-à-vis the head of sales: in terms of publicity, image and advertising
   - vis-à-vis the head of the technical department: in terms of fresh motivation for the employee suggestions scheme
   - vis-à-vis the head of the materials management department: in terms of reducing waste disposal problems by an ecological purchasing policy
   - vis-à-vis the head of finance: in terms of cost-saving, cost-neutrality or cost-transparency
5. Appeal to whatever motivates the departmental heads personally, e.g.:
   - where there is an obvious need for safety-first: in terms of

more rigorous environmental liability provisions, a greater likelihood of misdemeanours being detected and more stringent penalties
- where there is a perceptible need for a corporate spirit: in terms of the integrating effect of the environmentalist ideal on society, workforce and family
- where there is an evident need for public esteem: in terms of removal of the taint of the damaging environmental effects of business activity
- where there is a pressing need for self-realisation: in terms of the opportunity to do genuine pioneering work in the area where economics and ecology meet
- where there is a nagging reluctance to identify with "alternative ideas": in terms of the positive experience of other companies

6. Have no truck with the mechanistic application of motivation techniques or manipulatory wheeler-dealering, the kind of thing that runs counter to the principle of human respect and is easily seen through (which has an obvious demotivating effect).

Every decision must be psychologically prepared, underpinned and put to use

7. Prepare decisions on in-house environmental protection measures well in advance by providing information in good time and motivating members of the management team.
8. Before taking a decision on measures which could be controversial, wait for an opportune moment, e.g. the announcement of a successful year's trading, a special anniversary or a major order.
9. Continue to work on members of the management team who have been outvoted on an environmental protection issue, rather than treating them as defeated opponents.
10. Give wide in-house publicity to positive decisions on environmental protection measures, to ensure that the management team is seen to be acting in unison and to bind its individual members more strongly to the collective decision.
11. Where there is a positive response to a collective decision on environmental protection measures, stress the involvement of all concerned (and thus let everyone share in the success), both in the company and in the media.

12. Where there is a negative response to a collective decision on environmental protection measures (e.g. carping about the quality of recycled paper), stand by whichever members of the management team are under fire and thus strengthen team spirit.
13. Take every opportunity to thank and praise members of the management team for their environmentalist attitude, with a view to motivating them for future measures.

Draw up a strategy based on psychological priorities

14. Draw up a medium-term strategy (initially for your own use only) for the order in which in-house environmental activities should be placed on the agenda for a decision by the management team.
15. Bear in mind that the nature, extent and timing of the proposed activities should be in line with what may sometimes be only a slowly emerging environmental awareness in the management team.
16. Ensure that the following sequence is adhered to for decisions to be taken on environmental matters over a number of meetings (i.e. not all at once):
    - Measures laid down by law
    - Measures which will be of benefit to the company
    - Measures which will be of neither benefit nor detriment to the company
    - Measures which will impose a burden on the company

Decide on environmental protection measures laid down by law (phase 1)

17. Draw up and present for decision a programme aimed at implementing mandatory environmental protection measures, e.g.:
    - Acquire or construct a waste water treatment plant to comply with the legal threshold values.
    - Construct a low-noise factory building to reduce ambient noise to (and below) the legally permissible level.
18. Aim for unanimity in the management team, e.g. on the following grounds:
    - Contravention of the environmental protection laws is not a mere peccadillo.

- Companies acting illegally are liable to compensation claims or even closure of business.
- In the event of criminal proceedings, members of the management team are liable to fines and even prison sentences.

19. When it is time for a decision to be taken in the management team, ensure that all concerned are fully aware of the following:
    - Protection of the environment must be on the agenda of meetings of the highest management body
    - Protection of the environment is unavoidable
    - Protection of the environment has unanimity potential
20. When it comes to the decision, seek too to strengthen the feeling of corporate responsibility for the environment under the banner: "We are loyal to the law of the land. As far as protection of the environment goes, we will brook no compromise".
21. Make the transition from mandatory environmental protection to voluntary measures and launch phase two immediately after or even simultaneously with phase one.

Decide on environmental protection measures which will benefit the company (phase 2)

22. Draw up and present for decision a programme of "selfish" environmental protection measures, e.g.:
    - Reduce energy costs by installing control units in the heating system*
    - Reduce waste disposal costs by using compaction containers instead of open domestic refuse containers*
    - Reduce water costs by installing water-saving devices for WC cisterns*
    - Reduce raw materials, transportation and disposal costs by recycling heavy metals from electroplating sludges*
    - Reduce the legal liability risk by replacing leaky or potentially leaky oil tanks*
    - Boost turnover and improve profits by developing and marketing alternative products which are less polluting

* The asterisks indicate environmental protection measures which can usually be introduced easily and quickly to prevent or reduce costs.

23. Seek a unanimous vote in favour of at least some of the proposed measures, e.g. on the grounds that:
    - the planned environmental protection measures will pay for themselves quicker than other investment projects
    - environmental protection measures can avert more serious risks than comparable risk-reduction measures
    - an environmentalist marketing measure promises better turnover and profit growth than comparable marketing measures
24. When the time comes for a decision to be made, ensure that all concerned are fully aware of the following:
    - Protection of the environment must be on the agenda of meetings of the highest management body
    - Protection of the environment is not only unavoidable, but also lucrative
    - Protection of the environment has unanimity potential
25. Give another boost to the corporate sense of responsibility for the environment under the banner: "We are doing something for the environment and, if it benefits the company, all the better!"
26. Give the positive psychological influence of phase two several months to work and back it up by a series of success stories (e.g. water, energy and raw materials savings), before moving on to the psychologically more demanding third phase.

Decide on environmental protection measures which have a neutral effect on the company (phase three)

27. Draw up a programme for neutral environmental protection measures, i.e. measures which neither benefit nor burden the company (although they may be of medium- or long-term benefit) e.g.:
    - Install special notice boards for environmental protection information alongside the official notice boards for management and works council announcements.
    - Replace environmentally detrimental cleansers by biological alternative products which are comparable in price and function.
    - Extend the canteen menu to include organically produced dishes (at the same cost).
    - Allow environmental counsellors and consumer organisations to hold free information meetings.

28. Do not place the entire programme en bloc on the agenda: use discretion to spread the various points over several meetings.
29. Start by getting decisions taken on readily implementable activities (e.g. notice boards), and move on at subsequent meetings to activities requiring more organisation or which may be controversial for other reasons (e.g. environmental counselling in the canteen).
30. Aim to get a unanimous vote in favour from the management team, e.g. on the following grounds:

    - The measures will place virtually no burden on the company.
    - By enhancing staff motivation, the company is itself deriving benefit.
    - Planned environmental coaching of workers will result in the medium and long terms at least in a reduction in environmental protection risks and enhanced business opportunities, the net result being a quantifiable benefit for the company.
    - It is important to point out that, although this set of environmental protection measures may be only "benefit-neutral" for the company, the fact is that the company did derive material benefit from such measures at earlier stages (e.g. by energy-saving measures in the second phase).

31. Devote special attention to winning over members of the management team who take the view that any activity which is not geared strictly to profit maximisation should be dispensed with as a dangerous diversion.
32. Where necessary, have recourse to the "List of Arguments for Environmentalist Business Management" in Part C.
33. If it becomes evident that it is not going to be possible to obtain a unanimous vote in favour, consider withdrawing the proposal and reintroducing it as soon as environmental awareness seems to indicate more likelihood of the measure being passed unanimously.
34. Realise that a unanimous vote in favour of a particular measure at a later stage is often more useful in terms of spreading the environmental gospel in the company than an earlier decision, perhaps on a slender majority, bearing in it the seeds of dissension.
35. When it comes to a decision, keep on at members of the mana-

gement team to ensure that all concerned realise the following:

- Protection of the environment must be on the agenda of meetings of the highest management body.
- Protecting the environment is worthwhile even if it brings the company no tangible benefit.
- Even measures which do not bring the company any tangible benefit can obtain a majority or even unanimous vote in favour.

36. Work on the ecological corporate spirit under the banner: "Money is not everything. Protection of the environment is a worthwhile aim even in the absence of self-seeking motives."
37. Give the management team several months to get used to the idea of benefit-neutral environmental protection measures before moving on to the fourth – and psychologically most difficult – phase.

Decide on environmental protection measures which will place a burden on the company (phase 4)

38. Draw up, initially for your own guidance only, a programme of measures which will be of ecological benefit but will place a burden on the company – in the short term at least, e.g.:
    - systematic environmental protection training for trainees
    - application of high domestic environmental protection standards to production facilities run by subsidiaries abroad, regardless of what may be less demanding standards in those countries
    - apply environmentally benign building principles for the next new building project
    - subsidise a farm which can provide staff with cheap organically grown products
39. Embark on a phase of serious and thorough thought before taking any further steps:
    - In proposing measures which are of benefit to the environment but which place a burden on the company, the critical stage of environmentalist management has been reached.
    - The conventional view of things is now being turned upside down in that – for the first time – the environment is not serving the company, but – to some extent at least – the company is serving the environment.
    - Here (from the short-term perspective at least) the environ-

ment protection objective is in conflict with the profit motive – a company's lifeline.

- From now on, any further steps must be dictated not just by concern for the environment, but also by a sense of responsibility for the company and the people working for it.
- Before any such proposals can be presented to the management team for a decision, the vital material and organisational requirements on the one hand and the psychological requirements on the other must be fulfilled.

40. Consider carefully whether the material and organisational requirements are fulfilled.
    - Take a general and detailed look at the company's situation to see whether it is sound enough to be able to cope with even a very restricted and short-lived fall in profits.
    - Make sure that there is an effective financial early-warning system.
    - Ensure that the management team includes poeple who are guided purely by the profit motive, who can be relied on to advocate a strictly profit-oriented policy, and who will be prepared to call a halt if necessary.
    - Ensure that the person appointed as environment manager is as much aware of the cost-control principle as of the need for protecting the environment.
    - In the absence of any of the above preconditions, restrict decisions to phases one to three until all the requirements are fulfilled.
    - Work constantly on improving the company's profitability, e.g. by making special efforts in marketing and rationalisation to release financial resources for environmental activities.
41. Make sure that the psychological requirements are fulfilled so that the management team will vote in favour of the proposed measures. In particular, ensure that all participants in the meeting have a well-developed environmental awareness; if not, wait and work on the laggards in the meantime.
42. Once all the necessary conditions have been met, aim for a unanimous vote in favour of the proposed measures, e.g. on the following grounds:
    - The cost-increasing environmental measures come on one side of the balance sheet and are balanced out by successful energy- and water-saving measures on the other.

- The general situation of the company is such that it can afford to take on a public responsibility for the environment.
- In the medium and long terms, what may be seen initially as a financial sacrifice will probably turn out to be a useful investment.

43. Take the opportunity to prepare the ground for subsequent decisions by thanking all concerned for their sense of responsibility and for creating a corporate ecological spirit under the banner: "Protecting the environment is worth a few sacrifices."

Checklist No. 2: Corporate aims and strategies

If companies are to behave in an ecologically acceptable manner, they must make a critical analysis of their philosophy, formulate a set of objectives which take account of environmental questions and lay down appropriate strategies. An objective analysis of the situation (where do we stand?) must be taken as a starting-point to determine the company's goals (what do we want to achieve?) and decide on medium-term policy (what steps should be taken?).

Identify key ecological issues in the company's areas of activity (key issue analysis)

1. Analyse opportunities and risks in the company's operating environment and on the market (external factors), such as:
   - legislation (e.g. the laws on emission limits and waste disposal)
   - public awareness (e.g. press reports, demonstrations)
   - consumers' awareness (e.g. changes in attitude and behaviour)
   - competitors' activities (e.g. introduction of products which minimise ecological damage)
   - scientific and research developments (e.g. catalyst technology)
2. Analyse the company's strengths and weaknesses (internal factors), such as:
   - finance available for investment geared to environmental questions (e.g. development)
   - open-minded and flexible management attitudes
   - the company's range of products and its relevance to markets in the field of environmental protection (e.g. use of synergetic effects, access to markets arising from ecological concerns)
3. Draw up a consistent ecological strategy for the company, e.g. by:
   - systematic comparison of opportunities/strengths, risks/strengths, opportunities/weaknesses and risks/weaknesses
   - identification and assessment of the "critical" factors in the strategic balance (e.g. applicability of existing know-how to environmental markets; lack of adequate finance for the necessary investments)

Determine the company's objectives with due regard for ecological factors

4. Formulate models and principles for the company's strategy in the light of ecological considerations, e.g.:
   - Safeguard the market economy and free enterprise system by demonstrating their compatibility with ecological constraints.
   - Safeguard the company's existence by recognising general trends at an early stage and planning accordingly.
   - Seek competitive advantages by minimising environmental damage.
   - Adopt a dynamic approach to ecological challenges in all areas of the company's activity and help in the search for solutions.
   - Cooperate with business and academic partners to speed up the progress of knowledge in the environmental sector.
5. Lay down long-term objectives for the company as a whole in environmental matters, e.g.:
   - Capitalise on the goodwill of staff, the public and government which will result from an environmentalist commitment.
   - Take advantage of the lower costs resulting from energy savings, economical use of resources and other progress in environment-related technology.
   - Minimise risks arising from management or product liability, sudden changes in statutory limit values or surges in environmentally motivated demand.
   - Cooperate with trade associations, the media and government to generate further knowledge.
   - Influence legislation by lobbying activities at the pre-legislative stage.
6. Assess the relationships between the company's environmental and economic objectives.
   - Assess the implications of environmental objectives for turnover, costs and profits.
   - Identify major areas of conflict between these objectives (e.g. short-term higher costs, lower turnover, cash-flow problems).
   - Lay down long-term priorities within a system of objectives (e.g. environmental aims as main or secondary objectives and possible changes with time).

7. Clarify the ecological dimension in all departmental objectives.
   - Labour market: increase the company's attractiveness to ecologically concerned workers and reinforce staff loyalty.
   - Procurement: adopt an environmentalist posture in the purchase of raw materials, ancillary inputs and consumables.
   - Production: cut costs by saving energy, raw materials and water.
   - Marketing: take environmental considerations into account in logistics (e.g. transport by rail, not road).

Formulate ecologically sound strategies

8. Determine basic strategies.
   - Defensive or offensive stance? Keep the initiative: better to act than to react!
   - Action on a narrow or a wide front? Seek to concentrate effort on the specific areas in which the company is competent (e.g. as a specialist in the solution of particular environmental problems).
9. Plan environmentalist strategies for the company's various areas of activity.
   - Define areas of activity in product, market and technological terms (describing the product value, market segmentation and technologies with reference to environmental considerations) and lay down priorities for work on specific market segments.
   - Determine the company's basic attitude to other participants in the marketplace (competitors, distributive trades, customers), considering the scope for demarcation of functions or cooperation.
   - Lay down product and product range strategies (improve the environmental acceptability of the product range by introducing new products and changing or replacing existing ones).
   - Establish ecology portfolios and ensure that they are suitably balanced.
10. Formulate environmentalist department strategies.
    (See "marketing" checklist etc.)

Checklist No. 3: Marketing

Marketing means gearing the company to the market. All marketing instruments must be planned, coordinated and controlled in accordance with requirements to solve the customers' problems and achieve the company's long-term objectives (profit, security).

Within the general economic process, ecological factors are becoming important to the success of market-oriented management. The changing legal context in the form of more stringent environmental legislation and increased ecological awareness on the part of customers brings considerable risks and opens up new opportunities for the marketing of goods and services. Ecologically acceptable marketing concepts have to be developed not only for reasons of social responsibility but also to ensure that the company remains competitive.

The following checklist sets out the basic considerations to be taken into account when developing such concepts in the business sector.

Determine marketing objectives with due regard for ecological factors.
(See also "corporate aims and strategies" checklist.)

1. Ensure that the marketing concept fits into the company's philosophy and its system of objectives (e.g. safeguarding of long-term competitiveness).
2. Formulate marketing objectives in such a way that performance can be measured and monitored, both
   - in economic terms (e.g. capture of x per cent of specified new environment-related markets within a specified period) and
   - in terms of the company's profile (e.g. creation or reinforcement of the company's image and reputation as being capable of solving environmental problems in certain fields).
3. Determine and impose or agree on an order of priority for the objectives
   - according to product category or product,
   - according to customer category or customer, and
   - according to region.

Plan marketing activities in an integrated fashion

4. Product policy (see also "product development" checklist.)
   - Manufacture or offer products which minimise consumption of raw materials and which can be recycled (e.g. use raw materials as economically as possible, substitute abundant materials for scarce ones, minimise quantities of waste or alter its nature to reduce its impact).
   - Mark products to draw attention to their environmentally positive features (e.g. the German "blue angel" seal of approval).
   - Devise sensible packaging made from environmentally acceptable materials (e.g. increase reusability).
   - Ensure that the product is used in an acceptable manner by providing aftersales and advisory services (service packages, seminars).
5. Communications policy (see also "PR work" checklist)
   - Embrace the trend towards increasing consumer concern and reinforce it with advertising and public relations activities.
   - Enhance the image and reputation of the company for expertise in environmental questions by exposing selected target groups to ecological arguments and publicity.
   - Make sure that these claims are true and can be substantiated.
   - Allay public distrust of the business world in environmental matters by broadly based activities (e.g. through trade associations).
6. Distribution policy
   - Set up marketing channels by agreement between manufacturers and distributors in order to make recycling systems possible ("retrodistribution" channels).
   - Establish recycling centres and provide advice at the point of distribution in order to encourage a positive response from consumers.
   - Give preference to transport systems which carry reduced environmental costs in terms of energy consumption and pollution. (See also "company vehicles" checklist.)
7. Price and discount policy
   - If higher prices cannot be avoided as a result of ecologically sound manufacturing processes, make it clear to distributors and consumers how the costs are calculated (price

differentials based on ecological factors).
- Consider whether the additional cost of ecologically acceptable products can be spread by combined costing.

8. Check that all individual measures form part of an integrated package making a definite impact in environmental terms and adjust them as necessary.

Check and adjust marketing organisation and control (i.e. create structures and systems appropriate to the strategy pursued)

9. Ensure that all levels of management are sensitive to ecological issues. (See also "management motivation" and "staff motivation and training" checklists.)
   - Enhance awareness by means of information and training.
   - Foster an 'esprit de corps' and pride in setting an example in environmental matters.
10. Ensure that the company's organisation enables the strategies to be implemented.
    - Adapt the company structure.
    - Appoint a person to be responsible for all environmental questions (e.g. as the environment manager) at senior management level. (See also "in-house environmental protection arrangements" checklist.)
11. Develop monitoring and incentive systems.
    - Develop arrangements for environment control by means of additional instruments to check whether environmental objectives are being attained (monitoring systems).
    - Provide incentives for achieving or surpassing the environmental targets (e.g. bonus systems).

Checklist No. 4: In-house environmental protection arrangements

The function of such arrangements is to ensure that environmentalist attitudes are introduced, fostered and reinforced in a coordinated and interdisciplinary manner throughout the company. Intensive management is necessary because of increasing risks, the overall deterioration in the environmental situation and increasing concern on the part of the workforce and public, which make it essential to take anticipatory action.

The arrangements described here are intended to be additional to those already existing. In particular, the environment manager proposed under the Integrated System as a senior management-level coordinator and innovation-chaser has a much wider range of activities than the statutory "environment officer" who, under German law, is required in certain firms to look after water and air pollution and waste disposal problems (i.e. the "technical" aspects).

Appoint an environment manager

1. Issue a formal company standard laying down the job profile and list of duties for an environment manager. These include:
   - assistance in and coordination of conversion to environmentally more acceptable products
   - monitoring developments in environmental policy and establishing an early warning system with the help of in-house and external experts
   - liaison with works councils in all environmental matters
   - participation in environment committees inside and outside the company
   - monitoring new developments and products as part of a comprehensive environmentalist procurement policy
   - providing convincing presentation of the company's environment-related activities to the outside world, insofar as this is not done by other departments or partners/owners
   - arranging for precautionary pollution measurements and making proposals for commissioning consultants to investigate ways of saving energy and water
   - investigating the feasibility of allowing other companies to use spare capacity in the company's plant on a remunerative basis (e.g. waste disposal or recycling plant)
   - participating in training activities

2. Establish the environmental manager's position at senior management level.
   - This task should be entrusted to a particularly energetic and environmentally conscious member of the executive board.
3. Provide comprehensive information within the company on the duties, purpose and objectives of the new post.
4. Draw up an establishment chart clearly showing responsibilities and functions.
5. Provide the environment manager with active support.
6. Discuss and resolve conflicts between environmental and departmental objectives without delay. (See also "management motivation" checklist.)
7. Draw up a budget for environmental activities outside the company (e.g. support of associations for environmental protection).
8. Plan investment for environmental purposes separately within the overall investment programme and carry out a specific assessment of the extent to which objectives are met.
9. Ensure adequate liaison and discussion between departmental managers/directors/members of the executive board and the environment manager.
10. Give the environment manager the opportunity to draw attention to environmental problems and possible solutions by meeting bodies of workers (workforce meetings, information tours, etc.).

Plan environmental activities and assess progress

11. Make a study of weaknesses in all departments including subsidiaries and associated companies and draw up a plan of action indicating what is to be done, by whom and by when. In order to identify shortcomings, a systematic audit will be required of all known and predictable environmental problems affecting the company, assessing their relative importance. More particularly, a systematic analysis will be needed of the likelihood and repercussions of incidents, so that preventive arrangements can be made.
12. Wherever possible, incorporate specific objectives in the action plan, e.g.:
    - Eliminate within six months any unreasonable risks arising from the storage and handling of hazardous substances.

- Switch to materials less detrimental to the environment within twelve months.
- 20 per cent reduction in water consumption in electroplating operations by the end of the year.
- Optimum disposal of used oil within the next six months.

13. Draw up contingency plans.
All staff concerned with environmental protection within the company should be involved in contigency planning to enable them to act calmly, quickly and purposefully and to avoid the kind of panic which could easily lead to ill-considered action.
14. Ensure that the materials management department draws up a list of materials containing e.g. the following information:
    - inventory number
    - name
    - chemical designation
    - dangerous reactions and toxicity
    - ecological hazards
    - transport code
    - technical precautions
    - disposal
    - alternatives
    - annual consumption
    - unit price
    - supplier
15. Draw up an internal balance sheet setting out, and quantifying as far as possible, the advantages and disadvantages, if any, of environmental activities.

Set up a technical committee for environmental matters

16. The technical committee should deal with all environmental problems or questions affecting the company such as:
    - materials
    - energy supplies
    - water supplies
    - waste disposal
    - disposal of special-category wastes
    - scope for recycling
    - environmental problems in the production process
    - compliance with statutory limits for pollution, noise, dust
17. Ensure that the environment manager is represented on this committee.

18. Give the committee clear terms of reference.
19. Arrange meetings at regular intervals and ensure that minutes are kept.
20. Require the chairman of the committee to assess its performance.

Set up an interdisciplinary committee for environmental matters

21. In addition to the technical committee, set up an interdisciplinary committee with representatives from all company departments and the environment manager.
    This committee should deal mainly with wider, non-technical questions relating to the environment. The committee members should assist the environment manager in certain of his duties.
22. As in the case of the technical committee, lay down the terms of reference and frequency of meetings, ensure that minutes are kept and have the chairman assess performance.

Checklist No. 5: Staff motivation and training

A company stands or falls by the quality of its workforce. Their goodwill must be won and retained by fair and considerate management. They must be encouraged to be keen and creative.

If a company with well-established organisational structures and procedures is to adopt an environmentalist approach, the employees represent the greatest threat to the project but also the greatest potential aid to its success.

If the employees are not convinced, the project will fail no matter how well it has been prepared in other respects. On the other hand, if the workforce has once been won over to the idea of environmentalist management, the project will virtually run itself.

Staff will also become generally more enthusiastic if their normal work is better justified in their own eyes by the fact that they are at the same time safeguarding the environment. No-one can put "heart and soul" into his work unless he is sure that he is not thereby destroying nature, on which "heart and soul" depend.

Every aspect of staff motivation and training must reflect the awareness that in the long term a company can perform to high standards in environmental protection only by a consistently high standard of work in its traditional activities, thus providing the necessary basis, in terms of technology, scientific knowledge, personnel and equipment, for its environmental performance.

Concern for environmental standards must in practice always progress in step with an increasing awareness of standards of workmanship in the conventional sense, i.e. an inner commitment to work and products of a high quality.

Environmentalist management is easier if the management style is cooperative. To impose environmentalist ideas from above without any inner involvement of the workforce would not only be ineffective but would also nullify the humanistic dimension of the concept from the outset. Where it is proposed to introduce enlightened modes of thought and behaviour, this must be done in a sensitive manner, showing consideration towards the people concerned.

In view of the limited time available for staff motivation and training in the daily struggle for survival in a competitive world, these objectives might seem impossibly high. A great deal will indeed not be achievable until environmental problems and public concern have become even more acute. Failure to set ambitious targets, however, often means that realistic objectives are not achieved either.

Develop a motivation and training concept

1. Clarify who is to be motivated and trained:
   - Senior management (e.g. board of directors, senior executives, management team).
   - Middle management (e.g. department and section heads).
   - Other white-collar workers.
   - Blue-collar workers.
   - Trainees.
   - Employees of service companies who work frequently or regularly in the company (e.g. painters, plumbers, fitters and cleaning or waste disposal staff), although it is better to choose service companies with a sound environmental approach in the first place.
   - Former workers of the company (e.g. retired employees) to a limited extent (e.g. by providing home counsellors).
   - Employees' families – to a limited extent (e.g. by means of environmental counsellors for households).
2. Clarify the practical purpose of motivation and training.
   To impart the willingness and ability:
   - to work energetically and creatively towards the attainment of the company's environmental goals, to act with due regard for the environment at the workplace and at the same time to do a fully satisfactory job (e.g. grinding, turning, measuring) in the conventional sense
   - to show a proper concern for the environment on the way to work, at home and in all leisure pursuits
   - to exercise one's responsibility for the environment and a quality- and environment-conscious economy as a citizen (at local, regional or national level) by taking part in elections and citizens' initiatives
   - to defend the view – at work, at home, in the sports club or other private associations – that concern for the environment is as important as concern for standards of workmanship
3. Clarify the wider objective of motivation and training.
   To win over the "whole man/woman" to the environmentalist idea by directing motivation and training towards:

- feeling: strengthening the emotional attachment to the natural heritage
- thought: training in perception of interrelationships (e.g. a dwindling bird population means infestation with insects, hence use of pesticides, hence threat to groundwater, each link in the causal chain giving rise to further series of consequences with multiple interaction)
- sense of responsibility: demonstrating responsibility for one's own health, for one's fellow human beings, for plants and animals and for future generations and their living environment
- judgement: developing the ability to select, assess and use information on environmental matters in order to progress from a sense of responsibility to purposeful decisions
- action: encouragement to put decisions into practice to the benefit of human beings and the environment

Simultaneously developing feeling, thought, sense of responsibility, soundness of judgement and willingness to take action, and harnessing these faculties to the aim of high-quality work and products should be the ultimate objective.

4. Clarify what is to be conveyed by motivation and training.
   - The biosphere as an interrelated system and as the natural basis for all life, i.e. the precondition for its existence.
   - The threat to the ecological equilibrium and hence to man as a result of damage to water, soil, air, fauna and flora.
   - The scope for stopping or preventing environmental damage on the part of trade and industry, the energy sector, agriculture and private households.
     The points that need to be grasped here are:
     - how the Integrated System of Environmentalist Business Management works
     - that damage to the environment would be reduced considerably if all business companies were to adopt the system
     - that in the long term environmentalist management can be practised and promoted only by companies which maintain their competitiveness by offering high-quality products or services at prices appropriate to the market
   - The practical opportunities for the individual to stop or prevent environmental damage or to take other direct or indirect action to preserve the environment.

The individual may act in various capacities:

- as an employee (e.g. by precision measurements of pollutants at the workplace but also by fine calibration of workpieces since high-quality work and products help to safeguard the competitive position of the company and hence its superior environmental standards);
- as a private person (e.g. by saving energy, water and chemicals in the home);
- as a citizen (e.g. by cooperating with local special-category refuse collection schemes);
- as a propagandist in word and deed (e.g. in community associations, church groups, sports clubs, gardening clubs, at campsites and in touring parties).

5. Clarify the method of motivation and training.
   - Grading the persuasive process.
     In practice, it has proved effective to proceed in the following stages:
     - Arousing curiosity and interest among staff (e.g. by posting a newspaper report on a local pollution scandal directly affecting the workers on the company's notice board; displaying a catalytic converter with a description in a display cabinet; exhibiting a water barrel with the caption: "this is the amount of water you waste in period x by not using WC cistern water-saving devices").
     - Gradually raising the level of knowledge within the company (e.g. by setting up a special notice board marked "Environment news" for up-to-date information on environmental protection inside and outside the company).
     - Deliberate propaganda work to develop an environmental awareness which recognises the problems and seeks to make a specific contribution to solving them (e.g. by getting a forester to explain the forest die-back phenomenon to trainees on a field trip).
     - Practical encouragement and guidance for desirable behaviour at the workplace, at home and during leisure pursuits (e.g. by provision on the company's premises of facilities for the collection of used batteries, or by financing the activities of environmental counsellors who visit employees' homes at their request).
   - Optimum use of learning capacity.
     According to a teacher's rule of thumb, people retain:

- 10 per cent of what they read (e.g. column in the works newspaper);
- 20 per cent of what they hear (e.g. cassette from the company's cassette library);
- 30 per cent of what they see (e.g. use of biological paints by the company's painters and decorators);
- 50 per cent of what they hear and see (e.g. lecture and demonstration at an ecology session for trainees);
- 70 per cent of what they say themselves (e.g. workers' own descriptions of particular environmental problems at meetings of the interdisciplinary environment committee);
- 90 per cent of what they do themselves (e.g. economical use of powder in the washing machine after instruction by the home counsellor).

– Appealing to typical needs.
The needs most easily appealed to are:
- the need for material earnings to meet the cost of living and satisfy a wide range of requirements (e.g. through bonuses for attaining the company's environmental objectives or suggesting ecological improvements)
- the need for safety (e.g. through information on toxins present in food or on the importance of protective clothing at the workplace)
- the need for a sense of belonging (e.g. through educative activities which foster the development of a group spirit such as trainees' environmental seminars extending over several days)
- the need for status (e.g. through thanks, praise, recognition or award of insignia for exemplary conduct)
- the need for self-realisation (e.g. through staff participation in formulating the company's environmental objectives)

– These rules of thumb (grading of the persuasive process, maximum utilisation of learning capacity and incentives reflecting typical needs) should also be applied when instilling a general attention to quality in the company's activities (which must never be supplanted or eclipsed by environmental consciousness but must balance it as a complementary factor in a whole range of concerns).

6. Clarify who is to be responsible for motivation and training.

Depending on the motivation and training arrangements, this may be a job for:
- the person responsible for environmental matters at senior management level
- where appropriate, the company's statutory environment officer whose duties include waste disposal and the reduction of water and air pollution at technical level
- representatives of agencies responsible for the enforcement of environmental protection laws and obligations
- scientists (e.g. environmentally concerned doctors, chemists, physicists, home economists and nutritional scientists and ecologists)
- environmental counsellors for households and local authorities taking part in schemes introduced in a number of EEC Member States and modelled on the German AUGE scheme
- specially trained teachers from vocational schools
- representatives of consumer associations
- representatives of waste disposal companies, manufacturers of environment-related products or of companies which set an example in pollution abatement technology
- craftsmen who exercise their trade in such a way as to minimise damage to the environment – e.g. by returning to traditional methods – and who are able to give practical demonstrations
- inventors of technical solutions to environmental problems
- specialist journalists
- representatives of ecological citizens' initiatives or students' associations
- "victims" who can report at first hand how their health or property has suffered from damage to the environment
- public figures (with whom the workers may identify) who can speak about their own commitment to ecologically sound behaviour and thus set an example

7. Clarify what motivation and training methods should be employed.
   Possible methods include:
   - dissemination of information
   - social functions
   - staff involvement
   - introduction of incentives

- recognition, awards, etc.
- eliminating demotivation
- staff-supported environmental projects
- extension of apprentice training
- supplementing adult training and further education

Implement motivation and training measures

8. Disseminate information.
   - Distribute or display on notice boards press articles dealing with the environment.
   - Inform employees in good time of forthcoming press, radio or television reports on the company's environmental protection activities.
   - Have an environment column in the company newspaper.
   - A special issue of the newspaper on the environment.
   - Bring out another special issue on leisure activities, with articles by employees on ecological pastimes (e.g. organic gardening, protection of birds, bicycle tours, nature conservation), encouraging other employees to take up these activities.
   - Include well-illustrated occasional articles on such subjects as "How I gave up smoking", "I left my car at home" and "Cycling keeps you young".
   - Use the in-house newspaper to conduct prize competitions dealing with some aspect of the environment, e.g. "My best nature photograph", "Trees and woodland – a drawing and painting competition for everyone", "Young animals painted by our children".
   - Award prizes connected with the environment, e.g. a one-week holiday in a national park.
   - Publish the prize-winning entries in the newspaper, and consider enlarging them and using them to decorate walls at the plant.
   - If the company is part of an international group, involve the foreign companies in the competition; this not only introduces new motifs, but also helps to bring the members of the group closer together and spreads the idea of environmental protection beyond national boundaries.
   - Display in-house and external environmental information on the official notice board.
   - In addition to the management and works council notice

boards, create a special notice board for environmental information to make it clear that there is a "third element" affecting company matters and work relationships.
- Distribute material dealing with the environment, e.g. material published by the Federal Environmental Agency, the Ministry of Health, consumer organisations, AUGE and its offshoots in other European countries.
- Set up a company environment library (books, charts, environmental games), audio library (cassettes, records) or video library (slides, video films and cine films) for staff use.
- Install an electronic noticeboard in the canteen, with new tips each week for improving the environment (e.g. "Don't forget to use our wastepaper bank").
- At Christmas, give all departments posters of birds, plants, butterflies, etc. for use as wall decoration.
- At regular assemblies (e.g. works meetings, information meetings for management) and official meetings (e.g. economics committee, works council and foremen's meetings), report briefly on successes and shortcomings in environmental protection at the plant.

9. Social functions.
   - Touch upon the question of environmental protection in Christmas or New Year addresses.
   - Before Christmas, hold an "Environmental Quiz" in all departments, with bird feeding-tables, flower bulbs, wild-flower seeds, etc. as prizes.
   - Organise attractively presented consumer counselling shows during works outings.
   - Organise an "Environmental raffle" at works or office parties, with a bicycle as the main prize.
   - Whenever the occasion presents itself, hold a raffle for books, cassettes and videos dealing with the environment or for subscriptions to nature magazines.
   - Organise a bicycle excursion or rally for staff to help them rediscover cycling.
   - Organise an open day to introduce workers' relatives or a wider public to the company's environmental protection arrangements.
   - At a party for workers' children, arrange for environment counsellors or representatives of consumer organisations to demonstrate good children's toys (e.g. hand-carved

puppets) and offer healthy confectionery (instead of jelly-babies and the like) to show parents that alternative toys and foods are available.

- Before children's parties, open days and similar functions, always check whether it is possible to invite families living in the neighbourhood as well as employees and their families. This not only serves to spread the message of environmental protection but also – and particularly in small communities – has a very beneficial effect on the company's public image.
- Realise that social functions which bring together employees' and neighbourhood children under the environment banner are less expensive and more effective than major public-relations advertisements, especially as an original idea may well attract reporters and enter the news columns.
- Arrange for environmental counsellors to speak at senior citizens' functions (where coffee and tasty wholefood snacks should be provided), since old people are very eager to save housekeeping money by acting ecologically and they can help spread the ecology message in the large amount of free time they have.

10. Give staff a chance to get involved.
    - As a senior member of staff, ensure that, before the beginning of each financial year, all designated staff in their departments prepare a list of realistic environmental objectives for the year.
    - Discuss these objectives with the person responsible and check that they are consistent with the firm's philosophy and aims and with the departmental objectives (e.g. sales, technology, materials management, personnel, finance).
    - Try to ensure that employees themselves quantify their environmental objectives (as well as other objectives), e.g. "Reduce energy and water consumption by x per cent with no loss of output; y per cent increase in recycled input materials as a proportion of total purchases".
    - Urge staff to look for possible cost-cutting ecological measures within their areas of responsibility (see the asterisked measures in the checklists), and do not forget to congratulate them if successful.
    - Instruct employees to consult the appropriate environ-

mental checklists systematically when drawing up their list of objectives.
- Ensure that the economic objectives are worked out with the same degree of thoroughness as the ecological objectives, and that the employee is equally determined to attain both.
- Agree on a binding final version of the list with the employee concerned and strengthen his conviction that he has for the most part set his own objectives.
- Hold periodic (e.g. three-monthly) one-to-one interviews to discuss progress made towards attaining the economic and ecological objectives, deal with problems and, if necessary, revise the objectives.
- Make it perfectly clear that an end-of-year check (now including an "ecocheck") will be made with each employee to see whether he has achieved the goals jointly set and accepted, and that any shortcomings will have to be accounted for.
- Stress the importance of results and replace hierarchical monitoring by self-monitoring, to encourage staff to develop more initiative and obtain more job satisfaction.

11. Introduce incentive schemes.
    - Create an incentive for attaining or exceeding economic and ecological objectives by offering bonus or on-target payments.
    - Consider a scheme whereby the bonus for attaining economic objectives is reduced unless the ecological objectives are attained at the same time.
    - Ensure that the bonus formula does not allow under-target ecological performance to be offset by over-target economic performance, and vice versa.
    - If not already in existence, introduce a company suggestions scheme which gives workers a share of the savings made as a result of their suggestions.
    - Lay down in the rules governing the scheme that a higher payment than usual will be made for suggestions which cut costs and at the same time save energy, water or raw materials or help protect the environment in some other, specifically defined way.
    - Install special "environmental protection suggestions" boxes to encourage staff to make other environmental

suggestions which do not necessarily save money and are therefore not generally rewarded under the company suggestion scheme.

- Applaud such "environmental suggestions" with thanks, praise, mention in the staff newspaper, or, where the suggestion is a particularly good one or someone has made several such suggestions, with a badge of honour.
- Make an automatic cash bonus award for any "environmental suggestions" which, contrary to the author's expectations, turn out to reduce costs.
- Ensure that members of quality circles – in which employees make suggestions for improvements in a creative, competitive atmosphere without regard to hierarchical level or departmental boundaries – address themselves to ways of improving the environment too, and thus demonstrate that environmental protection is one aspect of quality.
- Consider setting up special "environmental circles" for particular problem areas.
- Make use of other creativity techniques, such as brainstorming, to find solutions to environmental problems.
- Select a social function – say, during the Christmas period – to honour those employees who have distinguished themselves by coming up with good suggestions (e.g. under the suggestions scheme or in the quality circles) and allow them to take part in an attractive raffle.
- Consider inviting spouses to the "inventors' celebrations" so as to give award winners the chance to gain status in the eyes of their spouses and to win also their support for the company's environmental protection programme.
- Announce that an employee's salary and promotion prospects will depend not only on his economic performance but also on whether he attains his environmental objectives.
- In all incentive schemes take particular care to ensure that the criteria on which rewards are based are clearly defined and uniformly and equitably applied.

12. Provide recognition.
    - Use praise, thanks and recognition for environmental awareness to motivate section heads, foremen, chargehands, workers, works council members and all employees to continue their efforts to protect the environment.
    - Select public occasions (e.g. meetings, excursions, parties) for presenting awards.

- Always ensure that exceptional performance in traditional fields is rewarded in the same way as achievements in the environmental sector.
- Honour employees who have distinguished themselves in the company in the environmental protection field by putting their names forward for awards from outside organisations.
- Through public-relations work ensure that reports on the company's environmental protection activities appear in the media so as to give staff a feeling of success and to strengthen their "group bonds" vis-à-vis the environment.
- Supply the media with a good information mix to get coverage of advances in environment technology, e.g. energy and water savings. (Many engineers and technicians feel that the media generally treat them as scapegoats, and are likely to be motivated by positive media response.)
- Include details of quality products and services in press releases dealing with the company's environmental protection activities, in the hope that the media will also publish some of these details and thereby provide publicity, at the same time giving credit to staff for their performance in their normal field of activity.

13. Eliminate demotivation.
    - Recognise that psychological preparation, moral support and the rewarding of success (i.e. psychological support for all major environmental protection measures) are as important to the ecologically aware manager as a rope is to a mountain climber.
    - Psychological preparation
        - Do not present the employee with a *fait accompli* or proceed without consulting him, as this may damage his self-respect; instead tell him in good time what has been decided and why.
        - Try to acknowledge his expertise, e.g. by consulting him as to the quickest, most effective and most economical way of implementing whatever has been decided.
    - Moral support
        - Provide moral support if a particular measure requires a change of habit (e.g. driving smoothly and avoiding short journeys to save petrol), if habitual standards are lowered

(the paper is no longer as white), or extra effort is required (the wastepaper bank is 40 paces away).
  - Use patience and perseverance to ensure that new methods are not spoilt by a return to old habits (e.g. throwing used batteries into the wastepaper basket).
- Reward success
  - Be generous with thanks and praise for an environmental protection measure that has been well carried out.
  - Act on the principle that recognition given in the presence of others is not only twice as effective but also motivates the others present to seek recognition by the same means.
- Tactfully eliminate opposition to environmental protection measures
  - Find out why agreed environmental protection measures are being postponed, "forgotten" or blocked.
  - Remember that opposition is rarely based on objective reasons but stems mostly from errors in dealing with others.
  - If personal efforts and objective arguments fail, act on the principle that an acceptable compromise can be more useful than an order imposed from above, which demotivates the employee and leaves him intractable.

14. Encourage staff involvement in environmental projects.
    - Adopt "selfless" environmental protection measures and make very clear within the company, and particularly to the works council, that the company or the shareholders have renounced some of their earnings in the interests of the environment without even a long-term return.
    - On the basis of this "first step", encourage every member of staff to make a small voluntary contribution, e.g. by paying a penny a day into an "environmental fund".
    - Match this by announcing that at the end of the year the company will pay into the fund an amount equal to that already in the kitty.
    - Manage the fund jointly, i.e. by giving management and staff equal voting rights.
    - For example, decide jointly to support a farm for the purpose of supplying the company canteen or staff with organically grown foodstuffs.
    - If employees wish to undertake voluntary environmental

protection work connected with the company outside working hours, e.g. by establishing a wetland habitat on company land, respond by providing money for the necessary materials, expertise and catering.
- With a particularly well motivated workforce, consider holding a secret ballot to determine whether part of the company's budget earmarked for staff bonuses should be used for a popular environmental protection project of immediate benefit to the employees.
- Potential projects would include the purchase and environmentally sound design of a company sports and recreation centre, which would then belong to the employees as members, or the initiation or support of a public campaign against a local coal-fired power station without adequate flue-gas desulphurisation equipment.
- Use the environment projects – made possible by joint sacrifices of shareholders and staff – to show that nationally too, progress in environmental protection can best be achieved through material restraint on the part of all sections of the community.
- Present the joint environmental protection projects to staff and the media at social functions, e.g. a garden party at the sports and recreation ground, with a view to encouraging other companies to undertake similar projects.

15. Extend apprentice training.
    - Take great pains to ensure that apprentices' training is geared towards the environment, since trainees are particularly receptive to ecological ideas and, being the new generation, can influence the course of industrial civilisation.
    - Establish and maintain a balance between economic and ecological effort.
        - Design the training programme such that the trainees can identify with the company's economic and ecological objectives and cultivate initiative and hard work in both fields.
        - In their practical work, encourage trainees to develop the same degree of application, thoroughness, self-discipline and quality awareness in conventional fields (e.g. measuring workpiece tolerances) and in the environmental field (e.g. measuring harmful substances).
        - In the classroom, convince trainees that their response to

problems involving the opposing forces of economics and ecology should not be a negative either/or but a positive one-and-the-other, that rather than take the easy way out in one direction or the other, they should double their efforts to do justice to both aspects.

- Ensure that this principle is seen to run like a thread through all lessons.
- Use imagery to get the message across, e.g.: "The economic and ecological ends of the bow have to be drawn to equal effect if we are to hit the target."
- Eradicate the misconception that apprentice training geared to the environment is a soft option and leave no-one in any doubt that the complexity of the work will make it harder but its usefulness will make it more rewarding.

– Make environmental protection an integral part of the training programme.

- Organise visits or field trips under the following three main headings:
  + "Discover and explore nature" (e.g. visits to a forestry department, wildlife park, nature trail, bird sanctuary or nature reserve)
  + "Discover and experience environmental devastation" (e.g. an "alternative" trip around a port, identifying the major polluters' outfall pipes, a visit to a special-category waste tip or a visit to an intensive feedlot unit)
  + "Discover and test possible solutions" (e.g. a visit to a model sewage treatment plant, a phosphate removal plant, a desulphurisation plant or an organic farm; another idea would be to collect mixed refuse and sort it, e.g. under the heading "Camping refuse and how it can be avoided")
- Undertake "learning-by-doing" projects, e.g.:
  + conduct simple soil, water and air analyses
  + help with the planting and seeding of the works site
  + with expert instruction, test silencer equipment on own motorbikes, mopeds or cars
- Organise environmental seminars lasting several days, which each trainee can attend once during his apprenticeship, addressed by experts in different fields in order to ensure that a balanced picture is presented.

- At intervals, e.g. every eight weeks, have an "Environment Friday".
- Extend theory teaching at the vocational school by prevailing upon the governors to devote more time in the syllabus to environmentally sound behaviour at the workplace.
- Incorporate environmental objectives into workshop teaching – e.g. for lathe operaters and toolmakers – by following:
  + in the first year (basic concepts of the trade): environmentally sound use of materials and consumables
  + in the second year (equipment fabrication for in-house use): construction of small environmental protection devices
  + in the third year (transfer to the actual workplace): environmentally sound behaviour at the workplace
- Try to get the examination regulations adapted accordingly, e.g. for trainee lathe operators and toolmakers:
  + try to ensure that the written examination at the vocational school goes beyond the different types of lathe, forms of gear and varieties of thread, measurement techniques and production tolerances, etc. to include such things as typical hazards to the environment produced by lubricants etc.
  + try to ensure that marking of the practical examination also takes into account any work steps relevant to the environment, in addition to appearance, dimensional accuracy, surface quality and operation of the workpiece
  + try to ensure that environmental protection is covered in the oral examination before the Chamber of Commerce and Industry examination committee

– Make sure that teachers and examiners receive the necessary training in environmental protection.

16. Supplement adult training.
    – Develop in-house and external training programmes to bring not only standards of workmanship, but also employees' business ecology knowledge and abilities up to a level where they can cope with the latest technical and other requirements and enable them at all times to meet the highest economic objectives.

- Here too, ensure that a balance is maintained between conventional and ecological teaching.
- Introduce ecology as an integral part of staff training.
  - Do not allow ecology training to degenerate into a separate course with no obvious links with occupational training; make it an essential component of normal training courses.
  - Do not combine the ecological components of regular courses into isolated "learning units". Bring out the ecological link at each normal learning step, e.g. teach the judicious use of oil and oil cans, instead of merely showing a video film on tanker disasters as an adjunct to the practical work.
  - Make all employees aware of the functional and ecological consequences of every work step and give them practical instruction and training so as to optimise the functional end ecological aspects of each step.
  - In this way ensure not only that all operational aspects are considered from the point of view of the environment (horizontal integration of the Integrated System), but also that each work step or process in a particular sector is judged just as much by its environmental impact as by quality (vertical integration).
- Take great care with the training of the training supervisors, e.g. the master craftsmen, who often combine an innate honesty with a craftsman's pride and whose sense of responsibility can be relied upon.
- Make full use of the services offered by existing institutions, e.g.:
  - employ environmental counsellors or representatives of consumer organisations to give talks after working hours on subjects of interest to private individuals (e.g. environmentally sound household management and nutritional advice);
  - encourage employees to go on environmental courses at a university or other educational establishment, with the fees paid by the company if the subject-matter taught can be applied in the company;
  - encourage employees to take correspondence courses on the same conditions.

Checklist No. 6: Working conditions

A "humane" working environment is an essential prerequisite for ecologically sound production. Workers can hardly be expected to be creative in the interests of the environment if they themselves are obliged to work under unsatisfactory conditions. The following checklist covers all the items needed to achieve suitable working conditions.

Avoid stress caused by environmental factors

Any attempt to avoid environmental stresses, whether arising from noise, light and colours, room climate or hazardous working materials, must always be based on the following principles:
- Firstly, implement measures to avoid stress (when technically possible, by altering production conditions and work processes).
- Secondly, isolate stress factors by containment (to reduce noise), de-dusting and detoxification systems (including waste water treatment and incineration plants), etc.
- Only where such measures are not feasible (or are unreasonably expensive), take personal protection measures at the workplace (ear protectors, dust masks, dosimeters, etc.).

1. Reduce noise (noise emissions and vibrations).
   - Reduce noise from the work process itself by selecting suitable procedures and optimising process conditions (e.g. choice of suitable equipment).
   - Reduce noise from subsidiary activities (which are given less attention than the main activities but are often a major component in total noise).
   - Shield off otherwise unattenuable noise sources.
   - Demarcate noise areas.
   - Ensure that personal protection devices are actually used.
   - Make sure that persons exposed to noise undergo health/medical check-ups.
2. Optimise lighting and colours.
   - Match lighting intensity to the type of work.
     The relevant regulations (in the Federal Republic of Germany, the Guidelines on Workplaces) specify the minimum lighting requirements for different activities.
   - Make sure that other parameters are complied with, e.g. lighting level, light intensity distribution, dazzle

suppression, light direction and shadow, light colour and colour reflection, as laid down in the appropriate provisions (in the Federal Republic of Germany, the Workplace Regulation).

- Employ indirect lighting at VDU workplaces.
  Lights (if possible white, but certainly as light as possible) should be directed at the ceiling; only indirect light will then fall on the screens, thus obviating reflections (and resulting in less eye strain).
- Use lamps whose light spectrum is close to that of normal daylight.
  Light has a great physiological and psychological effect on man. With fluorescent light tubes with a very limited light spectrum, combine different lamps to approximate to the spectrum of natural daylight.
- Use electronic devices or three-phase switching to avoid flickering of fluorescent lamps.
- Select colour schemes on the basis of the features of the room (size, machines installed, floor structure, ceiling design, pillars and beams, windows, access routes, etc.), existing colours (machines, materials, products, vehicles, etc.), the division into work areas and rest areas, the number and kind of people working there, as well as the jobs to be done and the working times.
  Colour can have a very marked effect: for example, a light colour can make a low ceiling appear higher and a dark colour can make a high ceiling appear lower; green gives the impression of reducing noise and gives maximum light in dim conditions since its wavelength is in the range to which the human eye is most sensitive.

3. Regulate the room climate.
   - Adjust the air temperature, relative humidity, air speed and heat radiation to comfortable levels.
     Air pressure, being difficult to adjust, is not considered here.
   - Pay particular attention to and avoid:
     - draughts (differences in local air speeds)
     - asymmetric distribution of heat radiation
     - floors that are either too cold or too hot
     - excessive temperature gradients between head and foot level
4. Avoid hazardous substances at the workplace.

- Minimise hazardous emissions by:
  - selecting suitable work processes, materials, additives, process materials, etc.
  - selecting suitable inert gases (if necessary and/or possible)
  - optimising operating parameters
- Measure whatever hazardous substances are produced and comply with the appropriate legal provisions.
  Further details are given in "Klima und Luft am Arbeitsplatz" (Workplace climate and air), published by the Institut für angewandte Arbeitswissenschaft (Institute for Applied Labour Studies) in 1986; among other things, steps must be taken to ensure that the MAK values (maximum workplace concentration) and TRK values (technical guide concentrations) are not exceeded, the latter values being laid down for substances for which it is not at present possible to set MAK values (carcinogenic and mutagenic substances).
- Bear in mind hazardous substances which are not produced by the production process or the resulting products: emissions from the building fabric, wastes, alcohol, cigarettes, preservatives, etc.
- Demarcate those areas in which hazardous substances are emitted.
- Ensure that personal protection equipment is used.
- Give persons exposed to hazardous substances medical check-ups.
- Ensure that there is adequate ventilation.
  Ventilation is absolutely essential, even with very low emissions of hazardous substances, in order to avoid any long-term effects.

Ensure that equipment (including EDP hardware) and workplaces are ergonomically designed

5. Ensure that controls operate reliably.
6. Make components easy to use.
7. Ensure that emergency shut-off switches are clearly marked and easily accessible.
8. Design controls and displays and workplace dimensions in accordance with anthropometric principles.
   Pay special attention to space and sequence of operations, height, room for knees and feet, supports and field of vision in

order to avoid forced postures and other uncomfortable (static work) or unnatural postures. As a general rule, static work and one-sided and excessive muscular exertion are to be avoided.

9. Ensure that VDUs have adequate luminance, do not flicker excessively, have a stable image, are free of reflection, provide adequate adjustment and have enough contrast.

Improve safety at work

10. Ensure that the safety regulations are observed (including the wearing of personal protection equipment).
11. Make sure that the emergency shut-off equipment can be operated quickly, easily and safely and that it operates automatically to preset limits.
12. Install safety fences, barriers, etc. to ensure that workers do not enter the danger area around automatic machines (including digital control equipment and industrial robots) and that any stray objects thrown out by the machine do not endanger personal safety.
13. Take additional precautions if normal safety equipment has to be removed for technical reasons such as installation or maintenance. In such cases, eliminate any danger to personnel (e.g. as a result of equipment operating at crawling speed or being switched to manual operation).
14. Wherever possible, install automatic anti-collision equipment.
15. Demarcate and clearly signpost access routes, etc.
16. Ensure that safety markings (colours, symbols) are always clearly visible.
17. Provide anti-dazzle equipment and spatter protection.

Ensure ergonomic design of EDP programs

18. Ensure that the software is suited to the job.
    - Avoid unnecessary strain on the operator.
      The software must help the user carry out his task without the extra burden of coping with the idiosyncracies of the system (such as additional management and routine operations – e.g. with text-processing systems, having to remember where or under what code certain passages of text have been stored).
    - Match the mask sequence to the normal work step sequence.

- Match the type and form of input to the job in question (e.g. graphic input).
- Ensure that data organisation does not require the active involvement of the user.
- Use programmable function keys for frequently recurring strings of commands.
- Ensure that response times are of appropriate duration (provide a programmable response delay system).

19. Ensure that the system is self-explanatory.
    - Make sure that the system is readily comprehensible. At the request of the user, the purpose, method of operation, performance and requirements of the system must be explained.
    - Match the form of input to the level of knowledge of the user.
    - Provide input aids geared to the situation/process in the form of texts, graphics or images (or combinations thereof).
    - Whenever possible, use physical objects (symbols) for input purposes ("rubber eraser" or "paper basket", depending on the type of deletion, a "brush" for infilling, virtual machines for task reallocation, etc.).
    - Provide facilities for adjusting the information density in a display.
    - Ensure that background processes can be made visible.
20. Provide as wide a range of control facilities as possible.
    - Allow the user to initiate/interrupt/continue the dialogue; the system should take over only in exceptional cases.
    - Provide a choice of dialogue status (beginner, expert, etc.).
    - Conduct test runs to ensure that other data input can be corrected.
21. Pay attention to reliability.
    - Aim to achieve as close a match as possible between system dialogue and user expectations.
    - Ensure that response times are uniform and can be calculated.
    - Ensure confirmation that an input command is being processed.
    - Make sure that information can be obtained at all times on the system status.
    - Ensure that given actions always achieve the same results.
22. Take steps for dealing with errors.

- Make error display readily comprehensible for correction purposes.
- Ensure that error messages show the cause of the error and, as far as possible, the manner of correction.

Provide training in good time

23. Provide training to familiarise staff with new systems.
    Group learning has already been successfully employed in numerous companies, and is a good solution.
24. Organise work to take account of what has been learned in training.
    The training process is facilitated if work is organised in a way which solicits the skills and knowledge already learned and allows new tasks to be allocated to staff on an individual basis.
25. Extend training to cover not only professional expertise but also social aspects and encourage staff to develop their own faculties.
26. Clarify the objective of training by explaining hierarchical and parallel systems in addition to the organisational system in which each individual worker finds himself (to enable workers to see relationships within the system).

Observe six basic rules when designing a work system

27. Match workers to the demands of the job.
    The aim is to avoid creating stress by making excessive or inadequate demands on staff.
28. Avoid monotony and a rigid work pace.
29. Give staff sufficient room and organisational freedom to carry out their tasks.
30. Make each activity include planning, decision-making and monitoring aspects in addition to executive aspects.
    Each worker must have time to organise his work and monitor his own activities and must be included in decision-making and planning in accordance with his particular abilities, interests and expertise.
31. Avoid social isolation.
32. Organise operations so as to include team work (quality circles, workshop circles, training workshop, etc.).

Checklist No. 7: Canteen food

Nutritional diseases cost some DM 40 000 million every year in the Federal Republic of Germany. Heart disease, metabolic diseases, indigestion, rheumatism, gout, diseases of the stomach and intestines, diabetes, various forms of cancer, etc. are often connected with the wrong kind of diet. Despite all the scientists' and doctors' warnings and all the bad publicity in the press and on the television, people still:

- eat too much and too quickly;
- chew too little;
- eat too much animal fat and too little vegetable fat;
- eat too much white bread, tinned food, sugar and salt as against too few fresh vegetables, salads, potatoes and pulses.

"If the doctors are to be believed, excess weight and the wrong kind of diet are the main causes of illness in our affluent, Western society, after smoking, alcohol and stress." (E.R. Koch, Krebswelt, Cologne 1981, page 113)

Many illnesses cause a great deal of personal suffering for the sick and their families. They lower the quality of life and may cause other, sometimes serious problems. The many working hours lost through illness seriously affect productivity and lead, of course, to higher and higher contributions to health insurance schemes and increases in other expenditure.

A change of eating habits is considered by many doctors to be basic therapy, and is often enough to relieve or cure many illnesses without tablets or other medicines. Millions of workers eat at their place of work every day, and so canteen food offers a unique opportunity for them to eat healthy and tasty food, prepared according to the basic principles of healthy eating and containing enough vitamins, minerals, trace elements, fat, protein and carbohydrates. It can also be habit-forming in that dietary habits acquired at work may spill over into the home.

In purely business terms, a healthy worker can be a productive worker, while a sick worker still has to be paid while out of action. This is a point worth stressing in connection with attempts to widen the canteen menu to include more wholefood dishes.

Provide information

1. Inform workers of the effects of bad eating habits through:
   - information bulletins/circulars;

- posters on notice boards;
- lectures by nutritionists (home economists and nutritional scientists, health advisers, environmental counsellors, etc.);
- short but informative brochures for distribution;
- interesting literature/books available for loan in each department;
- visits to organic farms/alternative farming ventures.

2. Send round a questionnaire to find out what interest there would be in an alternative menu.
3. Never make changes without first providing information. The nutritional field is an area riddled with preconceived ideas which can only be influenced by specific and, as far as possible, objective and scientifically well-founded information. If you wish to eat healthily and enjoy your food at the same time, you need information on what your body requires, on essential nutrients and on what goes to make up your food.
4. Enlist the help of the personnel department, the works council and the works doctor.
5. Check the canteen food.
   - Check with the supplier how much time elapses between production and delivery of the food. The longer the time-lag between when the food is cooked and when it is delivered or eaten, the greater the loss of vitamins and minerals.
   - Check whether the menus provide sufficient quantities of average mineral, vitamin and trace element requirements.
   - Check percentages of carbohydrates, fats and proteins.
   - Determine how much sugar and salt the menus contain. The German Nutritional Society warns that we eat too much in general, and in particular too much fat, too much sugar and too much salt.
   - Determine what food additives are used.
   - Ensure that no "irradiated foodstuffs" are eaten.
   - Urge the use of higher quality foodstuffs.

   Encourage preference of products grown under controlled cultivation.
6. Have wholefood menus prepared.

   "Wholefood" is prepared in such a way that as many vitamins, minerals and essential nutrients as possible are preserved. This entails careful preparation, short cooking times and serving dishes to customers as quick as possible.

- A wholefood meal would contain, for example:
  - Salad to start with, to stimulate the working of the bowels and ensure easier digestion;
  - a vegetarian main course, with organically grown whole cereals;
  - a dessert comprising fruit or milk products (for calcium).
- Wholefood cooking uses only fresh products, as far as possible organically grown, cold-pressed oils, seasalt and, for sweetening, honey.
  "Wholefood cooking can pamper the tastebuds even of gourmets."

7. Indicate the fat and salt content and number of joules or calories on menus.

Improve the range of dishes and drinks

8. Offer alternative dishes:
   - Raw vegetable salad dishes;
   - vegetarian meals.

   Vegetarians live longer than men and women with conventional living and eating habits, and fewer of them die of heart and circulatory diseases or cancer. These were the findings of a five-year study by the German Cancer Research Centre in Heidelberg.
9. Check whether it would be economically viable for the canteen to have its own kitchen.
10. Have a look at nearby restaurants and cafés and persuade them to pay more attention to "healthy eating" when producing their menus.
    A survey of over 1000 canteens and nearly 2000 restaurants showed that the food on offer was much too substantial, too fatty and lacking in vitamins: compared with recommended menus, the energy content was 36 per cent too high in canteens and 71 per cent too high in restaurants, the fat content was 58 per cent too high in canteens and more than twice as high in restaurants, while the vitamin content was 40 per cent too low in canteens and 30 per cent too low in restaurants! (R. Griesshammer, Der Öko-Knigge, Reinbek bei Hamburg 1984, p. 150)
11. Check the contents of the drinks dispensers and replace drinks with a high sugar content by mineral water, etc.
12. Check other dispensing machines and replace unhealthy

foodstuffs by more healthy ones or extend the range of healthier foods (e.g. fruit, wholemeal biscuits, wholemeal wafers, fruit slices, muesli bars, etc.).

Provide other stimuli

13. On special occasions, such as parties and works outings, provide health foods, at least as an alternative. Wholemeal products can provide very tasty and healthy snacks/between-meal nibbles/menus.
14. Do not attempt to do everything at once but make a simple and unobtrusive start – e.g. wholemeal pasta, whole-grain rice, fresh salad daily.
15. Offer alternative breakfast foods, e.g.
    - wholemeal rolls,
    - yoghurt/curd cheese with dextrorotatory lactic acid, both of which are nourishing and easily digestible,
    - muesli.
16. Whenever possible, offer non-alcoholic in preference to alcoholic drinks at works and office "do's" (mineral water, fruit juices – make sure that they have a low sugar content – vegetable juices, etc.).
17. Provide pleasant surroundings.
    Greenery, the right lighting and carefully laid tables all make an important contribution to pleasant surroundings.
18. At conferences, meetings, etc. where there are several participants, offer nuts, dried fruits and fresh fruit, together with wholemeal biscuits as an alternative to the customary white flour/sugar biscuits.
19. Provide honey instead of sugar for sweetening.

Checklist No. 8: Environmental counselling for employees' households

Environmentalists have calculated that private households account for some 30 per cent of the total environmental pollution in the Federal Republic of Germany. Even if a similar figure may not apply to all the EC countries, it can safely be assumed that private households are to a substantial extent responsible for environmental problems – in the broadest sense, e.g. by producing refuse (approximately 250 kg per person per year), using water (140 to 150 litres per person per day), consuming energy, producing effluent pollution in the form of washing powders, cleansers and various other products (more than 2 million tonnes per annum get into the sewage), polluting the air with the solvents and propellent gases in paints and varnishes, thinners, adhesives and sprays, not to mention having wood/coal/oil heating and producing ever-increasing amounts of exhaust gases from growing numbers of motor vehicles, and, finally, polluting the soil with pesticides, fertilizers and thawing salt.

Faced with this situation, the individual must wonder what he or she can do to protect our environment, which is after all the very basis of our existence. It is very simple. Protection of the environment starts with each person in that (almost) everyone can:

- save many litres of water every day by being careful with it;
- refuse to use pesticides;
- make do with less packaging and without plastic bags;
- use returnable bottles instead of disposable bottles or tins;
- use far fewer chemicals in the household;
- be more environmentally aware when driving;
- purchase articles which help to protect, or at least do not harm, the environment and avoid those which are positively harmful.

If a few million of the people of Europe were to take heed of these words, there would very soon be a considerable improvement in the environment and thus in the quality of life of each and every person.

It is vital for the population to be informed and enlightened. At present, there is an all too frequent lack of understanding of what is going on and of advice which can easily be put into practice.

It is here that every company can provide vital assistance, by giving its staff the opportunity to benefit from environmental counselling in their own homes.

Provide opportunities for environmental counselling in employees' households

1. Appoint environmental counsellors to advise staff, or request them from another body, providing financial support where appropriate.
2. Consider discussing the matter with another company and employing a joint counsellor for the two firms.
3. Contact environmental organisations and urge the appointment of environmental counsellors.
4. Make sure that the counsellor has first-class qualifications and is politically neutral and objective.
5. Introduce the counsellor officially to staff and explain in detail the meaning and purpose of environmental counselling.
6. Collect information on financial assistance from the State. In the FRG, for example, financial support is available through official "job creation programmes".
7. Organise meetings and discussions with environmental counsellors and workers, on such topics as:
   - the use of chemicals in the household;
   - how to avoid creating waste;
   - how to save water and energy;
   - environmentally benign building and do-it-yourself principles.
8. Draw up rules of thumb for objective advice on the environment, taking care not to violate the competition rules.
   - Make advice unbiased and avoid negative criticism.
   - Recommend only those products or services which have been tested by neutral, reliable experts and proved to be environmentally safe (e.g. those with the "Blue Angel" symbol authorised by the Federal Environmental Agency).
   - Make no claims which are untrue or whose veracity cannot be proven.
   - Praise ecologically beneficial products or services rather than criticise those which harm the environment (see P.C. Mohr, Vier Faustregeln für den Umweltberater, Hamburg 1985).
9. Ensure that the information made available to the counsellor as part of his work is handled confidentially.
10. Bring pressure to bear on the city or local authorities to appoint environmental counsellors.

11. Make staff more aware of environmental problems by providing information geared to their specific needs.
    As far back as 1973, an opinion survey conducted under the auspices of the Commission of the European Communities showed an extraordinary degree of interest in the problem of the environment. In subsequent years, protection of the environment and the fight against pollution remained one of the three most important problems for Europeans – after unemployment and poverty (see: The Europeans and their Environment, published by the Commission of the European Communities, Brussels 1982, p. 2).

Give workers tips/advice on practical environmental protection

12. Save energy
    - Maintain the right room temperature. 1° C less saves 6 per cent energy.
    - Do not use tumble dryers, or, if you must, use machines with low power consumption.
    - Install thermostat radiator valves (up to 15 per cent energy can be saved).
    - Seal/insulate windows.
    - Keep radiators free.
    - Install boilers with low power consumption.
13. Reduce water consumption.
    - Install flow restrictors on taps.
    - Install water-saving devices in toilet cisterns.
    - Install single lever mixer taps.
    - Repair leaking taps and toilet cisterns.
    - Shower instead of having a bath.

    These measures can easily yield a saving of 10 000 litres of water per person per year in the home.
14. Be more pollution-conscious when washing clothes.
    - Do not use the pre-wash.
    - Wash at 60°C instead of boiling.
    - Use one-third less washing powder per cycle.
    - Wash only full loads.
    - Do not use softener or detergent-impregnated clothes.
    - Use washing powder for delicate fabrics rather than heavy duty detergents.
    - Buy washing machines with lower water and power consumption.

- Treat stains separately.

15. Use cleaning products, etc. more sparingly.
    - Use green soap or a mild all-purpose cleanser rather than WC or bathroom cleansers.
    - Treat scale deposits with acetic acid.
    - Do not use deodorant blocks in toilet pans or cisterns.
    - Unblock pipes and U-bends with plungers or specially designed rods rather than with chemical agents.
    - Wash non-greasy dishes in hot water, without washing-up liquid.
    - Use more green or soft soap as an all-purpose cleanser.
    - Avoid cleansers with bleach or disinfectant.
    - Clean window panes with water and a dash of vinegar or alcohol.
    - Clean floors which are not specially dirty with clear water only; if they are more heavily soiled, use a little green soap or mild all-purpose cleanser.
    - Protect untreated furniture with beeswax, linseed oil or shellac.
    - Do not use disinfectants.
16. Avoid waste.
    - Do not buy products with unnecessary packaging.
    - Wherever possible, use reusable packaging, e.g. returnable bottles.
    - Avoid plastic packaging.
    - Do not put chemicals into the dustbin.
    - Reuse or collect paper.
    - Collect glass for recycling.
    - Put kitchen waste on a compost heap.
    - Take used oil to special collecting points.
    - Make sure that collecting points are set up for paper, glass, special category refuse and used oil.
17. Use biological paints, dyes and wood preservatives.
    - Use natural resin paints.
    - In the home, use natural resin latex paints or synthetic resin latex paints which are low in pollutants.
    - Inside, avoid using chemical wood preservatives as far as possible.
18. Do not use poisons in the garden.
    - Do not use chemical pesticides.

- Treat pesticide residues as special waste and do not put them in the dustbin.
- Use natural manure whenever possible, e.g. compost, green manure or vegetable fertilizer.
- Compost organic waste.
- Do not use peat – bark humus and compost are alternatives.

All these and many more practical tips are taken from the "Öko-Sparbuch für Haushalt und Familie", Munich 1986. Written by M. Gege, H. Jung, H.J. Pick and G. Winter, it shows how members of the household can, by being more aware of their environment,
- save a great deal of money;
- protect their health, and
- make their own contribution to improving the environment.

Checklist No. 9: Economising on energy and water

In the energy-intensive sectors of industry, energy costs are one of the decisive factors affecting competitiveness, and in those areas where energy consumption is lower, they can be rationalised. With prices rising, the same applies to water, which is an energy "carrier" in many heating and cooling systems, a process agent in many plants, and, last but not least, important as a "carrier" of sanitary waste.

Taking a look at energy and water consumption in a company can generate new ideas for optimising the manufacturing process. If energy and water are consistently well managed, there are bound to be savings in costs and raw materials.

Planning energy and water-saving measures

1. Do an internal audit.
   Do you know where the company consumes most electricity, heat and water?
2. List consumers in order of estimated quantities consumed.
3. Find out the total cost of bought-in energy and/or water consumed.
   Work out as far as possible the cost of the water and energy used by each operating unit.
5. Collect all the figures centrally.
6. Set up a small project group (with special emphasis on staff in production, planning and purchasing).

Set objectives for economising on energy and water

7. Appoint people to be responsible for energy and water in a particular workplace, area, workshop, or department.
8. Get together with the project group and an energy adviser to formulate objectives for each area.
9. Say what financial savings are possible and discuss the possible effects of the proposed measures.

Select energy and water-saving measures which pay off in the short term

10. Install flow restrictors on taps.*
11. Install automatic shut-off valves on showers.*
12. Check for losses from leaking pipes and discharge points and repair them.*

13. Use temperature regulators on rinsing baths.*
14. Provide extra insulation for hot water pipes.*
15. Clean the surfaces of heat exchangers frequently for maximum efficiency.*
16. For monitoring purposes, install manometers, thermometers, flowmeters, expansion valves and flow restrictors wherever economically feasible.*
17. Make water and cooling water pumps work as a function of the flow rate.*

Select energy- and water-saving measures which pay off in the longer term

18. Install recooling plants instead of using the public water supply.*
19. Use individual water heaters whenever there is a considerable potential heat loss through storage or long pipelines.*
20. Separate the water supply according to quality and quantity (drinking, service and industrial water).*
21. Use direct cooling with outside air or closed coolant circuits instead of once-through cooling.*
22. In wash and shower rooms, install automatic cut-off thermostat valves for mixing.*
23. Install water treatment plants to recycle washing, service and rinsing water.*

Organisational measures to back up energy- and water-saving measures

24. Check washing facilities, showers and toilets regularly to ensure that there are no leaks.*
25. Turn off water points which are not needed.*
26. Repair leaking taps immediately.*
27. Ensure that hot water leaves the heating plant or distributor at a temperature not above 50° C. Hot water should be available to the consumer at a temperature not above 45° C.*
28. Use minimal amounts of cooling water; the less water, the higher the outlet temperature.*

* The asterisks indicate environmental protection measures which can usually be introduced easily and quickly to prevent or reduce costs.

29. Reduce the freshwater requirements of cooling towers to a minimum. Turn off cooling water circuits when they are not required.*
30. Turn off service hot water circuits if they are not needed over a period of more than four hours.*
31. Turn off circulation pumps for service water outside operating hours.*
32. If possible, produce separate internal costings for town water, in-house water, well water and circulatory water. Work out a "fair" quantity and cost distribution in accordance with amounts consumed.*
33. Adjust quantities needed for WCs, showers and rinsing baths.*

Set priorities

34. Compile the measures discusssed above at one particular point within the organisation, divided up into the above groups, i.e.:
    - organisational measures
    - measures which pay off in the short term
    - measures which pay off in the longer term
35. Monitor progress periodically.
36. Compare targets with what has actually been achieved.
37. Inform the workers of results in a short report.
38. Demonstrate energy savings achieved to interested groups both within and outside the department.

Continue saving

39. Do not be satisfied with what has been achieved.
40. Move on to the next stage.

Checklist No. 10: Product development

The purpose of product development is to adapt a company's range of goods and services to the needs of the market. The "needs of the market" are in many cases synonymous with the "needs of the environment", certainly for all products whose possible consequences for the environment make them subject to regulations (e.g. vehicles, detergents) or are at least subject to more critical appraisal by the consumer (e.g. packaging). But even for products where the pollution potential is less obvious, product development should take account of environmental aspects, as it is here where decisions are taken on what materials and processes should be used, i.e. the matters of direct importance to the balance of nature.

The following checklist allows both ecological and economic aspects to be considered during the product development process.

Use value analysis for ecological as well as economic purposes

1. Check whether the manufacturing process involves the exploitative consumption of non-regenerable raw materials. Example: water and air consumption
2. Check whether large amounts of energy are required for manufacture:
   - energy requirement per working hour,
   - energy requirement per product unit.
3. Check whether consumption, use and maintenance by the user will involve high energy consumption or air, water or soil pollution.
4. Check whether the materials used for the product will allow it to be easily integrated into the ecological and raw materials cycles. Pay special attention to the following:
   - potential for reactivating destroyed products,
   - energy requirement for reactivation,
   - unusable wastes,
   - energy requirement for waste disposal.
5. Check whether materials and components lend themselves to recycling.
   - Askarel transformers containing PCBs can be disposed of only on special category tips.
   - In view of the pollutants they contain (heavy metals), fluorescent and discharge lamps should be collected and returned undamaged(!) to the manufacturer.

When deciding on the material composition and design of products, bear in mind the ecological repercussions of production, use and disposal

6. Avoid using substances which are detrimental to the environment and find substitutes for hazardous substances (in consultation with the materials management department).
   - Replace cyanide electrolysis by a cyanide-free equivalent.
   - Replace antimony oxide (used for making textiles and plastics flame-retardant).
   - Replace antimony sulphite (used for brake linings).
   - Replace arsenic oxide (used as a refining agent for glass) by antimony trioxide.
   - Replace lead in friction bearings by lead-free alloys.
   - Replace lead used for soldering by tin or other processes.
   - Replace cadmium used for coating by zinc and aluminium.
7. Aim for standardisation to reduce the range of parts used.
   - Use DIN and other standardised parts.
   - Increase the number of multi-purpose parts.
8. Take ecological aspects into account when selecting materials and equipment.
9. Observe legal requirements and regulations in development work, e.g.
   - screws to be exported to Sweden must not contain cadmium,
   - particle board may contain only small quantities of formaldehyde.
10. Design products to minimise the amount of materials needed.
    - Reduce thicknesses of walls and plates, but without running any risks.
    - Reduce waste in cutting and non-cutting processes (e.g. rectangular rather than round shapes).
    - Reduce waste by flush positioning of blanks.
11. In chemical engineering, select the process which offers the most ecological advantages.
    - Sulphuric acid can be obtained from gypsum, kainite, hydrogen sulphide or sulphide ores.
    - Cellulose can be manufactured by the calcium bisulphite process (high level of SO_2 emission) or the magnesium bisulphite process (low level of SO_2 emission, MgO emission).

12. Optimise energy-efficient design, bearing in mind all preliminary production stages and the energy required for disposal.
    - Dimensions: small is better than large.
    - Form: aerodynamics affects energy consumption.
    - Optimise material content.
      - Less weight saves energy.
      - Ceramic elements improve heat insulation.
      - Sintered ceramic elements reduce fuel requirements.
13. Design products to facilitate disposal, with minimal use of the environment as a waste dump.
    - Minimise packaging.
      - For large-diameter grinding wheels use hexagonal packing cases, which require 15 per cent less wood compared with square cases.
      - Use standardised packaging in order to make optimum use of space in transport media and stores.
      - Select packaging material with the lowest energy input requirement.
      - Design packaging for multiple use.
    - Develop long-life products.
      - Increase the functional and stylistic life of products.
      - Increase the material-related life.
      - Design products to facilitate repairs and service.

Checklist No. 11: Materials management

The materials management department of a firm is responsible for supplies. It ensures that the firm is able to produce and deliver goods economically, and covers all value-added stages from purchasing to sales. It is responsible for procuring both consumer and capital goods, which often account for upwards of 40 per cent of a firm's costs. The material and other products purchased can be harmful, neutral or beneficial to the environment. The following checklist sets out the points which an ecology-oriented materials management department should consider.

Analyse the current situation as regards environmental pollution caused by the firm's purchases

1. Prepare a balance sheet in respect of materials and energy
   - Record operational data.
     - Record the materials used for production.
     - Show materials transformations during the production process.
     - Give results in terms of form, quantity and composition.
   - Record ecological effects.
     - Observe emissions and their ecological impact site.
     - Identify the effects on the area concerned:
       + transport and dispersal pattern,
       + persistence (time required for biological degradation),
       + accumulation (transport and concentration in the food chain),
       + possible transformation processes.
   - Draw up targets.
     - Plan accordingly.
     - Give priority to ecological considerations.
     - Design in-house materials and energy cycles.
2. Calculate environmental parameters for materials management.
   - Establish environmental elasticities giving the percentage increase in "environment take" (e.g. emissions of dangerous substances from the factory, amount of special-category waste, etc.) attendant on a 1 per cent increase in a specific purchasing volume.
   - Establish the recycling rate as a quotient of the proportion of recycled material and total material consumption p.a.

Formulate an ecology-oriented purchasing strategy

3. Replace environmentally hazardous materials in the production process (see also checklists for production technology and product development).
   - Replace asbestos in brake and coupling linings, seals, floor coverings and chemical products used in building.
   - Replace cadmium used in electroplating (surface protection) by low-cadmium high-purity zinc, galvanic aluminising or aluminium vapour treatment.
   - Replace chlorinated hydrocarbons in cold cleaning solvent by substances which do not pollute the waste water.
   - Replace transformers containing PCBs by air-core or silicon-filled types.
4. Use more ecological materials for general purposes, e.g.
   - wallpaper made from recycled paper,
   - low-pollutant paints,
   - low-lead and low-chromate anti-corrosion coatings,
   - salt-free substances for spreading on roads and paths, etc. in winter,
   - environmentally safe drain-cleaning substances,
   - products made from recycled plastics (e.g. plant pots, garden furniture, signpost bases, floor coverings, building sheeting),
   - paper towels and paper cleaning tissues,*
   - recycled paper for stationary (forms, letter paper, envelopes, folders),*
   - returnable bottles in canteens,
   - reusable crates for foodstuffs in canteens,
   - water-saving cisterns and shower fittings (see also checklist "economising on water and energy"),*
   - replace conventional fluorescent lamps with energy-saving lamps (e.g. three-band fluorescent lamps, compact fluorescent lamps, single-socket fluorescent lamps, halide lamps, high-pressure sodium lamps).*
5. Replace unecological office materials, in particular filing and organisational aids made of synthetic materials, by articles made of natural materials, e.g.

* The asterisks indicate environmental protection measures which can usually be introduced easily and quickly to prevent or reduce costs.

- cardboard or wooden filing trays,
- folders made of cardboard,
- files made of cardboard without plastic lamination, with separable covers and lever mechanism,
- wooden filing card boxes,
- waste-paper baskets (wood, basketwork or recycled paper) with separate compartments to enable paper to be collected separately,
- rulers made of beechwood with metal insert,
- wooden or metal stamps, stamp pads and stamp holders,
- pens with refills, refillable ink pens, fountain pens, untreated pencils,
- solvent-free glues, pastes, glue-sticks,
- water-based correction fluid.

Do procurement market research with the aim of replacing unecological products

6. Specify product requirements and collect information on products.
   - Identify in-house use of products and note the problems (e.g. particle board containing formaldehyde used for the tops of washing machines and dishwashers).
   - Note product components and their characteristics (e.g. ecotoxicological effect of PCBs in transformers).
   - Identify special characteristics of products (e.g. storage life, problems involved in storage and transport).
7. Collect information from suppliers, in particular details of production processes (e.g. short bath or long bath process in the textile industry; use of economical rinsing process in electroplating; use of magnesium bisulphide process instead of calcium bisulphide process in paper manufacture).
8. Collect information on alternative products from suppliers and industries.
   - Consult information sources on alternative products (see information at the end of this checklist).
   - Consider using institutes active in environmental protection for market research.
   - Analyse ecology-oriented specialised literature and journals (see information at the end of this checklist).
9. Consult own R & D and engineering departments about the possibility of using alternative materials.

Send out enquiries based on the results of the procurement market research

10. Decide on the number of firms to which enquiries are to be sent.
    - Ascertain the status of the required item in the ecological ABC analysis.
    - Decide how many national and international suppliers to consult (separately depending on the ABC status, e.g. A-items: 10 suppliers of which 5 abroad; B-items: 6 suppliers of which 3 abroad; C-items: 3 suppliers of which 1 abroad).
11. Decide what form the enquiries should take.
    - Use recycled paper for enquiry forms.
    - Formulate enquiry with special reference to:
      - the production process,
      - means of protecting the environment from pollutants,
      - location of production facilities,
      - instruments for ensuring that legal requirements are met,
      - legal provisions, consumer protection and test requirements in the various countries.
12. Evaluate answers by reference to ecological and economic considerations.
    - Check that the details supplied are complete.
    - Check price, quantity, delivery conditions and technical data.
      - Note details of pollutants and energy consumption during use, including pollutant volume and emission levels, and name information sources for pollution level classification.
      - Note materials where disposal might have an adverse effect on the environment.
      - Note any limits exceeded and name pollution factors.
      - Compare resource consumption with that of a competing product with comparable performance and range of uses; note any potential for reducing consumption.
      - Note how production materials might be reused, and how recycled materials might be used in production.
      - Note details of product life, model changes and savings of raw material resources and labour.

- Note disposal details (household waste or special-category waste).

13. Rank offers in terms of environmental acceptability.
    - Select scale of assessment.
    - Fix criteria weightings.
    - Decide on what associative conditions (if...then) apply.
    - Establish scale for rejection.

Negotiate with suppliers

14. Ascertain whether suppliers are prepared to reveal data relevant to the environment.
15. Establish whether suppliers are prepared to use returnable packaging.
16. Agree on type of packaging taking account of ecological considerations.
17. Agree on packaging design and delivery method.
18. Request clearance certificates for the products.
19. Agree on supplier's contribution towards disposal costs (see also "law" checklist).
20. Cooperate with trade and specialist associations (see information at the end of this checklist).

Store materials to take account of the potential risk to the environment

21. Lock up dangerous chemicals and substances.
22. Apply ecological principles in stores (e.g. low-exhaust fork-lift trucks, reusable transport cases).

Optimise the movement of materials to avoid wastage of resources

23. Select the packaging units best suited to the production process.
24. Recycle packaging material which cannot be reused.
    - Collect paper and cardboard for recycling.
    - Reuse packaging materials for own purposes.*
    - Send plastic packaging for recycling.

Checklist No. 12: Production technology

Production and manufacturing technology covers all plant and machinery used for the transformation and processing of raw materials and semi-finished goods and generally plays a decisive role as far as emissions from a factory are concerned. Ecology-oriented innovations help to reduce pollution caused by a factory and have economic advantages in that they reduce the input of materials, water and energy and the disposal costs for waste and sewage. They may also improve product quality and reduce production waste. In the medium term, effective ecological measures can also bring about an improvement in the company's image in the eyes of neighbours, customers and authorities.

Use ecological materials and processes

1. Get rid of particularly hazardous raw materials, processes and parts of the production programme or replace them with others which cause less pollution (see also checklists for materials management and product development). For example:
   - instead of the solvent trichlorethylene, which is a notorious health hazard, use trichlorethane or perchlorethylene, which are less polluting and save energy,
   - replace cadmium or chrome coatings by zinc,
   - in electroplating processes, replace zinc electrolyte containing cyanide by cyanide-free or acidic electrolyte,
   - replace conventional paints by low-solvent paints (water-based), high-solid systems or powder coatings,
   - use low-emission energy sources, e.g. low-sulphur fuels or light heating oil or gas instead of heavy heating oil.
2. For wet processes reduce the temperature or switch to low-temperature processes, e.g. use cold cleaning solvents and cold bleaching and dying processes.*
3. Avoid dry processes and the cooling of workpieces. Avoid intermediate storage by switching from non-continuous manufacture to a continuous process.*
4. Prepare fuels for optimum combustion, e.g. homogenise heavy heating oil (mechanically breaking down the oil into very fine particles).

* The asterisks indicate environmental protection measures which can usually be introduced easily and quickly to prevent or reduce costs.

5. Use additives which improve the yield from raw materials and/or reduce emissions, e.g.
   - combustion-promoting additives, which act as catalysts to optimise and accelerate combustion processes,
   - use steel converters which are oxygen-blown rather than air-blown.
6. Interrupt or change production as little as possible if this means that the plant has to be cleaned or heated.

Use "clean technologies"

7. Prevent emissions during delivery, storage, crushing and mixing of dust-producing substances by means of hermetic storage, transport and production facilities.
8. Use technologies which achieve a better input-output ratio.
   - Convert combustion equipment, e.g. use fluidised-bed combustion in energy production or back-pressure furnaces in iron production.
   - Use modern painting systems, which reduce splashing and boost efficiency from some 50 per cent for normal air-spraying to more than 95 per cent for dipping, rolling or flow coating.
   - In wet processes reduce the input of chemicals by using a weaker concentration and/or a smaller bath volume.*
   - The volume of treatment baths can be reduced by avoiding unnecessary voids in treatment vessels and by using a suitable method of getting the liquid to the product (e.g. via jets) or the product through the liquid. Generally speaking, the average chemical concentration depends on the workpiece with the maximum requirements. The average can therefore be reduced by limiting the range of activities, by suitable production planning and/or by a measurement and control technology which adapts the concentration to specific requirements.
9. Use modern measuring and control technology.
   - Automatic monitoring and measuring of the concentration of treatment or process chemicals reduces material, personnel and environmental protection costs, ensures consistent product quality and reduces waste and plant downtimes.*
   - Automatic clean water injection for rinsing and washing processes, adapted to the conductivity of the water, not only reduces the amount of clean water needed, but also

increases the level of useful substances remaining in the waste water and thus facilitates recycling (cf. 14). With hot processing stages there is also a saving of energy.*
  - In drying processes, automatically controlled production speed and exhaust air humidity, etc. saves energy and improves machinery utilisation and quality.*
  - Optimising combustion processes reduces emissions and improves combustion efficiency in energy production.*

10. Increase the lifetimes of treatment baths by
    - using (ultra-)filtration, flotation, ion exchange, electrodialysis, adsorption, electrolysis or precipitation of impurities,*
    - pre-rinsing workpieces (e.g. with hot water).*
11. Reduce leakages and faults causing emissions, by
    - regular safety checks,
    - using emission-reducing sealing materials and methods,
    - more frequent maintenance of equipment, pipes, pipe connections, pumps and shut-off devices,
    - information and training for workers.
12. Remove water mechanically from workpieces, e.g. by squeezing.
13. Increase energy efficiency by insulating, sealing or covering equipment with a high working temperature, e.g. reduce the surface of hot treatment baths by means of styrofoam balls (see also checklist "economising on energy and water").

Recover useful materials and heat (see also "disposal and recycling" checklist)

14. Do not mix effluents containing different substances, as this makes it more difficult to recycle or recover useful substances.
15. Increase the concentration of noxious effluents by sealing the equipment (in the case of air emissions) or cutting down on rinsing and cleaning water (in the case of wet processes), in order to facilitate recycling.
16. Recycle the useful substances contained in effluents for production or convert them into other useful products.
    - Re-use effluents in the production process.*
      In the case of surface treatment, for instance, vaporisation losses in hot treatment baths should be replaced by high-concentration rinsing water. In paper manufacture the water obtained through water removal is used for the preparation of raw materials (to swell the fibres).

- Recover useful substances and use them for specific processing stages, e.g. recovery of
  - heavy metals, acids, etc. from effluents by means of decentralised ion exchangers, reverse osmosis, ultrafiltration and vaporising plates,
  - acids and organic solvents from the exhaust air by using adsorbers or absorbers.
- Use slightly soiled water for pre-rinsing.*
- Re-circulate water several times over.*

17. Recover heat.
    - Use heat exchangers to exploit the exhaust heat in cooling and production water and exhaust gases, and the exhaust heat which accumulates under factory roofs and in certain rooms.
    - Circulate hot exhaust air back into the production or combustion process.

Avoid emissions by post-production environmental protection measures

18. Enclose equipment to avoid the release of pollutants.
19. Use more effective environmental protection equipment.
    In metal surface treatment, the rigorous application of water-saving measures gives scope for replacing the extremely unreliable flow-through plants by safe and efficient charge plants.
20. Use environmental protection equipment which produces little waste.
    For example, desulphurisation equipment produces reusable substances such as sulphur, sulphur dioxide, sulphuric acid or gypsum instead of sludge, and creates a smaller amount of waste for subsequent dumping.
21. Ensure that pollutant treatment equipment is working properly.
    Concentrate on regular maintenance and checks and on monitoring and alarm systems for checking levels in chemical containers, cleaning efficiency and the functioning of measuring electrodes, injection elements and mixers.
22. Reduce effects of leaks and faults in waste water treatment plant, by
    - automatic emergency production shutdown in the event of a fault; emergency catchment tanks, etc.,
    - connecting all drains to the waste water treatment system.

23. Recycle or reprocess wastes (see also "disposal and recycling" checklist); e.g. send
    - used acid to metal processing plants for ore extraction,
    - concentrates containing heavy metals to central processing plants,
    - metal or metal-bearing wastes (aluminium, steel, lead, cadmium, chromium, copper, mercury, zinc) to secondary processing plants,
    - plastic wastes to the plastics industry,
    - waste paper and glass to collection points or users,
    - sewage sludge to be used as farm manure or, where heavy metal concentration is too high, for the recovery of useful substances.

Checklist No. 13: Disposal and recycling

The shortage of tip space, which is becoming more critical every year, and the fact that it is politically not on to set up new tip sites, have brought home the point that environmentally acceptable waste disposal and the extensive use of recycling have become important factors in decision-making at all levels of business activity. Many firms already take these aspects into account at the product development stage, in the development and selection of manufacturing processes and in the purchasing of materials (see appropriate checklists). The following checklist sets out the points which firms must consider when making decisions on how to deal with wastes in a way designed to protect the environment.

Make waste disposal and recycling subject to systematic planning

1. Carry out an analysis of the current situation regarding materials to be disposed of, in the form of a materials and energy balance sheet.
   - Name, describe and identify residues.
     - Specify individual types of material.
       Examples: wood, textile, paper, leather, asbestos.
     - In the case of mixtures list the origins.
       Examples: production process, manufacture of main product.
     - Give details of characteristics.
       Examples: material composition; dimensions; physical, chemical and biological characteristics.
     - List physiological characteristics.
       Examples: colour; appearance.
     - List medical characteristics.
       Examples: acute toxicity; long-term toxicity.
     - List production characteristics.
       Examples: manufacturing process; degree of processing.
   - Classify residues.
     Examples: degree of aggregation; size relationship; origin; use and disposal possibilities.
   - Use residues key for classification purposes.
2. Check potential for avoiding waste by eliminating creation of harmful residues during production (see "production technology" checklist).

3. Check potential for reducing waste by reducing creation of harmful residues during production.
4. Check potential for using physical and chemical processes to transform waste into harmless substances and energies.
   Examples: mixture of methyl alcohol, formic acid, acetic acid and ester is heated to 900–1000° C to form carbon dioxide and water.
5. Check potential for recycling waste and pollutants into own or external production (see also "production technology" checklist).
6. Check dispersal of wastes.
   - Test dilution effect (emission and air pollution).
   - Test concentration.
7. Check recycling potential in own and other companies (see also "production technology" checklist).
   - Ascertain how flexible the production organisation and process set-ups are in terms of coping with recycling requirements.
   - Estimate effects of recycling on income and expenditure.
   - Ascertain recycling potential in terms of the company's range of products and services.
     - Consider and analyse quantitative changes.
     - Analyse structural changes.
     - Study effects of design and packaging.
       + Do not use alloys which are unsuitable for recycling.
       + Reduce proportions of non-ferrous metals.
       + Use corrosion-resistant metals.
       + Ensure that the various components can be separated easily.
     - Bear in mind the varying nature of raw materials.
     - Consider the possibility of changing production processes.
   - Notify waste disposal exchanges of any substances which cannot be recycled in own production process.
     Examples: waste disposal exchanges organised by the VCI (German Chemical Industry Association) and the DIHT (German Chamber of Industry and Commerce).
   - Report residues to recycling information systems.
     Examples: DORIS – Dornier-Recycling-Informations-System; AWIDAT – Abfallwirtschaftsdatenbank des Umweltbundesamtes, Berlin.

– Play an active part in recycling management.

Ensure that recyclable materials are monitored by integrating the recycling principle into materials management and storage (see "materials management" checklist)

8. Set up residue management system to coordinate all recycling activities.
9. Organise collection and provide receptacles.
   – Reduce volume of waste by using compaction containers.
   – Set up used oil collection points.
   – Organise separate collections of paper, plastics and aluminium.
   – Collect solvents, solutions, acids and dyes.
   – Shred waste computer paper for use as packing material.
   – Convert unsuccessful photocopies into note-pads.*
10. Ask suppliers and manufacturers for product and safety information sheets (DIN 52900).
11. Allow employees to use collection points for any materials they might have for recycling.

Amend general terms of business in conjunction with suppliers (see "law" and "materials management" checklists)

12. Add to general purchasing conditions a clause making suppliers liable for the environmental acceptability of their products.
13. Add clauses guaranteeing that products purchased can be disposed of without undue expense.
14. Obtain confirmation that suppliers will take back disposable containers.
15. Add a clause requiring suppliers to provide full information on materials and product characteristics.
16. Add an exclusion clause ensuring that the purchasing firm is not liable in the event of the supplier infringing his legal obligations.

Check disposal companies

17. Check the bona fides of disposal companies.
18. Check that disposal companies are legally bound to insure themselves and that your own firm will not be liable in the case of improper disposal (see "insurance" checklist).

19. Ask to see waste disposal firms' permits.
20. Ask disposal firms what conditions have been imposed on them by the authorities and make spot checks that these are being met.
21. Keep internal records corresponding to the papers accompanying loads of waste for disposal.

Checklist No. 14: Company vehicles

The vehicles operated by a company are there to provide safe and reliable means of transport for the various departments. Cars and lorries play a major role in air pollution and are the cause of what may often be an unbearable noise nuisance for millions of people.

More pollutants enter the air from vehicle exhaust pipes than from all smokestacks in the Federal Republic of Germany put together. These include 6.2 million tonnes of carbon monoxide, 1.3 million tonnes of nitrogen oxides and 650 000 tonnes of hydrocarbons, including 50 000 tonnes of carcinogenic benzole. The effects on the health of people and the environment are well known: lung diseases, damage to the respiratory organs, blood count disorders, circulatory disorders and forest damage, to name only the most important.

This means that every litre of fuel not consumed by a vehicle and every reduction in the exhaust fumes released by combustion and in the noise caused by vehicles will be to the benefit of man and his environment. The following measures will be of assistance.

Buy low-pollution vehicles

1. Buy vehicles which are equipped with an efficient three-way catalytic converter. Numerous tests have shown that cars with catalytic converters generate some 90 per cent less noxious substances like carbon monoxide, hydrocarbons and nitrogen oxides. So long as soot filters are not available, diesel vehicles cannot be recommended as an alternative to cars equipped with catalytic converters. While it is true that diesel vehicles consume less fuel, they are also responsible for emitting carcinogenic hydrocarbon compounds. The extent of the cancer hazard is still a matter for discussion, but preventive environmental protection should err on the safe side. The fact remains, though, that a diesel car is still preferable to a petrol car without a catalytic converter.
2. Make exhaust and noise levels one of the company's purchasing criteria.
   - Compare exhaust levels, as there are considerable differences.
   - Obtain information from the Federal Environmental Agency.
3. Do not specify metallic paintwork.*

Aromatic hydrocarbons make metallic paints a health hazard during spraying; pollution is caused by solvent vapours.

4. For long journeys try to use 5-gear vehicles.*
5. Fit vehicles with low-noise and long-lifetime exhaust systems. Systems are available which keep noise below specific limits and are guaranteed service-free for two years or 75 000 km.
6. Use approved-quality remould tyres with the "Blue Angel" symbol.*
   In the Federal Republic of Germany more than 300 000 tonnes of old tyres pile up every year, and burning them pollutes the environment. Remould tyres use 80 per cent of the old tyre, with a significant saving in raw materials.

Re-equip existing vehicles and service them with environmental considerations in mind

7. Fit a catalytic converter or an exhaust recirculation system.
8. Fit petrol vehicles with transistorised ignition systems.*
   Conventional contact-breakers wear quickly, reducing engine performance and increasing petrol consumption. With a transistorised ignition system, you can be sure that the optimum values as originally set will be maintained for 40 000 km. Conversions sets are also available.
9. Use brake and clutch linings which do not contain asbestos.
10. Fit a device which cuts off fuel supply when the driver takes his foot from the accelerator pedal, saving up to 20 per cent fuel consumption.*
11. Fit a device to switch off the engine whilst waiting at traffic lights, etc.*
12. Have vehicles serviced regularly.
13. Check tyre pressure at regular intervals.*
    A 0.5 bar difference from the prescribed figure can increase fuel consumption by 5 per cent.
14. Change petrol vehicle sparking plugs regularly and if possible use broad-band plugs.*
    Sparking plugs play a major role in achieving optimum combustion of the fuel-air mixture.
15. Regular replacement of the air filter reduces fuel consumption by up to 10 per cent.

* The asterisks indicate environmental protection measures which can usually be introduced easily and quickly to prevent or reduce costs.

16. Adjust carburettor properly.
A badly adjusted carburettor can increase fuel consumption by up to 20 per cent, with a corresponding increase in exhaust fumes.
17. Wash engine only at garages or filling stations.
18. Dispose of used oil properly.
19. Use unleaded petrol.*
Manufacturers, automobile clubs and filling stations can provide information on whether unleaded petrol is suitable for a particular vehicle.

Adopt an environment-minded driving style

20. Do not drive aggressively or at high revs.*
Driving with a high engine speed consumes 25 per cent more fuel than a restrained driving style and produces twice as much carbon monoxide. Engine noise is also greater.
21. Drive smoothly and with foresight.*
Tests have shown a driver in a hurry to consume 40 per cent more fuel (and money) over a 28 km stretch of urban road with 32 sets of traffic lights – saving a mere 7 minutes.
22. Drive at a constant speed, even on motorways.*
On a test journey, a fast driver in a hurry needed 175 litres of fuel for 1550 km, whilst a slower driver consumed only 125 litres, a saving of 50 litres of fuel and 12.5 kg carbon monoxide emission. The difference in time for the journey was 1½ hours.
23. Change gear as soon as possible and use the most economical gear.*
Use first gear for setting off only and change rapidly into second, third and fourth gear.
24. Switch off the engine at traffic lights, level crossings, etc. where waiting time is longer than 30 seconds.*
25. Drive with foresight to make optimum use of synchronised traffic lights.*
26. Do not warm up a cold engine by letting it tick over; set off immediately, as the engine warms up more quickly when the vehicle is being driven and the automatic choke is switched off earlier.*
27. Do not fill the petrol tank up to the brim.
28. Use the choke carefully.*
When the outside temperature is 20°C do not use the choke. At 0°C push the choke half way in after 30 seconds and

completely in after 2–3 minutes. When the choke is out twice as many hydrocarbons and nine times as much carbon dioxide is produced. (See E.R. Koch, Umweltschutz zu Hause, Munich 1984, p. 233.)

29. Switch off fans in traffic jams.
When the fan is switched on up to 25 per cent more carbon monoxide and up to 36 per cent more hydrocarbons get into vehicles.

Plan journeys with environmental considerations in mind

30. Avoid short journeys.*
Short journeys consume a very large amount of fuel. When the engine is cold fuel consumption straight after setting off is around 40 litres per 100 km, after 1 km it is still around 20 litres per 100 km, and normal consumption is reached only after 4 km.
31. Use public transport for shopping expeditions into cities; use "park and ride" facilities.*
The German motoring association (ADAC) has calculated that on Saturdays when shops are open 75 per cent of vehicles driving through city centres are looking for a parking space.
32. Offer training in environmentally aware and economical driving, particularly in companies running lorries or a large number of cars and vans.*
33. Organise a competition to find the most economical drivers.*
34. Remove roofracks when not required.*
The additional fuel consumption of a family saloon travelling at a constant 130 km/h is over 12 per cent with an empty roofrack, up to 20 per cent with a loaded roofrack and covering sheet and up to 25 per cent with a loaded roofrack without a covering sheet.
35. Encourage car-pooling.*
If 4 people share a car for a daily journey up to 70 per cent of travelling costs can be saved, in addition to the substantial reduction in pollution.

Checklist No. 15: Building

One necessary aspect of company activity is investment in buildings for production, marketing, administration and other sides of the business. Regardless of its size, every structure impinges on nature in the broadest sense. Given that a building not only has to meet working requirements, but at the same time – and almost equally importantly – is required to present or improve the firm's image, market profile and status, as well as serving to boost its employees' morale, it would appear that investing firms really have no option but to consider both economic and environmental aspects when planning new buildings. The following recommendations show that the two aspects are not incompatible.

Preliminary planning

1. Consult an experienced specialist (architect specialising in environmentally benign building) from the outset.
2. Check the proposed site for negative factors and use only suitable sites.
   - Establish whether there is already any pollution (water, soil, air, climate) by inspecting the site and whatever environmental data is held by authorities, health departments, institutes, etc. and by taking measurements.
   - Have sites surveyed for a geopathogenic zones (fault zones) by a qualified geobiologist (diviner) or radiesthetist.

Formulate an environmentally aware building concept

3. Make the building harmonise with the landscape and with local building styles.
4. When fixing form and position of the building and arrangement of rooms, take account of topography, climatic conditions and direction (e.g. passive use of solar energy by means of windows facing south and closed facades facing north).
5. Bear in mind the results of the geobiological survey when planning the building layout.
   - Do not position workplaces above hidden fault zones.
   - Position roads, paths, storage areas and toilets, etc. above fault zones.
6. Plan internal organisation and working procedures so that
   - one workplace does not adversely affect another (e.g. noise, dust, fumes),

- waste disposal and recycling policy is practicable.
7. Incorporate variety into facade design.
8. Provide for green areas within the buildings.
9. Replace any vegetation which has to be destroyed by training creepers up facades and by "green" roofs.

Use minimum-pollution building materials

10. Observe the following points when selecting building materials:
    - pollution and health hazards during production (e.g. wastage of resources, energy consumption, emissions, toxic by-products),
    - pollution and health hazards attendant on use of the materials (e.g. painters exposed to solvent vapours),
    - pollution and health hazards involved in the subsequent use of the buildings (e.g. respiratory diseases caused by formaldehyde fumes),
    - pollution and health hazards involved in removing building materials (e.g. lung cancer caused by asbestos fibres; air pollution caused by burning plastics).
11. Where possible use natural materials with good physical characteristics (e.g. wood, clay, bricks and natural stone).
12. If the use of less ecological materials is unavoidable, use them only for specific purposes (e.g. use steel and reinforced concrete only for load-bearing and not for ordinary walls).
13. Ensure optimum heat insulation in all cases.

Take account of ecological aspects when planning fittings and installations

14. Formulate alternative plans for all sections, taking into account local factors (including cost-benefit and environmental impact assessment).
15. In connection with lighting give priority to health aspects (see also "working conditions" checklist).
    - Ensure that all workplaces have daylight.*
    - For windows use glass which lets through UV-rays.
    - Ensure that natural lighting is available for corridors and stairways.*
    - For additional artificial light at the workplace use lights which match the natural daylight spectrum.*

16. Avoid electrical installations which create hazards.
    - Restrict electrical installations to the necessary minimum.
    - Use star rather than ring circuits.
    - Use sheathed cables.
17. Plan heating, air conditioning and ventilation systems with an eye to energy saving and health protection criteria (see also checklist on "economising on water and energy").
    - Ensure that all windows at workplaces can be opened.
    - Restrict air conditioning to the strict minimum.*
    - Use low-temperature heating systems only.*
    - Give preference to radiant heat (e.g. hot air in underfloor cavity blocks) rather than fan heaters.
    - Exploit all heat recovery and heat-power combination possibilities.*
18. Plan plumbing installations to economise on drinking water (see also "economising on energy and water" checklist).
    - Avoid use of drinking water (groundwater) for production. Where possible use river water, sea water, rainwater or treated waste water.
    - Reduce drinking water consumption by using "grey" water (e.g. use waste water from showers to flush toilets).
    - Separate rainwater and dirty water.
    - Use rainwater for washing and cleaning.
    - Use rainwater to water gardens and grounds.
    - Channel rainwater through a pond.
    - Separate and reprocess industrial sewage water.
    - Equip toilet cisterns, showers, washbasins, etc. with water-saving devices.*
19. Give priority to reducing the volume of waste (see also "disposal and recycling" checklist).
    - Introduce a sensible and practical system of separate waste collections.
    - Eliminate hazards caused by special-category wastes.
    - Send waste for raw material recovery.
    - Compost and make use of organic wastes.

* The asterisks indicate environmental protection measures which can usually be introduced easily and quickly to prevent or reduce costs.

Make building surrounds as natural as possible

20. Store excavated topsoil carefully and use for landscaping.*
21. Keep surfaced areas (roads, parking spaces, yards) to the necessary minimum.
22. Do not seal surfaces by using concrete or asphalt, etc.; use interlocking sett paving or compacted gravel.
23. Use indigenous plants suited to the site.
24. Reduce energy requirement for the building by planting hedges and trees as wind shields.
25. Avoid excessive heat exposure by planting deciduous trees to the south of the building.
26. Use large pieces of land as wildlife habitat.
27. Do not use chemical plant protection substances.

Checklist No. 16: Finance

In a firm committed to environmentalist management, the question of finance is of strategic importance, quite apart from the classic aspects of conventional financing and auditing. The finance department can be seen as a "critical partner" of the technology and procurement departments in particular. The job of the finance department is to enter into a dialogue with the other corporate sectors and take a close look at whether the environmental protection element has been borne sufficiently in mind in the planning stage and in the product itself before any major investment decision is taken and before any major item is purchased. After all, integrated environmental protection makes sense in business terms too, leaving the use of environmental technology pure and simple as a second-best solution (not only in ecological terms).

Preventive environmental protection is a point to be borne in mind in respect of public financing aid too. Integrated environmental technology is the most important future-oriented aspect in the field of government aid for environmental protection. As a result, more and more manufacturers of non-polluting plant and products are receiving state aid. In other words, the finance department should check the environment angle out when planning its marketing strategy and not only in terms of adapting to environmental protection requirements.

As regards the financing of environmental protection measures in the United States, the United Kingdom and the Federal Republic of Germany, the situation is that the United Kingdom basically has only research and development programmes; in the United States the efforts of the federal authorities are concentrated on selected areas of the environment; in other words, the finance which is available in these two countries is mainly in the form of investment grants. The situation is different in the Federal Republic of Germany, where the generally high level of environment protection requirements is reflected in the funds available, which cover virtually all sectors of the environment and comprise a wide range of financing instruments, from marginally cheaper loans through special write-down arrangements to investment subsidies (the latter being granted only – in accordance with the "polluter pays" principle – in exceptional cases, eg. demonstration projects).

Do the right groundwork before investing in environmental protection.

1. Be sure about what is meant by investing in environmental protection.
   Generally speaking, this kind of investment is expected to bring about a reduction in the volume and noxiousness of waste water or air emissions or solid waste and to avoid damage to the soil or remove existing damage. The point of reference is normally the situation of the firm vis-à-vis the environment before the requisite investment is effected.
2. Whenever investment is planned, ascertain whether
   - it relates to environmental protection, or
   - it will increase pollution.
3. Whenever investment in environmental protection is being planned, ascertain whether
   - it is geared exclusively to protecting the environment, or
   - it will also enhance the firm's production capacity (i.e. integrated environmental protection).
4. Even under the pressure of environmental protection obligations, do not simply accept proposals for the acquisition of environmental protection technologies pure and simple, but find out whether
   - a similar or even better effect can be achieved by the earlier replacement of existing production plant and the acquisition of new, non-polluting machinery, and
   - environmental protection agencies are prepared, if necessary, to grant a longer stay of execution to facilitate an integrated approach.

   A great deal of tenacity required here, as environmental technologists and environmental agencies tend to prefer conventional solutions, i.e. those geared exclusively to protection of the environment.
5. If a particular investment is likely to increase pollution, find out whether
   - there is a lower-pollution alternative ("integrated environmental protection"),
   - all the likely costs caused by additional pollution have been properly included in project costing.

   There is a widespread tendency in practice for no account to be taken of such elements as the inevitable steep rise in the future in the costs of disposing of special-category waste; changes in environmental threshold limit values, which rarely remain in force for more than five years; entirely new investment constraints in the foreseeable future; savings in raw materials, auxiliaries and consumables by internal recycling; savings in energy and dumping costs by recycling.

6. Give preference to dynamic investment costing methods, e.g.
   - the capital value method, and
   - the internal interest rate method.

   In practice, static depreciation reference calculations and cost comparison calculations still predominate, according to a survey on recycling in industry. These usually discriminate against long-term projects, which only bear fruit in later years.
7. Introduce specific costing items for environmental protection. Proper costing in terms of environmental protection is not a sign of inadequate environmental awareness, but simply a basic precondition for investment decisions which are both rational and efficient in business and ecological terms. However, a sharp rise in environmental protection costs is not in the first instance a consequence of excessively high protection requirements, but rather a sign of an over-conventional approach to adapting to those requirements. The most common mistakes are:
   - Relying exclusively on end-of-pipe technologies (the result being an exponential increase in costs);
   - Paying attention only to the one part of the operation where the problem arises (with the result that the cost effect for every new environment problem is cumulative).

   The firm's financial management must keep a critical eye on environment protection cost trends and, should costs increase dramatically, call for a report on rationalisation potential. This can have a major effect on making staff more environment-and cost-conscious.

Make full use of environmental protection promotion programmes

8. Bear certain important basic principles in mind: Do not start investing before the aid application has been lodged.

   With some of the most attractive aid programmes, a start cannot be made on investing until state aid has been granted. Where time is of the essence, it is worth explaining the reasons and asking for leave to start earlier.

9. Take advantage of general aid schemes at national level.
10. In the United Kingdom, take a look at aid available for commercial research and development projects in the environment protection field.
    The Department of the Environment's Environmental Protection Technology (EPT) unit offers grants of 25 per cent or 50 per cent (for joint projects involving a number of firms) for projects which
    - aim to develop environmental protection technology
    - would not be feasible if funding were not available
    - are covered by selected priority areas.

    Unfortunately, though, the sum total of the funding available is not likely to be more than two million pounds a year.
11. In the United Kingdom, take a look at special waste recycling programmes.
    Commercial research and development projects concentrating on waste recycling are more likely to qualify for central and regional support programmes in the UK (contact the Department of the Environment in London, the Water and Environmental Protection Division in Cardiff and the Civil Engineering and Water Services Division in Edinburgh). Financial assistance is also available for waste recycling as a means of saving primary energy (Energy Technology Support Unit in Didcot, Oxon) or for improving the competitiveness of UK industry (Department of Trade and Industry in London and regional offices in Scotland and Wales). Here too, funds are only available for research and development projects. In all cases, the assistance takes the form of grants of up to 50 per cent of the investment costs, although again, the amount of money available each year is not likely to be very great.
12. Take advantage of all the counselling services offered by central or regional agencies or by cooperative institutions.
    The Department of the Environment's EPT unit in London offers general advice on environmental protection priorities (this is an important point in terms of business investment planning) and on marketing opportunities for environment-friendly projects and installations (important for firms with the requisite marketing plans). What may be even more important is the willingness of the EPT unit to arrange contacts with other firms working towards the same ends, or with government

specialists. Firms with up to 200 employees and with environmental protection problems (more specifically recycling) may qualify for counselling aid from the Department of Employment's Small Firms Service (further information from the local Small Firms Centres). Firms should also make use of the Local Enterprise Agencies' expertise.

13. In the USA, investigate the availability of government aid, especially in relation to waste water projects.
    Of more general and supra-regional importance in the USA is the Federal and State Construction Grants Programme, which was originally conceived only for government projects, but which since 1984 has also supplied financial aid for industrial waste water treatment installations designed not just for industrial waste waters. Funding takes the form of a grant towards investment costs up to a current maximum of some 55 per cent.
    In addition the States and local authorities can issue tax-privileged loans to finance measures to protect the environment.
    Given the powerful position of the states and frequently of the counties too in environmental policy matters, it would undoubtedly be worthwhile getting in touch with these authorities for full information on regional or local aid programmes for investment in environmental protection technology.
    These may also form a basis for incentive programmes; California, for example, a State noted for its vigorous environmental policy, offers the following schemes:
    - Industrial investment bonds floated by local or state agency for new development to provide capital infrastructure.
    - Capital Pollution Control Financing Services (waste control) which give loans and float bonds to buy equipment.
    - Clean Water Act grants.
    - University of California grants for "excellence" to industry groups.
    - Small business grants for study in hazardous waste reduction, recovery, and treatment technologies.
    - "Loan guarantee" by Small Business Development Corporation acting as loan broker for hazardous waste reduction projects.
14. Investigate the cost advantage of Emissions Trading in the USA.

For clean-air projects, substantial savings can often be made by joining forces ("bubble") or trading ("offset") with other firms. The advantage can even make up for what may sometimes be a substantial expenditure of time and effort on the bureaucracy involved in a bubble-project.

Financial advantages can also be obtained from "banking", which facilitates the sale of any part of emissions reduction which goes beyond the government requirement. Information is available here from the state environmental protection authorities and from the regional offices of the Environmental Protection Agency (EPA).

15. Get information on funding from European Community sources.
    - The Commission of the European Communities can grant subsidies for model projects (including in integrated environmental protection), but the kitty is small, there are lots of Member States and there are major environmental shortcomings everywhere.
    - The European Investment Bank in Luxembourg has interesting loan conditions for investment in environmental protection, both in ECU and in a variety of foreign currencies.

    Despite the fact that the European Investment Bank's loan interest conditions are not subsidised from public-sector budgets, they are often better than those offered by national banks as the Investment Bank can refinance its activities without any restrictions at all European finance centres and on the Eurodollar market, and is subject to fewer tax restrictions than many of the national commercial banks.

    The Commission of the European Communities has a programme of joint environmental activities, to which the following points apply. Applications for funding for demonstration projects should be addressed to the Commission of the European Communities in Brussels with copies for the national authorities, who are informed direct from Brussels. As in all progammes to do with demonstration installations, it is most important here to stress the demonstration or model character of the investment. The programme is funded to the tune of some 13 million ECU per year.
16. In an age of cross-border investment activities, take a look at what other countries have to offer.

When planning foreign investments, it is worth taking a look in good time at the way environmental protection technology is encouraged in other countries, especially within the European Community. A number of countries offer highly interesting programmes. We shall take a look here at what the Federal Republic of Germany has to offer.

- Special write-down facilities for environmental protection investments; it is particularly worthy of note that
  - environmentally benign production installations can in certain cases qualify for additional write-down provisions;
  - generally speaking, recycling plant can even qualify when the firm is paid for the scrap or residual substances delivered to the plant;
  - subsequent manufacturing costs may even have a productive effect; the important thing is just that the effects should arise exclusively from environmental protection reasons;
  - the high initial write-down rate (60 per cent) can be recovered over the 5-year depreciation period if it is not claimed in the first year.
- Low-interest loans from the ERP special fund, the Kreditanstalt für Wiederaufbau in Frankfurt and the Deutsche Ausgleichsbank in Bonn;
  - These may well offer the best loan conditions (normally up to two percentage points below the level payable on the capital market) for "normal" investments at national level;
  - They can also be granted for environmentally benign production plant;
  - They are uncomplicated and usually more favourable than loans available from commercial banks;
  - The rate of interest is stable over ten years or more and there is plenty of money available: something like DM 3500 million in 1988.
- Subsidies for demonstration installations from the investment programme run by the Federal Ministry for the Environment, Nature Protection and Reactor Safety in Bonn.
- Subsidies for research and development projects from funds available from the Federal Ministry for Research and Technology in Bonn.

   - Investment-boosting programmes run by the Federal States of Baden-Württemberg, Bavaria, Berlin, Hamburg, Hessen, North-Rhine-Westfalia, Rhineland-Palatinate and Schleswig-Holstein; these programmes are often more attractive than the national programmes, but the volume of funds is usually very limited, which means that they are often reserved for selected environment policy measures.
17. Take a good look at each Federal State's business aid programme if you are experiencing financing problems with environment-friendly products or production plant.
    Innovative production methods of this kind are often given higher priority in business development programmes so long as there are long-term market openings. But you will have made sure about that already (!).
18. Obtain additional information and clarify the most important aid concepts:
    - e.g. model/demonstration projects: already tried and tested at full scale, not yet used in an identical area under identical conditions, and of more than individual interest;
    - e.g. integrated environmental protection: less pollution by new production plant without any special additional environmental protection facilities.

Checklist No. 17: Law

Private law provides the businessman with the means of putting his personal ideas on ecological management into practice in his dealings with staff, suppliers and customers in the form of contractual agreements, e.g. to purchase or market only products with mainly pro-environmental characteristics.

Private law also give the businessman the right to protect himself against damage to his goods or to his firm, his land, water or water bodies resulting from atmospheric pollution and soil or groundwater contamination, and to demand legal compensation for the damage suffered. For instance, a company whose business it is to supply people with water can demand reimbursement of the cost of decontaminating water which has been polluted by oil or waste products. We are now seeing the introduction throughout Europe of a private-law product liability principle which, regardless of the negligence element, provides for liability for damage caused to the environment by a product defect.

At the same time, the state expects all businessmen to adopt an attitude of ecological awareness with its increasingly specific laws and regulations on the protection of the environment. Companies and businessmen may be subject to:

- claims for compensation
- plant closures
- fines
- prison sentences

The treaty of 25. 3. 1957 establishing the European Economic Community (EEC Treaty) also lays down powers and authority in the field of environmental protection legislation. With the entry into force of the Single European Act on 1 July 1987, protection of the environment has been placed on a firm footing with the European Community affirming responsibility for environmental protection. One of the aims of the Single European Act is to "preserve, protect and improve the quality of the environment, to contribute towards protecting human health and to ensure a prudent and rational utilisation of natural resources". What is now needed is acknowledgment of protection of the environment as a European constitutional principle.

Take steps to comply with official regulations

1. Comply with environmental laws dealing with the release of

substances into water and into air, and with noise abatement and waste disposal.

2. Appoint a member of the staff to check compliance with laws, regulations and official instructions on environmental protection and to follow developments in legislation (see also the "in-house environmental protection arrangements" checklist).
   - The member of staff must be well versed in technical and legal matters.
   - He or she must be informed of all existing laws, regulations and official instructions in the field, and must be given ongoing training facilities.
   - He or she must have direct access to the company's decision-makers.
   - He or she should present written reports at least once a year.
3. Introduce company guidelines for environmental protection, and in particular give every member of the management responsibility for taking action to prevent damage to the environment in his/her department (see also "in-house environmental protection arrangements" checklist).
4. Defer plant start-up until official approval has been granted. Take the plant out of operation as soon as the conditions for the granting of approval cease to exist.
5. Remember that the authorities must be given the requisite information to enable them to become involved in environmental problems. In legal terms, furnishing proof that the authorities had been notified and had raised no objection may clear the firm of liability and head off any legal sanctions.
6. Carry out measurements to check that thresholds are not being exceeded, and keep full records.
   Legislation may also stipulate that government agencies must be allowed to carry out measurements of, say, industrial noise emission or wastewater composition. There may, for example, be a statutory obligation in certain circumstances
   - to have pollution levels measured, the results passed on to the authorities and records kept;
   - in the case of certain plants subject to official approval and located in high-pollution areas, to submit an emissions statement containing details of the type, scale, temporal and spatial distribution of the air pollution released from the plant over a specific period.

Keep environmental damage and liability risks to a minimum

7. Mark all materials, especially poisonous ones which are dangerous to man, animals and plants, and store them separately (see also "materials management" and "disposal and recycling" checklists).
8. There is no such thing as a risk-free technical installation. It is up to management to adopt a confidence-boosting information policy and acquaint staff with the risks, e.g. by setting up a risks register listing all the parts of the plant which might be a potential threat to the environment.
9. Organise works inspections and draw up and apply safety regulations. If, for instance, an inspection visit were to bring to light the fact that a single-skin tank had no spill basin, the next step would be to draw up a safety regulation covering cases where containers, pipes or pumps spring leaks (as a result of material defects, wear, damage or incorrect operation), to ensure that leaking fluids cannot enter the public sewerage system.
10. In the event of an ecological accident, take immediate action to eliminate or prevent damage.
    - Shut down the plant, neutralise water pollution.
    - Inform authorities about the accident, as required.
    - Make no public statements until the repercussions of such statements have been properly assessed.
    - Inform the legal department or lawyer, bearing in mind possible liability claims or prosecution proceedings.
11. Avoid producer liability for pollution.
    - Companies marketing detergents: do not allow the statutory maximum quantities of phosphates to be exceeded.
    - Give special instructions for use to prevent any possible pollution by the company's products.
12. Make the company's suppliers sign legal agreements
    - to supply products with minimum negative impact on the environment,
    - to inform the company about any environmentally dangerous properties of the products,
    - to inform the company of possible immediate remedial action and methods of neutralising pollution (in the event of environmental damage occurring),
    - to take responsibility for waste materials originating from the product supplied.

13. When purchasing property or companies, include in the agreement a clause which makes the vendor responsible for the property being free of any potential pollutants, or demand a guarantee that no "inherited pollution" is being acquired in the deal.
14. Dispose of waste in compliance with the law; when using contractors, check their business policies and economic status.

Checklist No. 18: Insurance

The aim of company insurance is to insure the company against unquantifiable risks. The most serious risks to a company's financial situation and existence include damage to the environment and liability for such damage. Insurance against pollution and other such damage, however, is still at the experimental stage in all countries. Not enough statistical experience has been obtained yet, mainly because of the constant extension of statutory rules and the rapid development of measuring techniques. Various types of insurance are still being experimented with, aimed at attracting insurers to this market. The following recommendations reflect the position at the end of 1987.

Check what intrinsic damage could ensue from environmental risks

1. Check sickness, accident and life insurance schemes.
   Physical injury, for example, may be caused to the respiratory tract, eyes, skin or internal organs. Such damage may, like a disease, occur slowly and worsen, e.g. asbestosis, pneumoconiosis (covered by sickness insurance) – and frequently result in occupational incapacity and premature death (covered by statutory or mutual insurance schemes and life insurance); however, they may also occur as a result of accidents – as in Bhopal or Seveso – and thus result in permanent or "only" temporary injury (accident insurance, life insurance).
   Recommendation:
   A certain degree of basic protection is already provided on a statutory basis by the advanced social legislation in force in virtually all EEC countries; plants in special-risk sectors (asbestos, mining, chemical industries, etc.) should show social responsibility by supplementary company insurance schemes providing accident and life insurance for their staff.
2. Check fire and machinery insurance policies.
   Material damage, for example, may occur to buildings and installations as a result of acids, gases, vapours or soot following a fire (fire insurance, even if the machines themselves are not destroyed by the fire) and to machines, especially water pumps or filters, as a result of polluted water, contaminated oil or coolants (machinery insurance, technical insurance). Contamination by toxic substances generated by a fire can greatly increase the costs of clearing up.

In Anglo-american countries, an "all risk policy" will cover these risks.
Recommendation:
Property insurance is optional in most cases, with some exceptions for buildings and, in some areas, for machines. The cost of such policies should be reasonably commensurate with the (subjective) value of the property for the company.

3. Check stoppage insurance policies.
Site examination resulting from a spillage incident from a hazardous material container or from a fire can result in the firm being closed down by official order and prolong repair time.
Recommendation:
Key installations should be insured not just against loss of the equipment itself but above all against the loss-of-production damage arising from stoppages/destruction. On the other hand, for items such as cars, which can be replaced at any time, it is worth contemplating a policy with a retention clause or even no insurance at all. Loss-of-production policies are also optional and are intended to cover the risk of additional demands on the part of official authorities for environmental reasons.

Check possible risks to third parties caused by damage to the environment

4. Check third-party insurance.
Third-party insurance protects the businessman from third-party claims for damages, including harm to life and limb and, of course, to third-party property. It may also cover damage to common property such as air, water and soil.
5. Reconsider liability under private law.
The businessman may become liable under private law. Such liability may or may not be based on negligence and may even take the form of absolute liability. In all EEC countries, however, in order to press claims under private law, there must be a demonstrable causal link between the businessman's behaviour (omission or commission) and the damage which has occurred.
6. Consider the obligation to deal with damage under public law.
"Liability" may be linked with an undesirable state of affairs.

Because of the difficulty in proving either negligence or illegal action, or at least a link between cause and effect, this obligation to eliminate damage under public law is becoming increasingly important. For example, a landowner may be required to decontaminate his land even if it can be proven that he is not responsible for the contamination; the owner is liable for the "condition" of the property.

Recommendation:

Third-party insurance is in most cases optional; insurance is mandatory only in specific professions (doctors), certain sectors (nuclear industry) or on the basis of official regulations for individual cases (operators of waste dumps). In view of the incalculable cost of compensation for damage or its elimination, however, third-party insurance is indispensable. It must cover all conceivable areas of liability for the country in question and be constantly amended to keep pace with the latest legal developments; normal company third-party insurance is not entirely adequate. The need to amend policies is especially relevant in the universally controversial question of when damage starts to occur and, in this case, the inclusion or exclusion of "inherited" pollution.

7. Use special coverage.

   In Germany, most attempts to solve the specific problems of environmental damage and third-party insurance coverage apply the following concepts:

   - The risk of liability under the Water Resources Act can be insured against. This act makes the businessman absolutely liable for any changes in the condition of water and soil. This liability can be transferred to an insurer by means of a special policy with different clauses for the different types of liability (plant liability, residual-risk liability, etc.).
   - The risk of liability for pollution can be insured against by adding supplementary clauses to normal employers' liability insurance. According to § 14 of the Federal Law on Atmospheric Pollution and § 906 of the Civil Code (BGB), the businessman is liable for damage caused by emissions from his plant.

     Such emissions are understood to include not just dust but also odorous and noise emissions. This liability can be insured against as a supplementary clause to a normal employer's liability insurance policy.

- Radiation damage cannot be insured against. In most insurance sectors such damage is expressly excluded and is dealt with exclusively by the Atomic Energy Act.

Other Western countries have developed different liability laws which necessitate different insurance schemes. As there is not yet a uniform code of liability, utmost attention should be paid to the claims geared to the individual concepts.

Observe market trends

8. Find out about new insurance schemes.
   The normal type of employer's liability insurance for an industrial company does not provide adequate coverage for the two main areas of environmental liability: soil and water on the one hand and emissions on the other. It is even more important for specific environment insurance than for general liability that policies should be adapted to the changing scope of liability and keep pace with the latest trends in case law and administrative practice. However, earnings from this branch of insurance have declined so much as a result of a few major cases of environmental damage (USA: Love Channel; Italy: Seveso; India: Bhopal), and above all as a result of the unforeseen number of cases of water pollution from major or minor leaks that obtaining insurance coverage commensurate with the level of risk requires major efforts on the part of the policy holder and his brokers.
9. Make use of insurers' experience.
   With their experience and research facilities, insurers have substantial resources which should be made use of in the interests of ecological risk management.

Checklist No. 19: International business relations

Environment-oriented management must not stop at national borders. For one thing, people living abroad deserve just as much environmental and health protection as those at home. For another, damage to the environment in other countries often has repercussions on conditions in one's own country. Environment-oriented management also applies to exports, production in foreign countries and imports.

Things are likely to change quite considerably from 1992 on as regards import and export transactions between Member States of the European Community, 1992 being the scheduled completion date for the "European Internal Market", as enshrined in the "Single European Act" signed by the Heads of State and Government in 1985 (and since ratified by a number of countries, including the Federal Republic of Germany.

The Internal Market can only work smoothly, though, if the Member States manage to agree beforehand on Community product norms (including environmental norms). That is why the "Single European Act" states explicitly that agreement must be reached in good time on (high) environmental standards for products. This requirement puts welcome pressure on the politicians in terms of time and quality.

Under the terms of the "Single European Act", the Council of Ministers can in future adopt environmental standards by a qualified majority. This has the advantage that it will no longer be possible – as it has been under the unanimity voting system – for the country with the lowest standards to call the tune.

It is to be hoped that the Council will adopt very high environmental standards for products, for this would encourage companies in all Member States to develop ecologically sound alternative products. Given the worldwide growth in interest in low-pollution products this would in turn boost the competitiveness of European industry, open up new market sectors and help to conserve jobs.

In general terms, an environment-minded company should, in its international business relations set out to apply the following code of behaviour:

Keep exports environment-oriented

1. Ensure that goods intended for export meet the same quality

requirements and standards as those intended for the domestic market (unless there are more stringent requirements in the importing country).

2. Take steps to provide straightforward information and technical training programmes for purchasers and users to enable them to use, transport and store the goods without endangering the environment or human health, and to dispose of them safely.
3. Restrict or discontinue exports if this becomes necessary in the interests of the environment or human health in the importing country.

Keep foreign production environment-oriented

4. Ensure that the production facilities of foreign subsidiaries apply the same standards of plant safety, the same thresholds for pollution emission and the same requirements in other areas affecting the environment as the production plant of the parent company (unless more stringent requirements apply in the country of the subsidiary).
5. Restrict or discontinue manufacture of products if this becomes necessary for the protection of the environment or the health of the inhabitants of the country in which the foreign production plant is situated.
6. Use know-how transfer to raise the environmental technology status of all companies of an international group to that of the most advanced member of the group.
7. Ensure that the products made by foreign subsidiaries meet the same quality requirements and standards as those made by the parent company in the home country for the domestic market (unless more stringent requirements apply in the country of the subsidiary).

Keep imports environment-oriented

8. Find out whether the foreign producer of industrial goods or agricultural products applies the same standards of plant safety, the same maximum pollution emission levels and the same requirements in other areas affecting the environment as are prescribed in the home country for comparable industrial or agricultural production.
9. If the answer is negative, try to use the company's potential buying power to make the foreign producer adopt production

practices equivalent to those required by domestic legislation on environmental protection.

10. If attempts to exert influence on the producer, either directly or via the intermediate trade, are unfeasible or unsuccessful, try to obtain supplies from more ecologically-minded domestic or foreign producers.

It is worth noting that the German Chemical Industry Association (VCI) announced "guidelines for the chemical industry" on 10 July 1986 which, among other things, deal with the questions referred to in items 3–5 of the checklist, and state that: "If it becomes necessary for the protection of health and environment, the Chemical Industry will restrict marketing of products or discontinue their manufacure irrespective of economic interests." "The same principles regarding environmental protection and plant safety apply to German companies and their subsidiaries at home and abroad."

It is true that "the same principles" for environmental protection and plant safety do not necessarily mean "the same standards". Furthermore, the association's guidelines are not as binding on the association's members as a statutory obligation. After all, the pollution of the Rhine by chemicals in November 1986 showed that even at home, there is plenty of room for improvement in the formulation of, and compliance with, safety standards. Nevertheless, these guidelines are to be welcomed.

The question of what principles are to be applied in using technology transfer to raise foreign subsidiaries to the parent company's environmental technology level has been the subject of consultations within the European Chemical Association CEFIC (Conseil Européen des Fédérations de l'Industrie Chimique) for some time now. The results of these discussions will be of public interest.

It should also be pointed out that the VCI has, together with the Federation of German Wholesalers and Foreign Traders in Chemicals, drawn up a "Code of Behaviour for Exports of Dangerous Chemicals" which is in response to a series of OECD recommendations and which came into force on 11 March 1986. The Code deals in more detail – and in some ways less rigorously – with the group of questions referred to in items 1–3 and 7 of the checklist and is reproduced in full below.

The scope of application is restricted in several respects. It refers to a list of dangerous substances which is still incomplete. It does not refer to final products. It also contains important limitations in that it focuses, for example, on technical possibilities and proper handling (cf. item 1).

All in all, however, it is laudable and an example to others that an industrial federation should impose requirements on its members in addition to merely representing them to the outside world. This policy certainly serves to cultivate the federations's image and its long-term interests, but there is undoubtedly a moral component too.

Today's industry federations could learn a thing or two from the guilds of the Middle Ages, which managed to maintain their influence for centuries and gain the highest renown because they not only represented their members' interests but also acted as a moral authority for their members.

The checklists in this book could definitely help the industrial federations in developing an environmental protection code for their member companies, (see also the introduction to Part D: Checklists for Environmentalist Business Management). Although the scope for sanctions is limited, and the VCI admits that it will not exclude a member who violates the code of 11. 3. 1986, the moral and social pressure exerted by a code of behaviour is not to be underestimated, especially if conscientious efforts are made to check that it is being complied with and it is the subject of periodic public reports.

Code of Behaviour for Exports of Dangerous Chemicals of 11 March 1986

(formulated by the German Chemical Industry Association (VCI) and the Federation of German Wholesalers and Foreign Traders in Chemicals)

Foreword

The use of chemicals can create hazards for man and the environment. Governments, manufacturers and traders thus bear responsibility for ensuring the prevention as far as possible of any danger to human health and the environment stemming from the use of chemicals. This obligation applies to the use of chemicals in both the exporting and importing country.

To meet this responsibility, steps must be taken to help the importing countries to improve their monitoring of the proper use of imported substances, preparations or products and to assess any dangers to man and the environment associated with their use. This applies especially to Third World countries.

With the "Code of Behaviour for Exports of Dangerous Chemicals" described below, the chemical industry and chemical trade of the Federal Republic of Germany wish to contribute towards improving environmental and health protection in both the exporting and importing country.

Basic principle

1. Producers and traders shall show responsibility for the protection of human health and the environment by taking all the necessary steps within the technical means available to them to ensure that human health and the environment are not endangered by their substances, preparations or products when these are handled properly.

Quality and standards

2. Substances, preparations or products manufactured for export shall meet the same quality requirements and standards as applied by the manufacturer for comparable domestic products unless more stringent regulations or special local factors have to be taken into account.
3. Substances, preparations or products manufactured by subsidiaries in foreign countries shall meet the quality requirements and standards of the parent company unless more stringent statutory regulations or special local factors have to be taken into account.

Information

4. Manufacturers and traders shall provide customers with straightforward pertinent information, in their national language where possible, on the risks associated with the substances, preparations or products when these are handled properly, including any foreseeable misuse, if possible in the form of an overall assessment of the risk potential for man and the environment, as well as providing details of how they can be used safely, rendered innocuous and disposed of. This may take the form of safety data sheets, markings and customer information.
5. Manufacturers and traders shall cooperate as appropriate with

governments and international organisations in exchanging information on dangerous properties of chemicals, in which case the governments and international organisations must take into account the justified interests of the manufacturers and traders in not disclosing trade and company secrets.

6. Manufacturers and traders shall undertake to inform the competent Federal authority once a year via their federations whenever substances, whose use in the Federal Republic of Germany is banned or highly restricted, are exported for the first time, indicating the designation of the substance and recipient countries. Further information on assessing the substances' dangers will be provided to the authorities of the importing country if and when a justified request is made.

User training

7. Manufacturers and traders shall undertake, within the scope of their training of consumers and representatives of official bodies, to try to promote the proper use of products, especially in developing countries. Such training should cover the following topics: proper use, assessment of potential risks to man and the environment, prevention of risks, emergency measures in the event of accidents, transport and storage, waste disposal and general health and environmental protection.

Recalling of products

8. Manufacturers and traders shall inform their customers and the competent authorities immediately whenever it is discovered that there may be a risk to man and the environment in the proper use of the products. Such substances, preparations and products shall be recalled wherever possible.

Advertising

9. No advertising shall be conducted which runs counter to the aims of this code of behaviour.

Statistics

10. Manufacturers and traders shall keep and process, on their own responsibility, statistics on the type, quantity and country of destination of substances, preparations and products whose use is forbidden or highly restricted in the Federal Republic of Germany, but which have been exported by them.

11. The competent Federal authority shall be given information on the type and quantity of these substances, preparations or products and their countries of destination upon receipt of a request stating reasons.

Implementation

12. Manufacturers and traders shall undertake to carry out their own monitoring of compliance with this code of behaviour and report to the national authorities at specific intervals via their federations on compliance with the code.
13. The Chemical Industry Association and the Federation of German Wholesalers and Foreign Traders in Chemicals shall recommend compliance with this code of behaviour and the specified regulations to their member firms.
14. The code of behaviour shall be immediately applicable.

Checklist No. 20: Public relations work

The purpose of public relations work is to create permanent cross-links between the company and the public in order to build up and maintain confidence and understanding. This can include the provision of information by the company on the action it has taken to protect health and the environment in order to create an image which will help in achieving the company's targets. Such information also promotes environmental protection because it increases the public's awareness and encourages others to follow suit. The ideas expressed below may provide hints on how to conduct environment-oriented PR work.

Tell the truth, be clear and keep actions consistent with words

1. Only allow PR statements on environmental activities if they will stand up to checks.
   A company's claim to an above-averagely positive stance on the environment may result in investigations by the public and an increase in self-critical analysis by the company's own staff. Statements which cannot be proven are counter-productive.
2. Do not talk in general terms about the company's pro-environmental attitude. Concentrate on specific activities.
   Such statements are easier to understand and are more plausible. "Flowery" talk about the company's dedication to environmental protection often leads the public to believe the company prefers words to action.
3. Report on what the company has done rather than on what it plans to do.
   The image painted by the company in a PR statement must match the current situation. "Noble intentions" for the future are not accepted by the public and may even be seen as a smokescreen for the depressing reality.

It is better to put money into good work rather than into good reports on mediocre work

4. Take advantage of the fact that the media like reporting on new ideas and attitudes regarding environmental protection.
   - Involve PR staff in planning of environmental activities.
   - Use action which comes over well to the public to good effect by stretching it over a long period to ensure that it is repeatedly reported on by the media.

- Check whether material planned for ecology-related PR adverts or spots can be converted into specific ecological activities, the benefits or innovative character of which will be the subject of news items in the newspapers or programmes, with a much better publicity effect.

5. Involve the public in the planning and implementation of such activities, e.g.
   - allow company waste collection facilities to be used by local people where possible,
   - help to maintain and extend wildlife habitats near company premises, e.g. as part of apprentice training (see also "staff motivation and training" checklist),
   - join local ecological groups as a company or encourage members of the staff to join (unless the groups' aims are incompatible with those of the company),
   - extend the environmental counselling scheme for employees' households to local people (see also "environmental counselling for employees' households" and "staff motivation and training" checklists),
   - encourage other companies to give voluntary support for ecological management and enhance the effects of PR work by joining forces,
   - cooperate with other companies, authorities, public and scientific bodies to obtain a greater combined effect and at the same time gain a positive public reaction,
   - realise that ecological action carried out primarily for the cause itself usually has a better PR effect than mainly image-oriented action.

Always keep in mind all the important fields of action and target groups

6. Issue PR statements on, for example, the following ecological activities carried out by the company internally and externally (more details given in "overview" checklist):
   - progress in the disposal or recycling of waste materials, effluent and exhaust air, in the use of waste heat and in the reduction of noise levels,
   - improvements in working conditions by enhanced safety at work, more humane job conditions and healthier canteen food,

- success in research and technology in the field of safety and ecological compatibility of products, production processes, plant and waste disposal equipment,
- success in persuading other companies to increase in-house ecological activities and cooperation with other companies, with ecological associations or public bodies in achieving overriding ecological targets.

7. Choose, draft and disseminate PR statements such as to ensure that they are tailored to and reach the most varied target groups, i.e.
   - company staff and the people living in the immediate vicinity of the factory,
   - the company's customers and the public at large,
   - environment experts of official bodies, associations, institutes and other firms, and interested non-experts,
   - working people and pensioners, students and schoolchildren; incidentally, children should not be left out (for their own sakes and because they can motivate their parents),
   - people with a positive attitude, the sceptics, and members of critical citizens' initiatives.

IV. Pinpointing cost-reducing measures

Protecting the environment and making money at the same time – in other words, being both ecologist and entrepreneur – no doubt seems a Utopian dream. The fact is, though (as the checklists show), that there are plenty of commercial activities which serve the cause of environmental protection and are of benefit to the company, e.g. all the proposed means of saving energy, water and scarce raw materials reduce the pressure on the world's natural resources and on the firm's financial resources.

If every company were to put into practice only those environmental protection measures described in this book which can as a rule be introduced readily and at short notice with a view to avoiding or reducing costs (indicated by an asterisk in the text), the effect on the environment and the benefits for the firm would in themselves be very great.

Let us not forget, though, that firms which are prepared to go no further than the measures indicated with an asterisk may be missing the chance to make substantial savings elsewhere. There are any number of cases where giving systematic thought to the material flows in a firm and between the firm and its environment has mobilised rationalisation reserves which would have gone unnoticed had the firm not adopted an environmentalist approach.

Introducing the Integrated System of Environmentalist Business Management encourages key members of staff to think "laterally" or in terms of what effects their decisions will have on other spheres of life. The result is success in innovation and rationalisation in the firm's "conventional" business field. This knock-on effect is something which should not be underestimated.

Nor should we forget that there are plenty of measures which may not be immediately quantifiable, but which will indirectly at least reduce costs or even eliminate them entirely.

For instance, offering wholefood dishes on the canteen menu can have a major effect on staff health, reducing absence for sick leave and hence the cost of paying people who are too ill to work.

For businessmen setting out initially to practise protection of the environment in their firm with the aim of adopting measures which are readily practicable and will reduce their overheads, the following list sets out all the points marked with an asterisk in the checklists.

No. 1 Management motivation
(point 22)

No. 9 Economising on energy and water
(points 10, 11, 12, 13, 14, 15, 16, 17, 24, 25, 26, 27, 28, 29, 30, 31, 32, 33)

No. 11 Materials management
(points 4, 24)

No. 12 Production technology
(points 2, 3, 8, 9, 10, 13, 16)

No. 13 Disposal and recycling
(point 9)

No. 14 Company vehicles
(points 3, 4, 6, 8, 10, 11, 13, 14, 15, 16, 19, 20, 21, 22, 23, 24, 25, 26, 28, 30, 31, 32, 34, 35)

No. 15 Building
(points 15, 17, 18, 20)

E. The significance for Europe of environmentalist business management

The Commission of the European Communities intends to work towards a greater concern for the environment in the industrial policies pursued by the Community and its Member States. After all, manufacturing industry is – along with energy-generation, transport, agriculture and private households – one of the major polluters in Europe.

Greater consideration for the environment in industrial policy means much more than just tightening up the legislation on industrial emissions. What the Commission is really concerned about is making practicable models for environmentalist business management available to industry.

By presenting a model along these lines in Environment Year 1987, the Commission was in effect indicating quite clearly that it intended to go beyond the legislative process and provide unbureaucratic and pragmatic assistance for businessmen prepared to espouse environmentalist management techniques. By such activities the Commission demonstrates its concern with the kind of practical issues which really affect the people of Europe.

The Commission believes that the Integrated System of Environmentalist Business Management developed by Winter & Sohn and generally known as the Winter Model (here termed "the Model") can reasonably be taken as a guideline for a large number of companies in the European business community. The decision by the Commission to co-sponsor publication and distribution of this book must be seen in the light of the following considerations:

1. The aim is to pursuade as many European companies as possible to take up the idea of environmentalist management. If there are enough firms prepared to go beyond what the letter of the law requires, the result will be a major improvement in the environmental situation in the Community. Apart from the ecological aspect, the benefits for Europe will be of a medical, social, cultural and economic nature.
2. One of the means of achieving this is the publication and Euro-

pe-wide distribution of this book on the Integrated System in a number of languages. Lectures held in conjunction with the national chambers of trade and industry and business associations can provide effective back-up.

3. Experience has shown that it is possible to implement a project of this kind at a national level. In the Federal Republic of Germany, the Association of Young German Businessmen (BJU) has used Winter's experience to produce a "checklist for more environmental protection in companies", copies of which are distributed widely to businessmen, producing in many cases a change of business practice to the benefit of the environment. Lectures and seminars on the Integrated System have been held by a number of organisations, associations, chambers of trade and industry and universities. At the world's biggest environmental technology fair (ENVITEC) held in Düsseldorf on 18 February 1986, the Model was presented in full detail at a lecture organised by the Berlin health and environmental protection training centre, which is linked with the Federal Environmental Agency.
4. The Model has been very well received in the press, on radio and on television. The various political parties and social groupings have welcomed it, and Winter & Sohn were rewarded for the development and trial work on the Model with the BJU's environment prize on 6 June 1985, followed on 12 December 1986 by the environment prize awarded by the Schleswig-Holstein business studies and promotion association.
5. The Integrated System now has an international base. In its final draft of 10 January 1986, the conference on the protection of the River Rhine ("La Protection du Mileu Naturel Rhénan Bilan et Prospective") called on the Environment Committee of the Association for Trans-frontier Cooperation on the Upper Rhine ("Association pour la Cooperation Transfrontalière Rhin Supérieur") to "pursue its planning with a view to making the business community in the region aware of a comprehensive concept of business management integrating environmental requirements in all fields (production technology, materials management, personnel, marketing, waste disposal, etc.)." The resolution was based on a talk held on the Winter Model entitled "Compatibility between economics and the environment and Europe's heritage".

6. By circulating information on the Model, the European Community has achieved an effect going well beyond Environment Year 1987. Since its inception in the Federal Republic of Germany, the Model has steadily gained ground among interested businessmen Europe-wide, surely a sign that the time is now ripe for this kind of initiative.
7. Large numbers of people working in industry can benefit from the Model, which provides for environment-oriented training for all employees including apprentices, and the insitution of an environmentalist suggestions scheme on a cash bonus basis.
8. The Model can have an educational effect on broad sections of the population. By applying the system, companies are in effect setting an example for environmentally aware behaviour which can be copied by employees in their own homes. What is more, there is provision in the Model for employees to ask to receive advice in their own homes on ecological housekeeping by specially trained environmental counsellors who – initially at least – will be paid mainly by the company itself.
9. By encouraging "ecological" working conditions, the Model has a very strong social element to it. It also assists social integration by the common cause of improving the environment and living conditions for all.
10. The Model induces company management to take a closer look at environmental technology. As the Model comes to be used more widely in practice, the result is likely to be an increase in the number of jobs in the Community's environmental technology industry, while at the same time, the international competitiveness of this future-oriented sector of industry will be strengthened. If, however, the Community's industry were to fall behind the standard of environmental technology outside Europe, there would be a danger of the Community losing out in growth markets and hence sacrificing jobs to industrial powers outside Europe.
11. The Model can help to conserve jobs by encouraging companies to diversify in good time to keep pace with the growing demand for low-pollution alternative products. Without this kind of flexibility on the part of European firms, there would be a risk of the demand for such products being met by non-European suppliers quicker to react to market openings, while more and more jobs would be lost by European factories producing the conventional non-ecological products.

12. By helping to expand the range of low-pollution products (by stimulating demand), so that "dirigistic" government intervention is in many cases unnecessary, the Model is in step with the basically free-market form of most European economies.
13. From other angles too, there appears to be no conflict with the legislation in force in any of the Community's Member States.
14. The introduction of the Integrated System by a majority of companies in the European Community would greatly reduce the pollutant load on air, water and soil and help to solve many of the serious noise and waste heat problems.
15. If a large number of European companies were to espouse the Model and thus go beyond the legal requirements as regards noxious emissions, the effect would be to counter the alarming increase in environment-induced and way-of-life-induced illnesses in the people of Europe.
16. Less air pollution would also mean a slackening-off in the pace of forest die-back and of the rampant destruction of historic buildings and antiquities.
17. Another plus would be the boost given by the Model to town-planning and building. An example is Germany's first biologically designed industrial plant, part of Winter & Sohn's factory in Norderstedt.
18. Energy-saving and stewardship of natural resources are further consequences of the Integrated System. This bonus is particularly welcome in economic terms in the light of Europe's relative paucity of energy sources and other natural resources.
19. Nature conservation can also get a boost, as the Model also provides for environmental and ecological seminars and study trips for young apprentices and other trainess.
20. As the Model was developed in a medium-sized firm, it is of particular interest for the wide variety and large number of firms in this category, although it is perfectly suitable for use in large companies too.

By introducing a broad spectrum of the business community to the Integrated System, the Commission of the European Communities is acting as an important go-between in the drive to conserve our natural environment and hence the very basis of human civilisation in Europe. The company is the basic living cell of the business community organism. Unless the wide variety of individual firms and companies can be pursuaded to do their bit to protect the environment, business as a whole can never become environment-oriented, and without such an attitude, it will be impossible in the long run to conserve the vital natural basis of life itself in the countries of the European Community.

F. International organisations dealing with environmental management

There are quite a few international organisations which, if known, can be very useful for an environmentalist approach to business management.

The following chapter contains a selection of governmental organisations (I.) and industry-based non-governmental organisations (II.). The year of establishment, the main goals and activities and the most important publications of the various organisations are indicated as well as their current executive secretary (on July 1, 1988) and their address. The lists of organisations are in alphabetical order and do not claim to be exhaustive.

I. Governmental Organisations

1. European Economic Community (EEC)
2. Food and Agriculture Organisation of the United Nations (FAO)
3. Organisation for Economic Co-operation and Development (OECD)
4. United Nations Economic Commission for Europe (ECE)
5. United Nations Environment Programme (UNEP)
6. United Nations Industrial Development Organisation (UNIDO)
7. World Health Organisation (WHO)

II. Industry-based non-governmental organisations

Overall organisations:

1. Bureau International de la Récupération (BIR)
2. Business and Industry Advisory Committee to OECD (BIAC)
3. International Chamber of Commerce (ICC)
4. International Environmental Bureau (IEB)
5. Union of Industrial and Employers' Confederations of Europe (UNICE)

Organisations for a special branch of industry:

6. European Confederation of Pulp, Paper and Board Industry (CEPAC)
7. European Council of Chemical Manufacturers' Federations (CEFIC)
8. International Group of National Associations of Manufacturers of Agrochemical Products (GIFAP)
9. International Iron and Steel Institute (IISI)
10. International Petroleum Industry Environmental Conservation Association (IPIECA)
11. International Primary Aluminium Institute (IPAI)
12. Lead Development Association (LDA)
13. The Oil Companies' European Organisation for Environmental and Health Protection (CONCAWE)

I. Governmental organisations

The following lists can be helpful in finding the appropriate person to consult in developing a better environmentalist approach, amongst the international organisations dealing with environmental management.

1. European Economic Community (EEC)

The European Economic Community was created by a treaty signed in Rome on 25 March 1957 to establish a Common Market. The Commission of the EEC is the executive body. It has 22 Directors General dealing with different subjects. Among them are the following DG's that are relevant and useful for the development of an environmentalist approach in business management. We only mention activities that are relevant in the context of this book. Information on the numerous publications relating to the environment is available from the appropriate Directorates.

Address: Rue de la Loi 200, B-1049 Bruxelles, Belgium,
tel. (32.2) 235.11.11, telex COMEU B 21 877

Directorate General XI
Director General: Mr. Laurens Jan Brinkhorst
Adviser: Mr. Stanley Johnson

Assistant of the Director General: Mr. Hans Jankowski

DG XI of the EEC is responsible for environment, consumer protection and nuclear safety.

Directly attached to Director General are:
1. Legal aspects and application of Community Law
2. International Affairs
3. Relations with institutions and education in the field of environment
4. Finance and contracts

- **Directorate A** deals with nuclear safety, impact of industry on the environment and waste management.
  Main fields of activity are:
  1. Nuclear safety
  2. Monitoring of chemical substances, industrial hazard and biotechnology
  3. Waste management, clean technologies, protection of soils against pollution, prevention of noise pollution
  4. Economic aspects, employment and statistics

- **Directorate B** deals with the protection of water, air pollution control and conservation.
  Main fields of activity are:
  1. Protection and management of water
  2. Air pollution control
  3. Agriculture, nature conservation, coordination with other policies

- **Directorate C** deals with the protection and promotion of consumer interests.
  1. Commercial transactions and access to justice
  2. Physical protection and health
  3. Information, consumer education and statistical aspects of physical protection
  4. Promotion of consumer interests, coordination with other policies and representation of consumers.

Directorate General XII
Director General: Mr. Paolo Fasella

DG XII of the EEC deals with science, research and development. There are special Directorates for scientific and technical policy (A), means of action (B), technological research (C), nuclear safety research (D), biology (F), co-operation with non-member countries (G) and stimulation of scientific and technical development, design and evaluation of programmes (H).

- **Directorate E** deals with environment and non-nuclear energy sources.
  Main fields of activity are:
  1. Environment, recycling of waste
  2. Climatology and natural hazards
  3. Renewable energy sources
  4. Geothermal energy
  5. Rational energy use and energy system analysis
  6. Advanced fuel technology.

Directorate General XVII

Director General: Mr. Constantinos S. Maniatopoulos

DG XVII of the EEC is responsible for energy policy.
There are special Directorates for energy, policy, analyses and forecasts, and contracts (A), coal technology (B), oil and natural gas (C), nuclear energy (D), energy saving and alternative energy sources, electricity and heat (E), Euratom safeguards (F).

Network for Environmental Technology Transfer (NETT)

Secretary General: Mr. Frank Joyce

The Network for Environmental Technology Transfer is an independent, international non-profit-making association run by and for its members. The aim of NETT is to help the exchange of know-how between companies and organisations in the rapidly developing field of clean technology and waste technologies and to provide information on more efficient and cost-effective pollution control technologies. NETT was launched in 1988 with support from the Commission of the European Communities within the framework of the European Year of the Environment.

Address: Rue de la Science 5, B-1040 Bruxelles, Belgium,
tel. (32.2) 231.03.61, telefax 231.06.84.

2. Food and Agriculture Organisation of the United Nations (FAO)

Director General: Mr. Edouard Saouma

The Food and Agriculture Organisation of the UN was established on 16 October 1945 in Quebec to raise the levels of nutrition and standards of living of the peoples in the member countries to secure improvements in efficiency of production and distribution of all food and agricultural products and to contribute towards an expanding world economy. At a FAO Conference in 1985, Resolution 10/85 on an international code of conduct on the distribution and use of pesticides was unanimously adopted by FAO member countries. The code identifies potential hazards in the distribution and use of pesticides, including environmental hazards. It establishes standards of conduct and defines responsibilities for all those engaged in the regulation, distribution and use of pesticides. The code is supported by internationally accepted guidelines, which are referred to in the various articles of the code, and which provide the means of implementing the provisions of the code.

Publications:
FAO Monthly Bulletin of Statistics; Ceres – FAO Review of Agriculture and Development (6 times a year); FAO Plant Protection Bulletin (quarterly); Food and Agricultural Legislation (twice a year); Unasylva (forestry quarterly); FAO Commodity Review (annual); Fertilizer Yearbook; Production Yearbook; The State of Food and Agriculture (annual); Yearbook of Fishery Statistics; Yearbook of Forestry Products, Food and Nutrition (twice a year).

Address: Via delle Terme di Caracalla, I-00100 Roma, Italy,
tel. (39.6) 5.79.71, telex 610181 FAO I, telefax 61.02.48/514.61.72.

3. Organisation for Economic Co-operation and Development (OECD)

Secretary General: Mr. Jean Claude Paye

The Organisation for Economic Co-operation and Development was established on 30 September 1961 in Paris to help member countries promote economic growth, employment and improved standards of living, and to help promote the sound and harmonious development of the world economy. An Environment

Committee and various specialised groups are responsible for the economic and policy aspects of OECD's work on environmental affairs. Their work has led to agreements setting out guiding principles on the international trade aspects of environmental policies, and other agreements have been adopted concerning the use of environmentally dangerous chemicals, noise, waste, pollution, energy production, coastal management, the transboundary movement of hazardous waste and accidents including hazardous substances, transfrontier pollution and the polluter-pays principle.

Publications:
News from OECD (monthly); OECD Financial Statistics (monthly); OECD Observer (every 2 months); Indicators of Industrial Activity (quarterly); Pulp and Paper: Quarterly Statistics; OECD Economic Outlook (twice yearly).

Address: Rue André Pascal 2, F-75775 Paris CEDEX 16, France, tel. (33.1) 45.24.82.00, telex 620160, telefax 45.24.85.00.

4. United Nations Economic Commission for Europe (ECE)

Executive Secretary: Mr. Gerald Hinteregger

The United Nations Economic Commission for Europe was set up in 1947 by the UN Economic and Social Council, to study the economic and technological problems of the region and to recommend courses of action to member governments. One of the Principal Subsidiary Bodies is the Senior Advisers to ECE governments on environmental and water problems, with Working Parties on air pollution problems, on low- and non-waste technology and re-utilisation and recycling of wastes, on water problems, as well as on environmental impact assessment. ECE also provides the Secretariat for the Convention on long-range Transboundary Air Pollution and its related Protocols.

Publications:
Economic Bulletin for Europe (quarterly); Economic Survey of Europe (annual); Air Pollution Studies; Environmental Series; ECE 1947-1987.

Address: Palais des Nations, CH-1211 Geneva 10, Switzerland, tel. (41.22) 34.60.11, telex 289696, telefax 33.98.79.

5. United Nations Environment Programme (UNEP)

Executive Director: Dr. Mostafa K. Tolba

The UNEP was created in 1972, as a result of the Stockholm Conference on the Human Environment, to co-ordinate and catalyze UN activities in the field of the environment. It works with governments, national and international institutions and other parties concerned with the environment. In addition to a world-wide network of regional offices, certain programmes such as the International Register of Potentially Toxic Chemicals (IRPTC) and the Industry and Environment Office (IEO) are located in Geneva and Paris respectively.

Publications:
UNEP Annual Review, UNEP Reports and Proceedings Series, UNEP Reference Series, UNEP Executive Series, Uniterra Bulletin, IRPTC Bulletin.

Address: P.O.Box 30552, K-Nairobi, Kenya, tel. (2542) 33.39.30, telex 22068/22173, telefax 52.07.11.

Industry and Environment Office

Director: Ms. Jacqueline Aloisi de Larderel

The goals of the Industry and Environment Office, established by UNEP in Paris in 1975 to bring industry and government together for environmentally sound industrial development, are to encourage the incorporation of environmental criteria in industrial development plans; to promote the use of clean and safe technologies; to facilitate the implementation of procedures and principles in industry for the protection of the environment and to stimulate the exchange of relevant information and experience throughout the world.

Publications:
Industry and Environment Review; Technical Guides, Reports and Proceedings.

Address: Tour Mirabeau, Quai André Citroën,
F-75739 Paris CEDEX 15, France, tel. (33.1) 45.78.33.33,
telex 204997 F, telefax 45.78.32.34 Coframines for UNEP.

6. United Nations Industrial Development Organisation (UNIDO)

Director General: Mr. Domingo L. Siazon, jr.

The Industrial Development Organisation was established on 1 January 1967 and became a Specialised Agency of the UN in 1968. UNIDO's task is to provide industrial assistance to developing countries at their own request. It prepares industrial studies and conducts research by industry-sector as well as by country and for parts of countries; encourages the development and transfer of technology; maintains an industrial and technical information bank and industrial statistics; carries out empirical studies used in the industrialisation process. UNIDO has a mandate to assist and co-operate with non-governmental organisations as well as the public, co-operative and private sectors of industry.

Publications:
UNIDO Update (monthly); Industry and Development, Global Report (annual); Industrial Development Abstracts; Industry and Development Series; Transfer of Technology Series; Guide to Information Sources; Guide to Training Opportunities for Industrial Development; Annual Reports.

Address: Vienna International Center, P.O.Box 300, A-1400 Vienna, Austria, tel. (43.222) 2.63.10, telex 135617, telefax 23.21.56.

7. World Health Organisation (WHO)

Director General: Dr. Hiroshi Nakajima

The World Health Organisation was founded in New York in 1948 as a specialised agency of the United Nations. The objective of WHO is the attainment by all peoples of the highest possible level of health, which is a fundamental right of every human being without distinction of race, religion, political belief, economic or social condition. There is global consensus for a common social goal – health for all by the year 2000. People everywhere should have contact with health services enabling them to lead socially and economically productive lives. The benefits of international health work are reaped by all countries, including the most developed. WHO acts as the directing and coordinating authority on international health work. It ensures valid and productive co-operation in the field of health, and promotes research. WHO is a clearing house, absorbing, distilling, synthesizing and disseminating health information of all kinds.

Publications:
Bulletin of the World Health Organisation (bi-monthly); International Digest of the Health Legislation (quarterly); Weekly Epidemiological Record; World Health Statistics Quarterly; World Health Forum (quarterly); World Health (10 issues a year).

Address: Ave Appia, CH-1211 Geneva 27, Switzerland, tel. (41.22) 91.21.11, telex 27821, telefax 91.07.46.

II. Industry-based non-governmental organisations

With regard to industry-based non-governmental organisations a distinction is made between overall organisations (1.–7.) such as the International Chamber of Commerce, and organisations dealing with particular branches of industry (8.–13.). The value of their services for individual enterprises as well is often not sufficiently known.

Overall organisations:

1. Bureau International de la Récupération (BIR)

Secretary General: Mr. Francis Veys

Founded in 1948, the Bureau International de la Récupération is a non-profit-making organisation comprising the national associations representing firms and enterprises engaged in the recycling and reclamation of raw materials worldwide.

BIR covers four commodity divisions at present: scrap iron and steel, non-ferrous metals, paper stock, textiles. Special Committees include the Stainless Steel and Special Alloys Committee, as well as the Municipal Wastes Committee and Plastics Round-Table.

Publications: (for members only)
Proceedings of semi-annual meetings; General Membership Directory; Annual Report.

Address: Place du Samedi 13, Bte 4, B-1000 Brussels, Belgium, tel. (32.2) 217.82.51, telex 61965 BIR B, telefax 217.22.74

2. Business and Industry Advisory Committee to OECD (BIAC)

Secretary General: Ms. Yolande Michaud

The Business and Industry Advisory Committee was founded on 9 March 1962 in Paris to represent business and industry at OECD and to express opinions at OECD on all questions of common interest.

BIAC's activities in the environmental field are coordinated by the BIAC Environment Committee, the BIAC Chemicals Committee and task forces on accidents involving hazardous substances, and on hazardous wastes.

BIAC has frequent informal consultations with the OECD Secretariat on OECD programmes, and holds formal consultations with OECD Committees or working groups on the occasion of OECD meetings. Some of the recent OECD activities (1987–1988) on which BIAC has been consulted include: the systematic investigation of existing chemicals; chemical testing and assessment; chemicals export notification; accidents involving hazardous substances; the transfrontier movement of hazardous wastes; economic techniques and instruments in environmental policy.

Publications:
BIAC Guides for Manufacturers and Traders Exporting Chemicals (October 1985); numerous position papers on specific issues.

Address: Chaussée de la Muette 13/15, F-75016 Paris, France, tel. (33.1) 45.24.48.38/42.88.78.38, telex BIAC 6240403, telefax 42.88.78.38.

3. International Chamber of Commerce (ICC)

Secretary General: Mr. Hans König

The International Chamber of Commerce was founded in 1919 to establish a permanent non-governmental organisation of world business. The ICC represents the business community at international level, promotes world trade and investment based on free and fair competition, harmonises trade practices and terminology and provides a growing range of practical services to business.

Address: Cours Albert 1er 38, F-75008 Paris, France,
tel. (33.1) 45.62.34.56, telex 65077 ICC HQ, telefax 42.25.86.63, telegrams Incomerc Paris.

ICC Commission on Environment

Chairman: Mr. Karel Veldhuis
Secretary: Mr. Nigel Blackburn

The ICC has a Commission on Environment which determines ICC policy on environmental questions as regards initiatives and projects undertaken by intergovernmental organisations. It also undertakes "pro-active" initiatives such as the ICC Environmental Guidelines (a benchmark for company or sectoral codes) and a new standpoint on environmental auditing for publication at the end of 1988. The Commission also provides a forum in which member executives regularly meet representatives of UNEP and the specialised industry organisations mentioned in this chapter.

Publications:
Environmental Guidelines for World Industry; The Spirit of Versailles: The Business of Environmental Management; Cost-Benefit Analysis of Environmental Protection Measures.

4. International Environmental Bureau (IEB)

Director: Mr. Henrique Cavalcanti

The International Environmental Bureau, a specialised division of the International Chamber of Commerce, was established in 1986 and is funded independently by some 25 leading companies. The IEB works principally as a trans-industry clearing-house for environmental management information.

Publications:
Newsletter (issued 6 times a year); studies on protecting the environment; reports on clearing-house activities.

Address: Route de Chêne 61, CH-1208 Geneva, Switzerland, tel. (41.22) 86.51.11, telex 289556.

5. Union of Industrial and Employers' Confederations of Europe (UNICE)

Secretary General: Mr. Zygmunt Tyszkiewicz

The Union of Industrial and Employers' Confederations of Europe was established in 1985 and recognised as official spokesman for European business and industry vis-à-vis the European institutions. It is composed of 33 member federations from 22 European countries with a permanent Secretariat based in Brussels. UNICE's purpose is to promote the common professional interests of the firms represented by its members; to provide the framework within which member organisations can coordinate their European policies; to ensure that European decision-makers take UNICE's policies and opinions fully into account. It has a special Expert Commission on Environment.

Address: Rue Joseph II. 40, B-1040 Brussels, Belgium, tel. (32.2) 237.65.11, telex UNICE B 26013, telefax 231.14.45.

Organisations for a special branch of industry:

6. European Confederation of Pulp, Paper and Board Industry (CEPAC)

Managing Director: Mr. H.H. Kröner

CEPAC was founded on 23 April 1963 in Stresa to represent and defend the interests of the European Community's pulp, paper and board industry within the EC and worldwide, to act as a central source of information and industry statistics and to study all economic problems of interest to the industry.

Publications:
Key Statistics; Annual Statistics of the EC Pulp, Paper and Board Industry; CEPAC Annual Report; CEPAC Guide to the Classification of Paper and Board in Chapter 48 of the CCC Harmonised System and the EC Combined Nomenclature of 1988.

Address: Rue Washington 40, Bte 7, B-1050 Brussels, Belgium, tel. (32.2) 649.67.09/25, telex 65080 for CEPAC, telefax 641.92.75.

7. European Council of Chemical Manufacturers' Federations (CEFIC)

Director General: Mr. Hugo H. Lever

The European Chemical Industry Federation is the recognised voice of the European chemical industry – an industry which employs more than 2 million people and accounts for one third of world production.

Centrally located in Brussels, CEFIC is the forum where the European chemical industry coordinates its positions and approaches vis-à-vis the international bodies and authorities which have an influence on its business environment. Formed in 1972, it now has as members the National Chemical Federations of 15 European countries, and represents the interests of 34 major companies working in various sectors of the chemical industry. Issues which CEFIC tackles on its members' behalf include international trade, environment, health and safety, transport and distribution of chemicals, energy and raw material supplies, information and statistical surveys, and many other areas of interest to the European chemical industry.

Publications:
CEFIC Annual Reports; position papers; newsletters; the Chemical Industry of Western Europe prepared for the 21st century; publications relating to topics of particular interest to the chemical industry.

Address: Avenue Louise 250, Bte 71, B-1050 Brussels, Belgium, tel. (32.2) 640.29.05, telex 62444, telefax 640.19.81.

8. International Group of National Associations of Manufacturers of Agrochemical Products (GIFAP)

Director General: Mr. Hans G. von Loeper

Founded on 29 September 1967 in Brussels to represent the position of the member associations in all technical and scientific domains concerning industry with regard to international bodies (FAO, WHO, UNEP, UNIDO, DDO).

Publications:
GIFAP Bulletin (6 times a year); GIFAP Guidelines and Position Papers on key issues of concern to the Agrochemical Industry.

Address: Avenue Albert Lancaster 79 a, B-1180 Brussels, Belgium, tel. (32.2) 375.68.60, telex 62120 GIFAP B, telefax 375.27.93.

9. International Iron and Steel Institute (IISI)

Secretary General: Mr. Lenhard J. Holschuh

The International Iron and Steel Institute was the first of the international industry associations dealing solely with one industry. It was founded in 1967 in New York with headquarters in Brussels. Basically IISI is a non-profit-making research organisation dealing with various aspects of the international steel industry. Its aims are to provide a forum for free and open discussion of steel industry problems; to undertake research as directed; to collect, evaluate and disseminate statistics and information; to effect and maintain liaison with other organisations relating to steel; to promote the use of steel. The Standing Committee on Environmental Affairs was formed in 1973.

Publications:
Environmental Control in the Iron and Steel Industry (1978); Current Status and Problems of Environmental Control in the Japanese Steel Industry (1980); Environmental Affairs: A European Presentation (1981); Utilisation of Blast Furnace and BOF Slag (1984); Environmental Control Technology in the Steel Industry (1986); The Management of Steel Industry By-products and Waste (1987); Recycling and Disposal of Spent Materials from Acid Pickling and Coating Lines (1987).

Address: Rue Col. Bourg 120, B-1140 Brussels, Belgium, tel. (32.2) 735.90.75, telex 22639, telefax 735.80.12.

10. International Petroleum Industry Environmental Conservation Association (IPIECA)

Executive Secretary: Mr. Stanley Hope

The International Petroleum Industry Environmental Conservation Association is an association of petroleum companies and petroleum industry associations founded in March 1974. Its sphere of interest is environmental and associated health and development matters of worldwide or global concern as they may impact on the petroleum industry. Its principal purposes are to act as the industry's forum for considering these matters and to be its focus for interaction with UNEP and, selectively, other inter-governmental and international organisations active in this field.

Publications:
Technical Reports.

Address: College Hill 1 (1st floor), UK-London EC4R 2RA, United Kingdom, tel. (44.1) 248.34.47/48, telex 883281, telefax 489.90.67

11. International Primary Aluminium Institute (IPAI)

Secretary General: Mr. Peter Martyn

The International Primary Aluminium Institute was founded on 28 April 1972 in London, to promote and assist the development of primary aluminium and to provide a forum for exchanges of information and discussion. It also undertakes, sponsors or assists studies and research.

Publications:
Fluoride Emissions Control – Costs of New Aluminium Reduction Plants (1975); IPAI Environmental Recommendations for Siting and Operation of New Primary Aluminium Industry Facilities (1977); The Monitoring of Emissions from Aluminium Reduction Plants (1987); Review of the Petroleum Coke Situation and its Potential Impact on Sulphur Dioxide Emissions from Primary Aluminium Plants (1987); Environmental Legislation Survey (1981); Methods for Disposal of Residue from the Production of Alumina from Bauxite Ores (1982).

Address: New Zealand House (9th floor), Haymarket,
UK-London, United Kingdom, tel. (44.1) 930.05.28,
telex 917837 IPAI London, telefax 321.01.83.

12. Lead Development Association (LDA)

Chief Executive: Mr. F.D. Ward

The Lead Development Association was founded in 1946 and is supported principally by lead mining companies and lead metal producers. It is non-profit-making and exists to promote the use of lead in all forms and to represent the lead industry at national and international levels. The Association maintains an up-to-date library and provides technical advice on all aspects of lead, including health and safety and environmental issues.

Address: Berkeley Square 34, UK-London W1X 6AJ, United Kingdom, tel. (44.1) 499.84.22, telex 261286, telefax 493.15.55.

13. The Oil Companies' European Organisation for Environmental and Health Protection (CONCAWE)

Secretary General: Dr. J.-A. Terning

Founded in 1963 in The Hague to study environmental and health aspects of the processing, handling and use of oil in Europe. Its committees and working groups make studies of technical, economic and legislative aspects of environmental and health topics, supported by a library, a documentation system and statistical records.

Publications:
Technical Reports; Information Bulletins.

Address: Babylon-Kantoren A, Koningin Julianaplein 30–9, N-2595 AA The Hague, The Netherlands, tel. (31.70) 42.45.00, telex CONCAWE via SIPM 36000, telefax 42.45.13.

Epilogue

The young people of today are frequently alleged to lack the classic virtues such as diligence, meticulousness, constancy, circumspection, self-control, self-discipline, foresight and quality-awareness. This criticism is unfounded.

On the contrary, it is remarkable to see how much diligence many young people are prepared to put into acquiring a basic knowledge of ecology. Toxic substances are being measured with great meticulousness. Wild animals are being cared for and wetlands looked after with great constancy and circumspection. Self-control is being exercised in the observation of wild animals, while waste products are being sorted and disposed of with self-discipline. Foresight and quality-awareness are the watchwords in the purchase of low-pollution consumer goods and biological foodstuffs.

The classic virtues are still there, but are not always to be found where the businessman would like to have them. A lot of young people are asking themselves quite seriously what is the point in diligence and hard work. To pollute waste waters even more and to add yet more pollution to the beaches? Why, they wonder, should they get to work on time every morning just to help create more refuse and add more pollution to the community's drinking supplies? Why, they wonder, should they produce high-quality work just to generate profits for a factory whose inadequately filtered flue gases are polluting the environment and ruining people's health?

If the classic virtues are no longer found at the workplace as much as they used to be, it is mainly because people see no real point in the work they are doing. If young people (and, incidentally, many of the adults too) were to see more point in their work, the classic work virtues would soon reappear.

Work is perceived as being meaningful when it is not only a means of earning money but also – and primarily – serves to enhance the well-being of the country and its people. This is only possible, though, when profit-making does not result in contaminated groundwater, polluted rivers, poisoned air, damaged woodland, the extinction of animal and plant species and a poorer state of health.

A manufacturing company which manages to produce ecological products by low-pollution means can spare many of its workers the crisis of conscience resulting from the knowledge that they are earning their livelihoods by destroying life elsewhere.

In an environment-oriented company, the work process regains its old status as a means of enhancing the well-being of the community as a whole. A company which can give its employees a sense of doing the right thing can expect a better performance (and will get it from properly motivated staff).

It is wrong to think in terms of the Integrated System undermining the classic work virtues in a company – quite the opposite. By making work meaningful again, the company is in fact strengthening the classic virtues in both environmental and conventional work terms. The same degree of meticulousness is applied to measuring toxic substances as to making machine tools. The same circumspection is applied to dealing with hazardous waste as to handling fragile products.

It is up to us to create meaningful jobs by applying the environmentalist management technique, and it is up to us to consolidate the standard of living of our people while at the same time respecting and conserving the natural basis of all life.

Appendix I

Publications and Organisations

1. MANAGEMENT MOTIVATION

Publications

British

Clean-up: it's good business. Confederation of British Industry, Centre Point, New Oxford Street, London, WC1, tel. 01-379-7400, 1986.

American

Perlson, M.R., How to Understand and Influence People and Organisations, (Practical Psychology for Goal Achievement), AMACOM, New York, 1982.

The Journal of Environmental Economics and Management, Academic Press, Inc., 111 Fifth Avenue, New York, NY 10003.

Ziglar, Z., See You at the Top, Pelican Publishing Company, 25th edition, Louisiana, 1981.

German

Lay, R., Führen durch das Wort, 2. Aufl., München 1978.

Senn, J.F., Ökologie-orientierte Unternehmensführung, Frankfurt/M., Bern, New York 1986.

Organisations

British

Institute of Environmental Sciences Ltd, 14 Princes Gate, Hyde Park, London, SW7 1PU.

Royal Society of Arts (Environmental Secretary), 8 John Adam Street, London, WC2, tel. 01-930-5115.

American

The Center for Environmental Management, Tufts University, Medford, MA 02155, tel. (617)628-5000.

Thorne Ecological Institute, 5370 Manhattan Circle, Boulder, CO 80303, tel. (303)499-3647.

German

Bundesdeutscher Arbeitskreis für umweltbewußtes Management e.V. (B.A.U.M.), Christian-Förster-Str. 19, 2000 Hamburg 20, Tel. 040/40 77 21, 040/491 18 14.

2. CORPORATE AIMS AND STRATEGIES

Databases

International

Enviroline File 40, EIC/Intelligence, Inc., New York, vendor: DIALOG

Environmental Bibliography File 68, Environmental Studies Institute, Santa Barbara, CA, vendor: DIALOG.

Publications

International

Commission of the European Communities, European Better Environment Awards for Industry 1987, Brussels 1988.

European Environment Review, The Journal of European Community and International Environmental Policy and Law, Graham & Trotman Ltd, Sterling House, 66 Wilton Road, London SW1V 1DE, tel. 01-821-1123.

Joyce, Frank E., and Gunter Schneider (eds.), Environment and Economic Development in the Regions of the European Community, Avebury, Gower Publishing Company Limited, Gower House, Croff Road, Aldershot, Hants Gull 3 HR, England 1988.

British

Ashby, Eric, Reconciling Man with the Environment, Oxford University Press, Walton Street, Oxford, tel. 0865-56767, 1977.

Clean-up: it's good business. Confederation of British Industry, Centre Point, New Oxford Street, London, WC1, tel. 01-379-7400, 1986.

Elkington, John, with Tom Burke, The Green Capitalists, Industry's Search for Environmental Excellence, Victor Gollancz Limited, 14 Henrietta Street, London WC2E 8QJ, 1987, tel. 01-836-2006.

Elkington, John, Tom Burke and Julia Hailes, Green Pages, The Business of Saving the World, Routledge, 11 New Fetter Lane, London EC4P 4EE, 1988.

American

Beer, Stafford, Platform for Change, John Wiley & Sons Ltd, Chichester, New York, Brisbane, Toronto, corrected reprint 1978.

Brunner, David L. et al. (eds.), Corporations and the Environment: How Should Decisions Be Made? Paper from Symposium on Corporate Environmental Decision Making, sponsored by the Committee on Corporate Responsibility,

Graduate School of Business, Stanford University, CA, November 14–15, 1980.
Lund, Leonard, Corporate Organization for Environmental Policymaking, The Conference Board, Inc., New York, 1974.
Mayer, Frederick W., and Henry Lee (eds.), Environmental Risk Management: Research Needs and Opportunities, October 1986, # E-86-10, Energy and Environmental Policy Center, J.F.K. School of Government, Harvard University, Cambridge, MA.
Rowe, Allen J., Richard O. Mason, Karl E. Dickel, 2nd ed., Strategic Management & Business Policy: A Methodological Approach, Addison-Wesley Publication Company, 1985.

German

Arbeitsgemeinschaft für Umweltfragen e.V. (AGU), Umweltschutz und Technologie, Stenographisches Protokoll der Sitzung des 13. Umweltforums am 21. November 1985, Veröffentlichungen der AGU Nr. 28, Bonn 1986.
Binswanger, H.C., Arbeit und Umweltzerstörung, Frankfurt am Main 1983.
Brunowsky, R.-D., Wicke, L., Der Ökoplan (Durch Umweltschutz zum neuen Wirtschaftswunder), München, Zürich 1984; vgl. besonders S. 157ff.
Der Bundesminister des Innern, Abschlußbericht der Projektgruppe "Aktionsprogramm Ökologie", Argumente und Forderungen für eine ökologisch ausgerichtete Umweltvorsorgepolitik, Umweltbrief, Bonn, Oktober 1983.
Bundesverband der Deutschen Industrie e.V., Antworten auf eine Herausforderung, Berichte über praktizierten Umweltschutz in den Unternehmen, Köln 1978.
Bundesverband der Deutschen Industrie e.V., Industrie und Ökologie, Die Industrie nimmt zum Umweltschutz in der modernen Industriegesellschaft Stellung, BDI-Drucksache Nr. 172, Köln November 1984.
Bundesverband Junger Unternehmer der ASU e.V. (BJU), Umweltschutz als Teil der Unternehmensstrategie (eine Check-Liste des BJU für mehr Umweltschutz im Unternehmen), Mainz Juni 1985.
Dyllick, T., Beziehung zwischen Unternehmung und Umwelt, in: Die Betriebswirtschaft Nr. 3, 1986, S. 373ff.
Dyllick, T., Management der Umweltbeziehungen, in: Die Unternehmung, Nr. 3, 1988, S. 190ff.
Frank, H., Plaschka, G., Rößl, D. (Hrsg.), Umweltdynamik, Wien, New York 1988.
IG Metall, Mit uns für sinnvolle Arbeit und bessere Umwelt, Positionspapier der IG Metall "Umweltschutz im Betrieb", Frankfurt/M. Januar 1988.
Kieffer, K.W., Öko-Tagebuch eines Managers, Frankfurt/M. 1982.
Kirchenamt der Evangelischen Kirche in Deutschland und Sekretariat der Deutschen Bischofskonferenz, Gemeinsame Erklärung des Rates der Evangelischen Kirche in Deutschland und der Deutschen Bischofskonferenz, Verantwortung wahrnehmen für die Schöpfung, 2. Auflage, Gütersloh 1985.
Kreikebaum, H., Strategische Unternehmensplanung, Stuttgart 1981.
Lange, L., Umweltschutz und Unternehmensplanung, Wiesbaden 1978.
Liberales Institut (Hrsg.), Ökologische Marktwirtshaft als Lernprozeß, Zürich 1987. Bezugsquelle: Liberales Institut, Hottingerstr. 4, 8032 Zürich.
Mann, R., Das ganzheitliche Unternehmen, Bern, München, Wien 1988.

Meffert, H., Benkenstein, M., Schubert, F., Umweltschutz und Unternehmensverhalten, in: Harvard Manager, Heft 2, 1987, S. 32ff.

Nüßgens, K.H., Umweltschutz als eine Führungsaufgabe in Unternehmen, in: Fortschrittliche Betriebsführung, 23. Jg. (1974), Nr. 2, S. 111ff.

Oikos, Arbeitsunterlagen zur oikos-Konferenz Umweltorientierte Unternehmensführung, St. Gallen 1988, zu beziehen bei oikos – Umweltökonomische Studenteninitiative an der Hochschule St. Gallen, Dufourstr. 50, CH-9000 St. Gallen, Tel. 071/231915. Nähere Informationen erteilt Paschen von Flotow.

Öko-Institut, Projektgruppe ökologische Wirtschaft, Arbeiten im Einklang mit der Natur, Freiburg i.Br. 1985.

Pfriem, R. (Hrsg.), Ökologische Unternehmenspolitik, Frankfurt/M., New York 1986.

Senn, J.F., Ökologie-orientierte Unternehmensführung, Frankfurt/M., Bern, New York 1986.

Sprenger, R.-U., Umweltschutz und unternehmerisches Wettbewerbsverhalten, in: Umwelt und Energie, 1986, Nr. 1, Gruppe 12, S. 1ff.

Stahlmann, V., Umweltorientierte Materialwirtschaft, Wiesbaden 1988.

Stitzel, M., Ökologisch orientierte Unternehmensführung – Hemmung oder Förderung der Wettbewerbsfähigkeit der Unternehmung, in: Innovation und Wettbewerbsfähigkeit, Hrsg.: E. Dichtl, N. Gerke, A. Kieser, Wiesbaden 1987, S. 377ff.

Wicke, L., Die Ökologischen Milliarden (Das kostet die zerstörte Umwelt – so können wir sie retten), München 1986; vgl. besonders S. 172ff und S. 180ff.

Wicke, L., Umweltökonomie, München 1982.

Wicke, L., Offensiver betrieblicher Umweltschutz, in: Harvard Manager, 1987, Heft 3, S. 74ff.

Ernst Winter & Sohn (GmbH & Co) (Hrsg.), Umweltschutz als unternehmerische Aufgabe, in: Der Winter-Schneemann Nr. 10, 1979, S. 2; zu beziehen bei Ernst Winter & Sohn (GmbH & Co), Osterstraße 58, 2000 Hamburg 20.

Ernst Winter & Sohn (GmbH & Co) (Hrsg.), Winter-Modell: Pionierleistungen im Umweltschutz, in: Der Winter-Schneemann Nr. 20, Dezember 1985, S. 41ff; zu beziehen bei Ernst Winter & Sohn (GmbH & Co), Osterstraße 58, 2000 Hamburg 20.

Winter, G., Ein nationales Umwelt-Wiederaufbauwerk fände in Deutschland eine breite Unterstützung (Umweltbewußte Unternehmensführung – Die Wirtschaft steht vor einer neuen historischen Herausforderung), in: Handelsblatt Nr. 13 vom 18./19.1.1985, S. 21.

Organisations

American

Rocky Mountain Institute, 1739 Snowmass Creek Road, Old Snowmass, CO 81654-9199, tel. (303)744-8665, (303)927-3851.

Thorne Ecological Institute, 5370 Manhattan Circle, Boulder, CO 80303, tel. (303)499-3647.

German

Bundesdeutscher Arbeitskreis für umweltbewußtes Management e.V. (B.A.U.M.), Christian-Förster-Str. 19, 2000 Hamburg 20, Tel. 040/40 77 21, 040/491 18 14.

Bundesverband Junger Unternehmer der ASU e.V. (BJU); Bundesgeschäftsstelle: Mainzer Straße 238, 5300 Bonn 2, Tel. 0228/34 30 44.

3. MARKETING

Publications

International

European Environment Review, The Journal of European Community and International Environmental Policy and Law, Graham & Trotman Ltd, Sterling House, 66 Wilton Road, London SW1V 1DE, tel. 01-821-1123.

British

Elkington, John, with Tom Burke, The Green Capitalists, Industry's Search for Environmental Excellence, Victor Gollancz Limited, 14 Henrietta Street, London WC2E 8QJ, 1987.

Elkington, John, Tom Burke and Julia Hailes, Green Pages, The Business of Saving the World, Routledge, 11 New Fetter Lane, London EC4P 4EE, 1988.

Elkington, John, and Julia Hailes of Sustain Ability, The Green Consumer Guide, Victor Gollancz, 14 Henrietta Street, London WC2E 8QJ, 1988.

American

Fisk, Georg, Marketing and the Ecological Crisis, Harper & Row Inc., 10 East, 53rd Street, New York, 1974.

Environmental Concerns Force Global Change In the Market, Chemical Week, Vol. 42# 18, McGraw-Hill, Inc., New York, May 14, 1988, p. 22–39.

Henion, Karl E., and Thomas C. Kinnear (eds.), Ecological Marketing, American Marketing Association, National Workshop on Ecological Marketing, Austin, Texas, 1976 (university microfilm).

Michman, Ronald D., Linking Ecology and Public Policy with Marketing Planning, Akron Business and Economic Review, Fall 1985.

Murphy, Patrick E., and Eugene Laczniak, Marketing & Ecology: Retrospect & Prospect, Business & Society, Fall '77, Volume XVIII No. 1, p. 26–34. Roosevelt University, Walter E. Heller College of Business, Chicago.

Perry, Donald L., Social Marketing Strategies: Conservation Issues & Analysis, Goodyear Publishing, Pacific Palisades, California, 1976.

Pollution Engineering Magazine, Pudvan Publishing Company, Northbrook, IL 60062, tel. (312) 498-9840.

Zeithaml, C.P., Zeithaml, V.A., Environmental Management: Revising the Marketing Perspective, in: Journal of Marketing, Vol. 48 (1984), Spring, p. 46, Harper & Row, Inc., 10 East, 53rd Street, New York.

German

Belz, C., Stillstand des Öko-Marketing, in: Thexis Nr. 3, 1988.

Burghold, J., Implikationen eines ökologisch orientierten Marketing, dargestellt am Beispiel der Absatz-Marktprogrammerstellung in der Konsumgüterindustrie, Augsburg, 1988, (Das Literaturverzeichnis umfaßt ca. 400 einschlägige deutsch- und englischsprachige Quellen)

Hasitschka, W., Ökologisches Marketing, in: Marketing ZFP, 6. Jg. (1984), Nr. 4, S. 245ff.

Hillmann, K.-H., Umweltkrise und Umweltwandel, 2. Auflage, Würzburg 1986.

Liese, H.-J., Markt und Umwelt, München 1986.

Meffert, H., Gestaltung und Durchsetzung ökologiegerechter Marketingkonzeptionen, in: Strategische Unternehmensführung und Marketing. Beiträge zur marktorientierten Unternehmenspolitik, Hrsg.: H. Meffert, Wiesbaden 1988.

Meffert, H., Bruhn, M., Schubert, F., Walther, Th., Marketing und Ökologie – Chancen und Risiken umweltorientierter Absatzstrategien der Unternehmungen, in: Die Betriebswirtschaft, Heft 2, 1986, S. 140–159.

Meffert, H. Kirchgeorg, M., Ostmeier, H., Analysekonzepte und strategische Optionen des ökologieorientierten Marketing, in: Thexis, 1988, Heft 3, S. 5ff.

Meffert, H., Wagner, H., (Hrsg.), Marketing und Ökologie – eine Bestandsaufnahme, Arbeitspapiere der Wissenschaftlichen Gesellschaft für Marketing und Unternehmensführung e.V., Nr. 25, Münster 1985.

Meyer, W., und das Lehr- und Forschungsteam Marketing an der Universität Augsburg (Hrsg.), Ökologie und Marketing, Ökologische Herausforderungen und wirtschaftliche Problemlösungen, Arbeitspapiere zur Schriftenreihe Schwerpunkt Marketing, Band 9, Augsburg 1985.

Raffée, H. Wiedmann, K.P., Die künftige Bedeutung der Produktqualität unter Einschluß ökologischer Gesichtspunkte, in: Qualität – Die Herausforderung, Hrsg.: Lisson, A., Berlin u.a. 1987, S. 349–377.

Raffée, H., und Wolfgang, F., Bedarfslenkendes Marketing von Elektrizitätsversorgungsunternehmen, Arbeitspapiere des Institutes für Marketing der Universität Mannheim, Nr. 3, Mannheim 1980.

Ruppen, L., Marketing und Umweltschutz, Diss. 1978, Fribourg

Schreiber, R.L., Marketing und Werbung im Dienst der Ökologie, ZV + ZV 18/1985, S. 20ff.

Senn, J.F., Ökologie-orientierte Unternehmensführung, Frankfurt/M., Bern, New York 1986.

Stahlmann, V., Umweltorientierte Materialwirtschaft, Wiesbaden 1988.

Thome, G., Produktpolitik und Ökologie, München 1981.

Umweltbundesamt (Hrsg.), Umweltfreundliche Beschaffung, Handbuch zur Berücksichtigung des Umweltschutzes in der öffentlichen Verwaltung und im Einkauf, Wiesbaden und Berlin 1987.

Wiedmann, K.P., Ökologisches Bewußtsein und unternehmerisches Marketing, Arbeitspapiere des Instituts für Marketing der Universität Mannheim, Nr. 28, Mannheim 1984.

Organisations

American

The Center for Environmental Management, Tufts University, Medford, MA 02155, tel. (617)628-5000.
NutraClean, 149 Franklin St., Suite B, Oakland, CA 94607, tel. (415) 832-1415.

German

Bundesdeutscher Arbeitskreis für umweltbewußtes Management e.V (B.A.U.M.), Christian-Förster-Str. 19, 2000 Hamburg 20, Tel. 040/40 77 21, 040/491 18 14.

4. IN-HOUSE ENVIRONMENTAL PROTECTION ARRANGEMENTS

Databases

German

UMPLIS (Informations- und Dokumentationssystem Umwelt beim Umweltbundesamt Berlin), Bismarckplatz 1, 1000 Berlin 33, Tel. 030/8903-555.

Publications

British

Clean-up: it's good business. Confederation of British Industry, Centre Point, New Oxford Street, London WC1, tel. 01-379-7400, 1986.
Ekins, Paul, ed., The living economy: a new economics in the making, Routledge and Kegan Paul Ltd., Broadway House, Newtown Road, Henley-on-Thames, Surrey, tel. 0753-39435, 1986.
Elkington, John with Tom Burke, The Green Capitalists, Industry's Search for Environmental Excellence, Victor Gollancz Limited, 14 Henrietta Street, London WC2E 8QJ, 1987.

American

Hazardous Waste Reduction: A Critical Ounce of Prevention, Presentation at European Conference on Industry and Environmental Management, October 12, 1987, Interlaken, Switzerland. Presented by Joanna Underwood, Executive Director of INFORM, New York.

German

Deutsche BP Aktiengesellschaft (Hrsg.), BP Umweltschutz-Enquête 1986 (BP-Enquête über die Arbeit deutscher Umweltschutzbeauftragter), Hamburg 1986. Für Rückfragen: Dr. Klaus Repenning, Umweltschutzbeauftragter, Tel. 040/635 26 90.

Gorges, H.A., Organisation im Umweltschutz, in: Handbuch des Umweltschutzes (Loseblattsammlung), herausgegeben von J. Vogl, A. Heigl, K. Schäfer, Band 5, München 1977.

Institut für ökologische Wirtschaftsforschung (IÖW), Zur Reform des betrieblichen Umweltbeauftragten, Schriftenreihe, Oktober 1988.

Schneider, G., Die Notwendigkeit einer vorausschauenden Umweltplanung unter besonderer Berücksichtigung der europäischen Umweltpolitik, in: Umweltschutz der achtziger Jahre, herausgegeben vom Institut für Umweltschutz der Universität Dortmund, Berlin 1981, S. 31–37.

Senn, J.F., Ökologie-orientierte Unternehmensführung Frankfurt/M., Bern, New York 1986.

Stahlmann, V., Umweltorientierte Materialwirtschaft, Wiesbaden1988.

Stahlmann, V., Das Institut des Umweltbeauftragten und seine Reformierbarkeit, IOeW-Schriftreihe, Juni 1988.

Ernst Winter & Sohn (GmbH & Co) (Hrsg.), Winter-Modell: Pionierleistungen im Umweltschutz, in: Der Winter-Schneemann Nr. 20, Dezember 1985, S. 41ff.; zu beziehen bei Ernst Winter & Sohn (GmbH & Co), Osterstraße 58, 2000 Hamburg 20.

Zimmermann, M., (Hrsg.), Umweltberatung in Theorie und Praxis, in: Stadtforschung aktuell, Bd. 18, Basel, Boston 1988.

Organisations

German

Bundesdeutscher Arbeitskreis für umweltbewußtes Management e.V. (B.A.U.M.), Christian-Förster-Str. 19, 2000 Hamburg 20, Tel. 040/40 77 21, 040/491 18 14.

Verband der Betriebsbeauftragten für Umweltschutz e.V., Alfredstr. 77–79, 4300 Essen, Tel. 0201/77 20 11.

5. STAFF MOTIVATION AND TRAINING

Databases

American

Occupational Safety & Health Administration, Training & Education System, Office of Management Data Systems, U.S. Dept. of Labor, OSHA, 200 Constitution Ave., NW, Washington, DC 20210, tel. (202)523-7008.

German

DOMA, Dokumentation Maschinenbau, Ostbahnhofstr. 3, 6000 Frankfurt/Main 1, Tel. 069/4308-232.

Publications

British

Bingham, Gail, Resolving environmental disputes: a decade of experience. The Conservation Foundation, 11a West Halkin Street, London, SW1, Tel. 01-235-1793, 1986.

Elkington, John, with Tom Burke, The Green Capitalists, Industry's Search for Environmental Excellence, Victor Gollancz Limited, 14 Henrietta Street, London WC2E 8QJ, 1987.

The Environmentalist (Environmental Education), Science and Technology Letters, 12 Clarence Row, Kew; Surrey, TW9 3NL.

American

Applied Industrial Hygiene (monthly), Applied Industrial Hygiene, Inc., American Conference of Governmental Hygienists, 6500 Glenway Avenue, Cincinnati, OH 45211-4438, tel. (513)661-7881.

German

Kayser, B., Bericht über Aktivitäten der Umwelterziehung in Bund, Ländern und überregionalen Institutionen, herausgegeben von der UNESCO – Verbindungsstelle für Umwelterziehung im Umweltbundesamt, Berlin August 1984.

Knittel, B./Gege, M., Konzept für die Ausbildung zum Umweltberater für Haushalt, Familie und Kommunen, Hamburg 1986. (Noch nicht veröffentlicht, zu beziehen durch: Aktionsgemeinschaft Umwelt, Gesundheit, Ernährung e.V. (A.U.G.E.), Christian-Förster-Str. 19, 2000 Hamburg 20, Tel. 040/40 26 97).

Ökomedia Institut (Hrsg), Medienkursbuch Ökologie, Freiburg 1985.

Opaschowski, H.W., Freizeit und Umwelt, Band 6 der Schriftenreihe zur Freizeitforschung, herausgegeben von B.A.T. Freizeitforschungsinstitut, Hamburg 1985.

Schwab, K./Kroos, H., Moderne Unternehmensführung im Maschinenbau, herausgegeben vom Verein Deutscher Maschinenbau-Anstalten e.V., Frankfurt/Main-Niederrad 1971.

Senn, J.F., Ökologie-orientierte Unternehmensführung, Frankfurt/M., Bern, New York 1986.

Ernst Winter & Sohn (GmbH & Co.)(Hrsg.), Winter-Modell: Pionierleistungen im Umweltschutz, in: Der Winter-Schneemann Nr. 20, Dezember 1985, S. 41ff.; zu beziehen bei Ernst Winter & Sohn (GmbH & Co.), Osterstraße 58, 2000 Hamburg 20.

Organisations

British

National Association for Environmental Education, West Midlands College of Higher Education, Gorway, Walsall, WS1 3BD.

American

Midwest Center for Occupational Health & Safety, St. Paul-Ramsey Medical Center, 640 Jackson Street, St. Paul, MN 55101, tel. (612)221-3992.

The Minerva Education Institute, Xavier University, Cincinnati, OH 45207, tel. (513)745-3057.

German

Aktionsgemeinschaft Umwelt, Gesundheit, Ernährung e.V. (A.U.G.E.), Christian-Förster-Str. 19, 2000 Hamburg 20, Tel. 040/40 26 97.

Bundesdeutscher Arbeitskreis für umweltbewußtes Management e.V. (B.A.U.M.), Christian-Förster-Straße 19, 2000 Hamburg 20, Tel. 040/40 77 21, 040/491 18 14.

6. WORKING CONDITIONS

Databases

British

HSE Line, Library and Information Services, Research and Laboratory Service, Broad Lane, Sheffield, S3 7HQ, tel. 0742-768141.

American

Environmental Health News, (Occupational Safety and Health reports from OSHA, NIOSH, TSCA, EPA), tel. OSH 212-752-4530

Occupational Safety & Health Administration Training & Education System, Office of Management Data Systems, Occupational Safety & Health Administration, U.S. Department of Labor, 200 Constitution Avenue, NW, Washington, DC 20210, tel. (202)523-7008.

German

Dokumentation über Arbeitsmarkt- und Berufsforschung, Institut für Arbeitsmarkt- und Berufsforschung der Bundesanstalt für Arbeit, Regensburger Straße 104, 8500 Nürnberg 1.

Dokumentation über Arbeitsschutz, Bundesanstalt für Arbeitsschutz, Postfach 17 02 02, 4600 Dortmund 1.

Dokumentation über Humanisierung des Arbeitslebens, Institut der Deutschen Wirtschaft, Gustav-Heinemann-Ufer 84–88, 5000 Köln 51.

Publications

British

Croner's Health and Safety at Work (published yearly). Croner Publications Ltd, Croner House, 173 Kingston Road, New Malden, Surrey KT3 3SS, tel. 01-942-8966.

Environmental Health (Journal of the Institute of Environmental Health Officers), Chadwick House, Rishworth Street, London, SE1 0QT, tel. 01-928-8006.
Health and Safety Executive, Baynards' House, 1–13 Chepstow Place, London W2 4TF, tel. 01-229-3456, selection of free leaflets.
PM International Newsletter (newsheet covering health at work, energy management, accident prevention, industrial security and pollution control), Wealden Press Ltd, South Park, Lodge, Mayfield Lane, Wadhurst, East Sussex, TN5 6JE, tel. 089-288-2366, selection of free leaflets.

American

Applied Industrial Hygiene (monthly), Applied Industrial Hygiene, Inc., American Conference of Governmental Hygienists, 6500 Glenway Avenue, Cincinnati, OH 45211-4438, tel. (513)661-7881.
Hudgins, Randall and Ruth Ruttenberg, Occupational Safety and Health in the Chemical Industry, Council on Economic Priorities, St. Martin's Press, 1981.
Indoor Air Facts, No. 3: Ventilation and Air Quality in Offices, Office of Air & Radiation, U.S. EPA, Washington Feb. 1988.
Indoor Pollutants, Committee on Indoor Pollutants, Board on Toxicology & Environmental Health Hazards, National Research Council, National Academy Press, Washington, DC, 1981.
Indoor Pollution News, Burall Publications, Inc., A Subsidiary of The Bureau of National Affairs, Inc., 2445 M Street, NW, Washington, DC 20037, tel. (202) 452-7889.
Levy, Barry S., and David H. Wegman (eds.), Occupational Health: Recognizing and Preventing Work-Related Disease, Little, Brown & Company, Boston, 1983.
Polakoff, Phillip L., Work & Health, It's Your Life: An Action Guide to Job Hazards, Press Associates, Inc., Washington, DC, 1984.

German

Below, F. v., Borges, A., Hildebrandt, F., Moderne Fabrikorganisation – Stand und Entwicklungstendenzen, Berlin, Heidelberg, New York, Tokyo 1985.
Fischer, C. und R., Chemie im Büro, Hamburg 1988.
Hackstein, R. Heeg, F.J., Below, F.v. Arbeitsorganisation und neue Technologien, Berlin, Heidelberg, New York, Tokyo 1986.
Heeg, F.J., Qualitätszirkel und andere Gruppenaktivitäten – Einsatz in der betrieblichen Praxis und Anwendung, fir-Reihe Forschung für die Praxis – Band 1 (Hrsg. R. Hackstein), Berlin, Heidelberg, New York, Tokyo 1985.
IG Metall, Arbeitsschutz ist Umweltschutz (eine Dokumentation bestehend aus Artikeln aus METALL und "Der Gewerkschafter" seit 1983), zusammengestellt von Werner Hoffmann, Frankfurt/M. November 1987.
Institut für Angewandte Arbeitswissenschaft e.V. (Hrsg.), Klima und Luft am Arbeitsplatz – Meßtechnisches Taschenbuch für den Betriebspraktiker, Köln 1986.
Katalyse, BUND, Öko-Institut, ULF, Chemie am Arbeitsplatz, Hamburg 1987.
Öko-Institut, Projektgruppe ökologische Wirtschaft, Arbeiten im Einklang mit der Natur, Freiburg i.Br. 1985.

Umweltbundesamt (Hrsg.), Umweltfreundliche Beschaffung, Handbuch zur Berücksichtigung des Umweltschutzes in der öffentlichen Verwaltung und im Einkauf, Wiesbaden und Berlin 1987.

Organisations

American

American Society of Heating, Refrigerating & Air-Conditioning Engineers (ASHRAE), 1791 Tullie Circle, N.E., Atlanta, GA 30329, tel. (404)636-8400.

Midwest Center for Occupational Health & Safety, St. Paul-Ramsey Medical Center, 640 Jackson Street, St. Paul, MN 55101, tel. (612)221-3992.

The Minerva Education Institute, Xavier University, Cincinnati, OH 45207, tel. (513)745-3057.

National Institute of Occupational Safety and Health (NIOSH), 200 Independence Avenue, SW, Room 714B, Washington, DC, 20201, tel. (202)472-7134.

Occupational Safety & Health Administration (OSHA), U.S. Department of Labor, 200 Constitution Avenue, NW, Washington, DC 20210, tel. (202)523-7008.

Office of Air & Radiation, U.S. Environmental Protection Agency, Washington, DC 20460.

William Mc Donough Architects, 116 E. 27th Street, New York, NY 10016, tel. (212)481-1111.

British

The Department of Social Insurance and Industrial Welfare, The Trades Union Congress, Congress House, Great Russell Street, London WC1, tel. 01-636-4030.

The Health and Safety Executive, Baynards House, 1–13 Chepstow Place, Westbourne Grove, London W2 4TF, tel. 01-229-3456, government agency.

German

Berufsgenossenschaftliches Institut für Arbeitssicherheit (BIA), Lindenstraße 80, 5208 St. Augustin 2.

Förderung von Projekten zur menschengerechten Ausgestaltung der Arbeitswelt: Deutsche Forschungs- und Versuchsanstalt für Luft- und Raumfahrt e.V. (DFVLR), Projektträger "Humanisierung des Arbeitslebens (HdA)", Südstraße 125, 5300 Bonn 2.

Gesellschaft für Arbeitswissenschaft (GfA), Geschäftsstelle, Ardeystr. 67, 4600 Dortmund 1.

Institut für Arbeitswissenschaft der RWTH Aachen, Wüllnerstr. 5, Pontdriesch 14–16, Kreuzherrnstr. 4, 5100 Aachen.

Kommission zur Reinhaltung der Luft des Vereins Deutscher Ingenieure (VDI), Graf-Recke-Str. 84, 4000 Düsseldorf 1.

MAK-Werte: Kommission zur Prüfung gesundheitsschädlicher Arbeitsstoffe der Deutschen Forschungsgemeinschaft, Geschäftsstelle der Deutschen Forschungsgemeinschaft (DFG), Kennedyallee 40, 5300 Bonn 2.

Technische Regeln für gefährliche Arbeitsstoffe: Ausschuß für gefährliche Arbeitsstoffe (AgA) beim Bundesminister für Arbeit und Sozialordnung, Bundesanstalt für Arbeitsschutz und Unfallforschung, Postfach 170202, 4600 Dortmund 17.

Verein Deutscher Sicherheitsingenieure e.V. (VDSI), Postfach 120764, 6200 Wiesbaden, Tel. 06121/60 04 00.

7. CANTEEN FOOD

Publications

British

Elkington, John, Tom Burke and Julia Hailes, Green Pages, The Business of Saving the World, Routledge, 11 New Fetter Lane, London ECP 4EE, 1988.

Elkington, John, and Julia Hailes of Sustain Ability, The Green Consumer Guide, Victor Gollancz, 14 Henrietta Street, London WC2E 8QJ, 1988.

Guide to Healthy Eating, free from the Health Education Authority, 78 New Oxford Street, London, WC1A 1AH.

Hanssen, Maurice with Till Marsden, The New E for Additives, Thorsons Ltd., Dennington Estate, Wellingborough Northants, tel. 0933-440 033.

American

Carper, Jean, Total Nutrition Guide, Bantam Books, New York, 1987.

Goldbeck, Nikki and David, The Goldbecks' Guide to Good Food: Your Complete Shopping Guide to the Best, Most Healthful Foods Available in Supermarkets, Natural Food Stores, And By Mail, Nal Books, New York, 1988.

Vander, Arthur J., Nutrition, Stress, and Toxic Chemicals, The University of Michigan Press, Ann Arbor, 1981.

Wurtman, Judith J., Managing Your Mind & Mood Through Food, Harper & Row Publishers, New York, 1988.

German

Gasper, H., Kämper, U., u.a., Chemie in Lebensmitteln, Frankfurt/Main 1982, herausgegeben von der Katalyse-Umwelt-Gruppe Köln e.V.

Gege, M., Jung, H., Pick, H.J., Winter, G., Das Öko-Sparbuch für Haushalt und Familie, München 1986.

Haas, R., Die Dr. Haas-Leistungsdiät – für Sport, Beruf und Fitness, München 1985.

Heinze, U., Linden, W. u.a., Was wir alles schlucken – Zusatzstoffe in Lebensmitteln –, Reinbek bei Hamburg 1985, herausgegeben von der Katalyse-Umwelt-Gruppe, Köln e.V.

Kapfelsberger, E./Pollmer, U., Iß und stirb, Köln 1983.

Koch, E.R., Krebswelt, Köln 1981.

Mackarness, R., Allergie gegen Nahrungsmittel und Chemikalien, Stuttgart 1982.

Umweltbundesamt (Hrsg.), Umweltfreundliche Beschaffung, Handbuch zur Berücksichtigung des Umweltschutzes in der öffentlichen Verwaltung und im Einkauf, Wiesbaden und Berlin 1987.

Organisations

British

Health Education Authority, 78 New Oxford Street, London WC1, tel. 01-631-0930.

American

NutraClean, 149 Franklin St., Suite B, Oakland, CA 94607, tel. (415)832-1415.

German

Aktionsgemeinschaft Umwelt, Gesundheit, Ernährung e.V. (A.U.G.E.), Christian-Förster-Str. 19, 2000 Hamburg 20, Tel. 040/40 26 97.

8. ENVIRONMENTAL COUNSELLING FOR EMPLOYEES' HOUSEHOLDS

Publications

International

AUGE, Feasibility Demonstration Project for Household and Community Environmental Advisors, Project Report and Summary, Commission of European Community Contract No. 6613(86)01, Aktionsgemeinschaft Umwelt, Gesundheit, Ernährung e.V., D-2000 Hamburg 20, Sillemstraße 36.

ECO-CONSEIL, Institut pour le conseil en environnement, Le temps des éco-emplois, Projet-pilote européen de création de postes de conseillers en environnement auprès des communes et des ménages (Label de l'Année Européenne de l'Environnement 3 176), Rapport intérimaire sur la réalisation du projet-pilote en Alsace et sur ses perspectives de développement. Obtainable from: ECO-CONSEIL, Institut pour le conseil en environnement, Siège – tél.: 88 60 16 19, 6, rue d'Arras, 67000 Strasbourg. For further information please contact Mrs. Esther Peter-Davis, director of the Institute, same telephone number.

British

Nature Conservancy Council, Northminster House, Peterborough, PE1 1UA, tel. 0733 40345, a range of publications.

Elkington, John, and Julia Hailes of Sustain Ability, The Green Consumer Guide, Victor Gollancz, 14 Henrietta Street, London WC2E 8QJ, 1988.

American

Bierman-Lytle, Paul, Building a Healthy House, Everything Natural, September/October 1986. Newsletter is defunct, get article from the Masters Corporation, P.O.Box 514, New Canaan, CT 06840, tel. (203) 966-3541.

Collins, Card C. (ed.), Our Food, Air and Water: How Safe Are They?, Facts on File Publications, New York, 1984.

ENVIRON: A Magazine for Ecologic Living, Wary Canary Press, Box 8820, Ft. Collins, CO 80525, tel. (303)223-8816.

Goldbeck, Nikki and David, The Goldbecks' Guide to Good Food: Your Composite Shopping Guide to the Best, Most Healthful Foods Available in Supermarkets, Natural Food Stores, And By Mail, Nat Books, New York, 1988.

Healthy Home section in Practical Homeowner (monthly), Rodale Press, Inc., Emmaus, PA.

Hershkowitz, Allen, Joanna Underwood & Maarten de Kadt, Garbage: Practices, Problems & Remedies, INFORM, Inc., New York, 1988.

The Natural Choice: Non-Toxic Home Products, LIVOS Plant Chemistry, 614 Agua Fria Street, Santa Fe, NM 87501, tel. (505)988-9111.

Water Wheel: Your Guide to Home Water Conservation ECOS, Inc., Damonmill Square, Concord, MA 01742, tel. (617)369-3951.

German

Aktionsgemeinschaft Umwelt, Gesundheit, Ernährung e.V. (A.U.G.E.) (Hrsg.), Aktuelles Aktionsprogramm zum Modellprojekt Umweltberatung für Haushalt, Familie und Kommunen; Bezugsquelle: Aktionsgemeinschaft Umwelt, Gesundheit, Ernährung e.V., Sillemstr. 36, 2000 Hamburg 20, Tel. 040/40 26 97.

Autorengruppe, koordiniert und überarbeitet von R. Grießhammer, Chemie im Haushalt, Reinbek bei Hamburg 1984; herausgegeben von: Öko-Institut Freiburg, Katalyse-Umweltgruppe, Köln, Verein für Umwelt- und Arbeitsschutz, Bund für Umwelt und Naturschutz Deutschland e.V. (BUND).

Der Bundesminister für Jugend, Familie und Gesundheit, Chemie im Haushalt und Innenraumbelastung, Antwort der Bundesregierung auf eine große Anfrage, Bundestags-Drucksache 10/4285 vom 19.11.1985.

Gege, M., Jung, H., Pick, H.J., Winter, G., Das Öko-Sparbuch für Haushalt und Familie, München 1986.

Grießhammer, R., Der Öko-Knigge, Reinbek bei Hamburg 1984.

Koch, E.R., Umweltschutz zu Hause, München 1984.

Mihailescu, A., Umwelt-Sünden-Katalog, München 1983.

Mohr, P.C., Vier Faustregeln für den Umweltberater, Hamburg 1985; Bezugsquelle; Aktionsgemeinschaft Umwelt, Gesundheit, Ernährung e.V. (A.U.G.E.), Christian-Förster-Str. 19, 2000 Hamburg 20, Tel. 040/40 26 97.

Mohr, P.C., Umweltberatung durch Privatpersonen und Behörden, ein Beitrag zu den Rechtsgrundlagen der Umweltberatung für die privaten Haushalte, Natur und Recht, Erscheinungsjahr 1988, genauer Zeitpunkt noch ungewiß.

Umweltbundesamt (Hrsg.), Umweltfreundliche Beschaffung, Handbuch zur Berücksichtigung des Umweltschutzes in der öffentlichen Verwaltung und im Einkauf, Wiesbaden und Berlin 1987.

Ernst Winter & Sohn (GmbH & Co) (Hrsg.), Winter-Modell: Pionierleistungen im Umweltschutz, in: Der Winter-Schneemann Nr. 20, Dezember 1985, S. 41ff; zu beziehen bei Ernst Winter & Sohn (GmbH & Co), Osterstraße 58, 2000 Hamburg 20.

Organisations

American

Master's Corporation, P.O. Box 514, 12 Curtis Avenue, New Canaan, CT 06840, tel. (203)966-3541.

German

Aktionsgemeinschaft Umwelt, Gesundheit, Ernährung e.V. (A.U.G.E.), Christian-Förster-Str. 19, 2000 Hamburg 20, Tel. 040/40 26 97.

9. ECONOMISING ON ENERGY AND WATER

Databases

International

Energyline. (Energy policy US and international), EIC Intelligence Inc., 48 West 38th Street, New York, NY 10018, USA, 0101, tel. 212 944 8500.

American

DOE Energy File 103, 104, U.S. Department of Energy, Washington, DC, vendor: DIALOG.

Energy & Environmental Database, Center for Energy & Environmental Information, Oak Ridge National Lab, vendors: DIALOG, SDC, BRS.

German

Dokumentation Maschinenbau, Ostbahnhofstr. 13, 6000 Frankfurt/Main, Tel. 069/4308-215/227.

Publications

British

Burberry, Peter, Building for Energy Conservation, The Royal Institute of British Architects, Finsbury Mission, 39 Moreland Street, London, EC1V 8BB, 1978.

Department of Energy, Energy Efficiency in Buildings, Information Division Distribution Unit, Room 1312 Thames House South, Millbank, London, SW1P 4QJ, 1985.

Department of Trade and Industry, A Brief Guide to Support and Advice for Recycling (Business Advice for Smaller Firms, Technical Advice, Help with energy costs, Research and Development Support for new Technology in the collection and disposal of waste, Research and Development Support for new Technology using waste as a fuel, Support for Innovation, EEC Support for R & D, DTI Support for R & D), available from Department of Trade and Industry, Minerals and Metals Division 3, Room 1014, Ashdown House, 123 Victoria Street, London SW1E 6RB.

Department of Trade and Industry, Folder: The Government Focus on Reclamation containing A Brief Guide to Support and Advice for Recycling; Watch your Waste – organisations to contact; Watch your Waste – a new video about reclamation. Obtainable from Department of Trade and Industry or Confederation of British Industry, Centre Point, 103 New Oxford Street, London WC1A 1DU, tel. 01-379 7400.

Elkington, John, Tom Burke and Julia Hailes, Green Pages, The Business of Saving the World, Routledge, 11 New Fetter Lane, London EC4P 4EE, 1988.

Elkington, John, and Julia Hailes of Sustain Ability, The Green Consumer Guide, Victor Gollancz, 14 Henrietta Street, London WC2E 8QJ, 1988.

Langley, K.F., Industrial Energy Efficiency in the UK up to the Year 2000, Information Office, Energy Technology Support Unit, Building 156, Atomic Energy Research Establishment, Harwell, Oxon, OX11 ORA 1985.

Parker, Colin, and Roberts, Tim, Energy from Waste, ERL, 106 Gloucester Place, London, W1H 3DB; tel. 01-486-1211, 1985.

American

Energy Conservation Indicators, Energy Information Administration, Publishing # DOE/EPA, 0441, Washington D.C., 1986.

Gillette Water Conservation Program: Water Conservation & Audit Tips: The Gillette Company, Prudential Tower Building, Boston, MA 02199, tel. (617) 421-7000.

Water Use Management for Dollars and Sense: Guidelines for Establishing Water Management Programs for Industry, Business, and Hotels & Motels, Resource Management Associates, Inc., West Barnstable, MA 02668, 1982.

German

Borch, G., Fürbock, M., Mansfeld, L., Winje, D., Energiemanagement, Bd. I–VI, Berlin, Heidelberg, New York, Tokyo 1986.

Bundesverband Junger Unternehmer der ASU e.V. (BJU), Umweltschutz als Teil der Unternehmensstrategie (Eine Check-Liste des BJU für mehr Umweltschutz im Unternehmen), Mainz 1985.

Technologie-Nachrichten Nr. 381 – 1.8.1986, An den Eichen, 5202 Hennef-Lichtenberg.

Umweltbundesamt (Hrsg.), Umweltfreundliche Beschaffung, Handbuch zur Berücksichtigung des Umweltschutzes in der öffentlichen Verwaltung und im Einkauf, Wiesbaden und Berlin 1987.

VDMA-Referat Energie, Maßnahmen zur Energieeinsparung im Betrieb, Frankfurt/M. 1982.

Organisations

British

The Association for the Conservation of Energy, 9 Sherlock Mews, London W1M 3RH, tel. 01-935-1495.

Department of Environment, Energy Efficiency Office, Distribution Unit, Room 1312, Thames House, South Millbank, London, SW1P 4QJ. Offer advice and a range of publications, tel. 01-211-5779.

American

Air Pollution Control Association, P.O.Box 2861, Pittsburgh, PA 15230, tel. (412)232-3444.

Council on Economic Priorities, 30 Irving Place, New York, NY 10003, tel. (212)420-1133.

Current Awareness Publications from Office of Scientific and Technical Information, National Technical Information Service, U.S. Department of Commerce, 5285 Port Royal Rd., Springfield, VA 22161, tel. (703)487-4650.

Government Institutes, Inc., 966 Hungerford Drive, # 24, Rockville, MD 20850, tel. (301)251-9250.

INFORM, 381 Park Ave. South, New York, NY 10016, tel. (212) 689-4040.

National Energy Information Center, U.S. Department of Energy, 1 FO48 Forrestal Bldg., 1000 Independence Ave. NW, Washington, DC 20585.

NYSERDA, Rockefeller Plaza, Albany, NY 12223, tel. (518) 465-6251.

Office of Deputy Assistant Secretary for Renewable Energy Technology, U.S. Department of Energy, 1000 Independence Ave. SW, Washington, D.C. 20585, tel. (202)586-9275.

Rocky Mountain Institute, 1739 Snowmass Creek Road, Old Snowmass, CO 81654-9199, tel. (303)744-8665, (303)927-3851.

German

Bundesdeutscher Arbeitskreis für umweltbewußtes Management e.V. (B.A.U.M.), Christian-Förster-Str. 19, 2000 Hamburg 20, Tel. 040/40 77 21, 040/491 18 14.

Bundesverband Junger Unternehmer der ASU e.V. (BJU), Bundesgeschäftsstelle: Mainzer Straße 238, 5300 Bonn 2, tel. 02 28/34 30 44.

Verband Deutscher Maschinen- und Anlagenbau e.V. (VDMA), Technische Abteilung, Bereich Umweltpolitik, Lyoner Straße 18, 6000 Frankfurt/Main, tel. 069/6603-325.

10. PRODUCT DEVELOPMENT

Publications

International

Commission of the European Communities, European Better Environment Awards for Industry 1987, Brussels 1988

British

Department of Trade and Industry, A Brief Guide to Support and Advice for Recycling (Business Advice for Smaller Firms, Technical Advice, Help with energy costs, Research and Development Support for new Technology in the collection and disposal of waste, Research and Development Support for new Technology using waste as a fuel, Support for Innovation, EEC Support for R & D, DTI Support for R & D), available from Department of Trade and Industry, Minerals and Metals Division 3, Room 1014, Ashdown House, 123 Victoria Street, London SW1E 6RB.

Elkington, John, with Tom Burke, The Green Capitalists, Industry's Search for Environmental Excellence, Victor Gollancz Limited, 14 Henrietta Street, London WC2E 8QJ, 1987.

Elkington, John, Tom Burke and Julia Hailes, Green Pages, The Business of Saving the World, Routledge, 11 New Fetter Lane, London EC4P 4EE, 1988.

Elkington, John, and Julia Hailes of Sustain Ability, The Green Consumer Guide, Victor Gollancz, 14 Henrietta Street, London WC2E 8QJ, 1988.

American

Stahel, W.R., Hidden Resources – Product life as a variable: the notion of utilization. Science and public policy, August 1986.

German

Blom, F., Beschaffungsmarktforschung: Warum? Wo? Wie?, Nürnberg 1982.

Börlin, M., in Zusammenarbeit mit Walter R. Stahel, Wirtschaftliche Strategie der Dauerhaftigkeit, Betrachtungen über die Verlängerung der Lebensdauer von Produkten als Beitrag zur Vermeidung von Abfällen, herausgegeben vom Schweizerischen Bankverein, Schweiz, November 1987.

Raffée, H., Wiedmann, K.-P., Die künftige Bedeutung der Produktqualität unter Einschluß ökologischer Gesichtspunkte, in: Qualität – Die Herausforderung, Hrsg.: Lisson, A., Berlin u.a. 1987, S. 349–377.

Senn, J.F., Ökologie-orientierte Unternehmensführung, Frankfurt/M., Bern, New York 1986.

Strebel, H., Umwelt und Betriebswirtschaft, Berlin 1980.

Studien- und Fördergesellschaft der Schleswig-Holsteinischen Wirtschaft e.V., Wirtschaft und Umweltschutz in Schleswig-Holstein, Rendsburg 1984.

Thome, G., Produktpolitik und Ökologie, München 1981.

Umweltbundesamt (Hrsg.), Umweltfreundliche Beschaffung, Handbuch zur Berücksichtigung des Umweltschutzes in der öffentlichen Verwaltung und im Einkauf, Wiesbaden und Berlin 1987.

Ernst Winter & Sohn (GmbH & Co) (Hrsg.), Winter-Modell: Pionierleistungen im Umweltschutz, in: Der Winter-Schneemann Nr. 20, Dezember 1985, S. 41ff; zu beziehen bei Ernst Winter & Sohn (GmbH & Co), Osterstraße 58, 2000 Hamburg 20.

Organisations

British

The Design Council, 28 Haymarket, London SW1Y 4SU, tel. 01-839 8000.

The Ecological Materials Research Institute, Brunel University, Shoreditch Campus, Egham, Surrey TW2 0JZ, tel. 0787-21697.

German

Bundesdeutscher Arbeitskreis für umweltbewußtes Management e.V. (B.A.U.M.), Christian-Förster-Str. 19, 2000 Hamburg 20, Tel. 040/40 77 21, 040/491 18 14.

11. MATERIALS MANAGEMENT

Databases

German

UMPLIS (Informations- und Dokumentationssystem Umwelt beim Umweltbundesamt Berlin, Bismarckplatz 1, 1000 Berlin 33, Tel. 030/8903-555.

Publications

British

Department of Trade and Industry, A Brief Guide to Support and Advice for Recycling (Business Advice for Smaller Firms, Technical Advice, Help with energy costs, Research and Development Support for new Technology using waste as a fuel, Support for Innovation, EEC Support for R & D, DTI Support for R & D), available from Department of Trade and Industry, Minerals and Metals Division 3, Room 1014, Ashdown House, 123 Victoria Street, London SW1E 6RB.

Department of Trade and Industry, Folder: The Government Focus on Reclamation, containing: A Brief Guide to Support and Advice for Recycling; Watch your Waste – organisations to contact; Watch your Waste – a new video about reclamation. Obtainable from Department of Trade and Industry or Confederation of British Industry, Centre Point, 103 New Oxford Street, London WC1A 1DU, tel. 01-379-7400.

Elkington, John, Tom Burke and Julia Hailes, Green Pages, The Business of Saving the World, Routledge, 11 New Fetter Lane, London EC4P 4EE, 1988.

Matus, Materials Selector, The Engineering Information Company Ltd, 15 Ingate Place, London, SW8, tel. 01-622-8155.

Vogler, John, Work from Waste, Intermediate Technology Publications and Oxfam, 103–105 Southampton Row, London, WC1B 4HH, tel. 01-436-9761, 1981.

American

Regulations, Recommendations & Assessments Extracted from RTECS (Registry of Toxic Effects of Chemical Substances), Government Printing Office, 1986.

German

Blom, F., Beschaffungsmarktforschung: Warum? Wo? Wie?, Nürnberg 1982.

Grochla, E., Grundlagen der Materialwirtschaft, 3. Auflage, Wiesbaden 1978.

Stahlmann, V., Umweltorientierte Materialwirtschaft, Wiesbaden 1988.

Strebel, H., Umwelt und Betriebswirtschaft, Berlin 1980.

Umweltbundesamt (Hrsg.), Umweltfreundliche Beschaffung, Handbuch zur Berücksichtigung des Umweltschutzes in der öffentlichen Verwaltung und im Einkauf, Wiesbaden und Berlin 1987.

Organisations

British

Chemical Industries Association, 93 Albert Embankment, London SE1 7TU, tel. 01-735-3001.

The Ecological Materials Research Institute, Brunel University, Shoreditch Campus, Egham, Surrey TW2 0JZ, tel. 0787-21697.

The Materials Information Centre, The Design Council, 28 Haymarket, London, SW1Y 4SU, tel. 01-839-8000.

The Reclamation Association, 16 High Street, Brampton, Huntingdon, Cambridgeshire PE18 8TU, tel. 0480-55249.

American

Advanced Technology Center, New Jersey Institute of Technology, Martin Luther King Boulevard, Newark, NJ 07102, tel. (201)596-3434.

Center for Hazardous Materials Research, University of Pittsburgh, 320 William Pitt Way, Pittsburgh, PA 15238, tel. (412)826-5320.

German

Aktionsgemeinschaft Umwelt, Gesundheit, Ernährung e.V. (A.U.G.E.), Christian-Förster-Straße 19, 2000 Hamburg 20, Tel. 040/40 26 97.

Bundesdeutscher Arbeitskreis für umweltbewußtes Management e.V. (B.A.U.M.), Christian-Förster-Straße 19, 2000 Hamburg 20, Tel. 040/40 77 21, 040/491 18 14.

Bundesverband Materialwirtschaft und Einkauf e.V. (BME), Waidmannstr. 25, 6000 Frankfurt/M. 70.

12. PRODUCTION TECHNOLOGY

Databases

German

Dokumentation Maschinenbau, Ostbahnhofstr. 13, 6000 Frankfurt/Main 1, Tel.: 069/43 08-215/227.

UMPLIS (Informations- und Dokumentationssystem Umwelt beim Umweltbundesamt Berlin), Bismarckplatz 1, 1000 Berlin 33, Tel.: 030/89 03-555.

Publications

International

Commission of the European Communities, European Better Environment Awards for Industry 1987, Brussels 1988.

United Nations Economic Commission for Europe, Compendium on Low- and Non-waste Technology: Summaries of Manuscripts 1–20, UNECE, Geneva, tel. 010-41-22-34-60-11, 1981.

British

Department of the Environment, Environmental Protection Technology, A new scheme to encourage innovation in the field of environmental protection technology, produced by the Central Office of Information 1987.

Department of Trade and Industry, A Brief Guide to Support and Advice for Recycling (Business Advice for Smaller Firms, Technical Advice, Help with energy costs, Research and Development Support for new Technology using waste as a fuel, Support for Innovation, EEC Support for R & D, DTI Support for R & D), available from Department of Trade and Industry, Minerals and Metals Division 3, Room 1014, Ashdown House, 123 Victoria Street, London SW1E 6RB.

Department of Trade and Industry, Folder: The Government Focus on Reclamation, containing: A Brief Guide to Support and Advice for Recycling; Watch your Waste – organisations to contact; Watch your Waste – a new video about reclamation. Obtainable from Department of Trade and Industry or Confederation of British Industry, Centre Point, 103 New Oxford Street, London WC1A 1DU, tel. 01-379 7400.

American

Approaches to Source Reduction of Hazardous Wastes: Practical Guidance from Existing Policies & Programs, Environmental Defense Fund, New York, 1986.

Pollution Prevention Pays Program, Environmental Engineering & Pollution Control, 3M Corporation, Box 33331 Building 21-2W-07, St. Paul, MN 55133.

Sarokin, David J., et al., Cutting Chemical Wastes, INFORM Inc., New York, 1985.

Serious Reduction of Hazardous Waste, Summary, Office of Technology Assessment, Washington, September 1986.

Waste Reduction Always Pays Info Kit (WRAP), Environmental Quality Department, Dow Chemical U.S.A., Willard H. Dow Center, Midland, MI 48674, tel. (517)636-2953.

German

Arbeitsgemeinschaft für Umweltfragen e.V. (AGU), Umweltschutz und Technologie, Stenographisches Protokoll der Sitzung des 13. Umweltforums am 21. November 1985, Veröffentlichungen der AGU Nr. 28, Bonn 1986.

Bundesverband der Deutschen Industrie e.V., Antworten auf eine Herausforderung, Berichte über praktizierten Umweltschutz in den Unternehmen, Köln 1978.

Hartinger, L., (Hrsg.), Taschenbuch der Abwasserbehandlung, Band 2, Technik, München/Wien 1980.

Maas, Ch., Determinanten von Umweltschutzinnovationen – Theoretische Überlegungen und erste empirische Evidenz, Diskussionspapier 108 der Wirtschaftswissenschaftlichen Dokumentation, Technische Universität Berlin, Berlin 1986.

Maas, Ch., Ewers, H.-J., Wirkungen umweltpolitischer Maßnahmen auf das Innovationsverhalten von Galvanik-Betrieben – Ergebnisse explorativer Fallstudien, IIUG/dp 83-12, Wissenschaftszentrum Berlin 1983, insbesondere Seiten 166–194 und die dort angegebene Literatur.

Umweltbundesamt (Hrsg.), Luftreinhaltung '81, Entwicklung – Stand – Tendenzen, Materialien zum Zweiten Immissionsschutzbericht der Bundesregierung an den Deutschen Bundestag nach dem § 61 Bundes-Immissionsgesetz, Berlin 1981.

Vogl, J., Heigl, A., Schäfer, K., (Hrsg.), Handbuch des Umweltschutzes, Loseblattsammlung, München (div. Jg.).

Organisations

British

Chemical Industries Association, 93 Albert Embankment, London SE1 7TU, tel. 01-735-3001.

The Institute of Waste Management, 3 Albion Place, Derngate, Northampton NN1 1UD, tel. 0604-20426/8.

The Reclamation Association, 16 High Street, Brampton, Huntingdon, Cambridgeshire PE18 8TU, tel. 0480-55 249.

American

Center for Hazardous Materials Research, University of Pittsburgh, 320 William Pitt Way, Pittsburgh, PA 15238, tel. (412)826-5320.

ChemCycle Corporation, 129 South St., Boston, MA 02111, tel. (617) 451-0922.

National Roundtable for State Waste Reduction Programs, P.O. Box 27687, Raleigh, NC 27611, tel. (919)733-7015.

US EPA Center for Environmental Research Information, 26 Martin Luther King, Cincinnati, OH 45268, tel. (513)569-7391.

German

Bundesdeutscher Arbeitskreis für umweltbewußtes Management e.V. (B.A.U.M.), Christian-Förster-Str. 19, 2000 Hamburg 20, tel. 040/40 77 21, 040/491 18 14.

Verband Deutscher Maschinen- und Anlagenbau e.V. (V.D.M.A), Technische Abteilung, Bereich Umweltpolitik, Lyoner Straße 18, 6000 Frankfurt/Main 71, Tel.: 069/66 03-325.

13. DISPOSAL AND RECYCLING

Databases

German

AWIDAT, Abfallwirtschaftsdatenbank beim Umweltbundesamt, Bismarckplatz 1, 1000 Berlin 33, tel. 030/8903-1.

Publications

British

Department of Trade and Industry, A Brief Guide to Support and Advice for Recycling (Business Advice for Smaller Firms, Technical Advice, Help with energy costs, Research and Development Support for new Technology in the collection and disposal of waste, Research and Development Support for new Technology using waste as a fuel, Support for Innovation, EEC Support for R & D, DTI Support for R & D), available from Department of Trade and Industry, Minerals and Metals Division 3, Room 1014, Ashdown House, 123 Victoria Street, London SW1E 6RB.

Department of Trade and Industry, Folder: The Government Focus on Reclamation, containing: A Brief Guide to Support and Advice for Recycling; Watch your Waste – organisations to contact; Watch your Waste – a new video about reclamation. Obtainable from Department of Trade and Industry or Confederation of British Industry, Centre Point, 103 New Oxford Street, London WC1A 1DU, tel. 01-379 7400.

Elkington, John, Tom Burke and Julia Hailes, Green Pages, The Business of Saving the World, Routledge, 11 New Fetter Lane, London EC4P 4EE, 1988.

Materials Reclamation Weekly, Maclaren Publishers Ltd., P.O. Box 109, Maclaren House, Scarbrook Road, Croydon, CR9 1QH, tel. 01-688-7788.

Parker, Colin, and Tim Roberts, Energy from Waste, ERL, 106 Gloucester Place, London, W1H 3DB, tel. 01-486-1211.

Porteous, Andrew, Recycling Resources, Refuse. Longman Group UK Ltd., 5 Bentinck Street, London WC1, tel. 01-935-0121.

Royston, Michael, Pollution Prevention Pays. Pergamon Press plc, 33 Holborn, EC1, tel. 01-822-2345, 1979.

Vogler, Jon, Work from Waste. Intermediate Technology Publications and Oxfam, 1981.

Wastes Management (Journal of Institute of Wastes Management), Institute of Wastes Management, 3 Albion Place, Northampton, NN1 1UD, tel. 0604-20426.

Wilson, David, Waste Management, Oxford University Press (Publishing), Walton Street, Oxford, Oxon, OX2 6DP, tel. 0865-56767, 1981.

American

Coming Full Circle, Successful Recycling Today, Environmental Defense Fund, 257 Park Avenue South, New York 10010, 1988.

Recycling: The Answer to Our Garbage Problem, Citizens Clearinghouse for Hazardous Wastes, Inc. Arlington, VA. (See bibliography.)

Waste Minimization: Environmental Quality With Economic Benefits, U.S. EPA, Office of Solid Waste & Emergency Response, 1987.

Wilczynski, Edward J. and Donna M. Watson (eds.), Marketing & Financing Aspects of Resource Recovery, U.S. Dept. of Commerce, Office of Environmental Affairs, January 1980.

German

Blohm, F., Recycling und Umweltschutz, in: Beschaffung aktuell 1/86. Ministerium für Ernährung, Landwirtschaft, Umwelt und Forsten Baden-

Württemberg (Hrsg.), Altlastenhandbuch (Teil I: Altlastenbewertung, Teil II: Untersuchungsgrundlagen), Stuttgart 1987; Bezugsquelle: Landesanstalt für Umweltschutz Baden-Württemberg, Griesbachstraße 3, 7500 Karlsruhe 21.

Panz, R.G., Recycling, Wiesbaden 1980.

Stahlmann, V., Umweltorientierte Materialwirtschaft, Wiesbaden 1988.

Strebel, H., Umwelt und Betriebswirtschaft, Berlin 1980.

Umweltbundesamt (Hrsg.), Umweltfreundliche Beschaffung, Handbuch zur Berücksichtigung des Umweltschutzes in der öffentlichen Verwaltung und im Einkauf, Wiesbaden und Berlin 1987.

Organisations

British

Chemical Industries Association, 93 Albert Embankment, London SE1 7TU, tel. 01-735-3001.

The Institute of Waste Management, 3 Albion Place, Derngate, Northampton NN1 1UD, tel. 0604-20426/8.

The Reclamation Association, 16 High Street, Brampton, Huntingdon, Cambridgeshire PE18 8TU, tel. 0480-55249.

American

Government Institutes, Inc., 966 Hungerford Drive, # 24, Rockville, MD 20850, tel. (301)251-9250.

Hazardous Waste Treatment Council, 1440 New York Avenue, NW, Suite 310, Washington, DC, tel. (202)783-0870, (202)966-6020.

INFORM, 381 Park Avenue South, New York, NY 10016, tel. (212)689-4040.

North East Industrial Waste Exchange, (plus monthly magazine), an Information Clearinghouse for Waste w/Reuse Value, 90 Presidential Plaza, Suite 122, Syracuse, NY 13202, tel. (315)422-6572, tel. (800)237-2481.

Office of Solid Waste & Emergency Response, Office of Solid Waste; Waste Minimization Staff, U.S. EPA, WH 565, 401 M Street, SW, Washington, DC 20460, tel. (202)382-4610.

US EPA Center for Environmental Research Information, 26 Martin Luther King, Cincinnati, OH 45268, tel. (513)569-7391.

German

BPS – Bundesverband privater Sonderabfallbeseitiger und Rückstandsverwerter e.V., Gurlittstr. 31, 2000 Hamburg 1.

VAB – Vermittlungsstelle der Wirtschaft für Altlastensanierungs-Beratung e.V., Kirchstr. 2, 5000 Köln 50 (Rodenkirchen), Tel.: 0221/39 20 46 or 0221/39 20 47.

14. COMPANY VEHICLES

Databases

German

UMPLIS (Informations- und Dokumentationssystem Umwelt beim Umweltbundesamt Berlin), Bismarckplatz 1, 1000 Berlin 33, Tel. 030/89 03-555.

Publications

British

The National Advisory Unit for Community Transport, Keymer Street, Beswick, Manchester, M11 3FY, tel. 061-273-6038. Various books and leaflets.

American

Current Awareness Publications from Office of Scientific and Technical Information, National Technical Information Service, U.S. Department of Commerce, 5285 Port Royal Rd., Springfield, VA 22161, tel. (703) 487-4650.

INFORM Study on Natural Gas & Methanol as Alternative Transportation Fuels (to be published in early 1989), INFORM 381 Park Avenue South, New York, NY 10016, tel. (212)689-4040.

German

Bundesministerium für Umwelt, Naturschutz und Reaktorsicherheit (Hrsg.), Was Sie schon immer über Auto und Umwelt wissen wollten, Stuttgart, Berlin, Köln, Mainz, 1987; Bezugsquelle: Umweltbundesamt, Bismarckplatz 1, 1000 Berlin 33.

Faber, G., Energie-Sparbuch für Autofahrer, 6128 Höchst 3.

Umweltbundesamt (Hrsg.), Umweltfreundliche Beschaffung, Handbuch zur Berücksichtigung des Umweltschutzes in der öffentlichen Verwaltung und im Einkauf, Wiesbaden und Berlin, 1987.

Organisations

British

Campaign for Lead Free Air (CLEAR), 2 Northdown Street, London, N1 9BG, tel. 01-278-9686.

National Society for Clean Air, 136 North Street, Brighton BN1 1RG, tel. 0273-26313.

American

American Gas Association, Marketing Services, 1515 Wilson Blvd., Arlington, VA 22209, tel. (703)841-8400.

Brooklyn Union Gas Company, 195 Montague Street, Brooklyn, NY 11201, tel. (718) 403-2525.

Office of Mobile Sources, Motor Vehicle Emissions Laboratory, US Environmental Protection Agency, 2565 Plymouth Road, Ann Arbor, MI 48105, tel. (313)668-4200.

German

Bundesdeutscher Arbeitskreis für umweltbewußtes Management e.V. (B.A.U.M.), Christian-Förster-Str. 19, 2000 Hamburg 20, Tel.: 040/40 77 21, 040/491 18 14.

15. BUILDING

Databases

British

ACOMPLINE (urban policy and development), Research Library of the London Residuary Body, County Hall, London, SE1 7PB.

Publications

British

Burberry, Peter, Building for Energy Conservation, The Royal Institute of British Architects, Finsbury Mission, 39 Moreland Street, London, EC1V 8BB, 1978.

The Department of Energy, Energy Efficiency in Buildings, Information Division Distribution Unit, Room 1312, Thames House South, Millbank, London, SW1P 4QJ, 1985.

Elkington, John, Tom Burke and Julia Hailes, Green Pages, The Business of Saving the World, Routledge, 11 New Fetter Lane, London, EC4P 4EE, 1988.

Project Appraisal, Beech Tree Publishing, 10 Watford Close, Guildford, Surrey, GU1 2EP, tel. 0483-67497.

Sharland, Ian, Woods Practical Guide to Noise Control, The Royal Institute of British Architects, Finsbury Mission, 39 Moreland Street, London, EC1V 8BB, 1972.

American

Alvarez, Mark, Healthy Building, Practical Homeowner, Rodale Press, February 1987, p.30–34.

Crowther, Richard L., Indoor Air: Risks and Remedies, Richard L. Crowther FAIA, 1986.

Indoor Pollution News, Burall Publications, Inc., A Subsidiary of the Bureau of National Affairs, Inc., 2445 M Street, NW, Washington, DC 20037, tel. (202)452-7889.

The Natural Choice: Non-Toxic Home Products, LIVOS Plant Chemistry, 614 Agua Fria St., Santa Fe, NM 87501.

Perlman, Ellen, Researchers, Designers Take Steps to Heal Sick Buildings, Buildings Design Journal, Communications Channels, Inc., Atlanta, GA, February 1987.

German

Albrecht, R., Paker, L., Rehberg, S., Reiner, Y., Umweltentlastung durch ökologische Bau- und Siedlungsweisen, Bd. I: Planungsvorschläge und bauliche Maßnahmen, Bd. II: Auswirkungen auf Baustoffverwendung, Energiebedarf, Luft und Klima, Abfallbeseitigung und Wasserhaushalt, Lärm, Flächenbedarf, Kosten und Arbeitsmarkt; herausgegeben vom Umweltbundesamt, Wiesbaden/Berlin, 1984.

BUND-Umweltzentrum, Umweltfreundliches Bauen, (BUND-Informationsmappe), Stuttgart, 1985; Bezugsquelle: BUND, Rotebühlstraße 84/1, 7000 Stuttgart 1.

Der Bundesminister für Jugend, Familie und Gesundheit, Chemie im Haushalt und Innenraumbelastung, Antwort der Bundesregierung auf eine große Anfrage, Bundestags-Drucksache 10/4285 vom 19.11.1985.

Grote, H., Bauen mit Kopf, Berlin 1988.

Katalyse Umweltgruppe/Gruppe für ökologische Bau- und Umweltplanung (Hrsg.), Das ökologische Heimwerkerbuch, Reinbek 1985.

Krüger, K.-H., Babylonische Signale der Unvernunft, (Artikel über den Umschwung in der Bürohaus-Architektur), Der Spiegel, Nr. 4 vom 21.1.1985, S.140 ff.

Krusche, P., Altzhaus, D., Gabriel, I., Weig-Krusche, M., Ökologisches Bauen, herausgegeben vom Umweltbundesamt, Wiesbaden/Berlin, 1982.

Schneider, A., Gesünder Wohnen durch biologisches Bauen III, Institut für Baubiologie und Ökologie, Neubeuern 1984.

Umweltbundesamt (Hrgs.), Umweltfreundliche Beschaffung, Handbuch zur Berücksichtigung des Umweltschutzes in der öffentlichen Verwaltung und im Einkauf, Wiesbaden und Berlin 1987.

Ernst Winter & Sohn (GmbH & Co.) (Hrsg.), Winter-Modell: Pionierleistungen im Umweltschutz, in: Der Winter-Schneemann Nr. 20, Dezember 1985, S.41ff; zu beziehen bei Ernst Winter & Sohn (GmbH & Co.), Osterstraße 58, 2000 Hamburg 20.

Organisations

International

Internationales Institut für Baubiologie, Heilig-Geist-Straße 54, 8200 Rosenheim, Tel.: 0 80 31/170 91.

American

The College of Environmental Design, University of Colorado, Boulder, CO 80309, tel. (303) 492-7711.

Master's Corporation, P.O. Box 514, 12 Curtis Avenue, New Canaan, Ct. 06840, tel. (205)966-3541.

William McDonough Architects, 116 E. 27th Street, New York, NY 10016, tel. (212) 481-1111.

German

Bund Architektur und Baubiologie e.V. (BAB), Kreuzbergweg 22, 5300 Bonn 1.

Bundesdeutscher Arbeitskreis für umweltbewußtes Management e.V. (B.A.U.M.), Christian-Förster-Str. 19, 2000 Hamburg 20, Tel.: 040/40 77 21, 040/491 18 14.

Bundesverband Gesundes Bauen und Wohnen e.V., Postfach 18 20, 3300 Braunschweig, Tel.: 05 31/8 28 40.

Institut für Baubiologie und Ökologie, Holzham 25, 8201 Neubeuern, Tel.: 0 80 35/20 39.

16. FINANCE

Publications

British

Department of the Environment, Environmental Protection Technology, A new scheme to encourage innovation in the field of environmental protection technology, produced by the Central Office of Information 1987.

Department of Trade and Industry, A Brief Guide to Support and Advice for Recycling (Business Advice for Smaller Firms, Technical Advice, Help with energy costs, Research and Development Support for new Technology in the collection and disposal of waste, Research and Development Support for new Technology using waste as a fuel, Support for Innovation, EEC Support for R & D, DTI Support for R & D), available from Department of Trade and Industry, Minerals and Metals Division 3, Room 1014, Ashdown House, 123 Victoria Street, London SW1E 6RB.

Department of Trade and Industry, Folder: The Government Focus on Reclamation, containing: A Brief Guide to Support and Advice for Recycling; Watch your Waste – organisations to contact; Watch your Waste – a new video about reclamation. Obtainable from Department of Trade and Industry or Confederation of British Industry, Centre Point, 103 New Oxford Street, London WC1A 1DU, tel. 01-379 7400.

American

The Journal of Environmental Economics and Management, Academic Press, Inc., 111 Fifth Avenue, New York, NY 10003.

German

Bürger-Service Band I, Förderfibel, wird kostenlos herausgegeben vom Bundesministerium für Forschung und Technologie, Referat Presse und Öffentlichkeitsarbeit, Postfach 20 07 06, 5300 Bonn 2.

Der Bundesminister für Umwelt, Naturschutz und Reaktorsicherheit (Hrsg.), Investitionshilfen im Umweltschutz, Bonn 1986 (Stand vom 1.9.1986); Bezugsquelle: Der Bundesminister für Umwelt, Naturschutz und Reaktorsicherheit, Postfach 12 06 29, 5300 Bonn 1.

Hoffmann, V., Die Programme zur Förderung von Umweltschutzinvestitionen und Umweltschutzförderung durch Sonderabschreibungen, in: Umwelt und Energie, Rudolf Haufe Verlag, Hindenburgstr. 64, D-7800 Freiburg i.Br.

Weitere Informationen über die Finanzierungshilfen des Bundes und der Länder an die gewerbliche Wirtschaft finden sich in der jährlichen Sonderausgabe der Zeitschrift für das gesamte Kreditwesen (ZfGK), Verlag Fritz Knapp, Neue Mainzer Str. 60, 6000 Frankfurt/M.

Organisations

International

Commission of the European Communities, Directorate-General for the Environment, Consumer Protection and Nuclear Safety, Rue de la Loi 208, B-1049 Brussels.

European Investment Bank, 100, Boulevard Konrad Adenauer. L-1115 Luxembourg.

OECD Environment Committee, Group of Economic Experts, 2, rue André-Pascal, 75775 Paris, Cedex 16.

British

Department of the Environment, Romnay House, 43 Marsham Street, London SW1 3PY.

Department of the Environment Enquiries Unit, 2 Marsham Street, London, SW1, tel. 01-212-4693.

American

State

California Department of Commerce, Office of Business Development, 1121 L Street Suite 600, Sacramento, CA 95814, tel. (916)322-5665.

California Pollution Control Financing Authority, 915 Capitol Mall Rm. 280, Sacramento, CA 95814, tel. (916)445-9597.

Federal

Environmental Protection Agency, Waterside Mall, Washington DC 80460.

Office of Environmental Affairs, U.S. Department of Commerce, Washington, DC 20230.

German

Bundesdeutscher Arbeitskreis für umweltbewußtes Management e.V. (B.A.U.M.), Christian-Förster-Str. 19, 2000 Hamburg 20, Tel.: 040/40 77 21, 040/491 18 14.

17. LAW

Databases

International

Enlex (at development stage) (Environmental issues in EC Member States), Italian Supreme Court, Computer Documentation Centre, Rome, tel. 010-396-656-8597.

German

Juris – Juristisches Informationssystem für die Bundesrepublik Deutschland, Bundesministerium für Justiz, 5300 Bonn 2.

Publications

International

European Environment Review, the Journal of European Community and International Environmental Policy and Law, Graham & Trotman Ltd., Sterling House, 66 Wilton Road, London SW1V 1DE, tel. 01-821-1123.

The Law and Practice Concerning Occupational Health in the Member States of the European Community; Environmental Resources Ltd., 106 Gloucester Place, London, W1H 3DB, tel. 01-486-1211.

British

Haigh, Nigel, EEC Environmental Policy and Britain, Longman Group UK Ltd., 5 Bentinck Street, London, WC1, tel. 01-935-0121.

Journal of Energy and Natural Resources Law, Sweet and Maxwell Ltd., 11 New Fetter Lane, London, EC4P 4EE, tel. 01-583-9855.

The Law and Practice Relating to Pollution Control in the United Kingdom; Environmental Resources Ltd., 106 Gloucester Place, London, W1H 3DB, tel. 01-486-1211.

American

Dimento, Joseph F., Environmental Law and American Business: Dilemmas of Compliance, Plenum Publishers, New York, 1986.

Novick, Sheldon et al. (eds.), Law of Environmental Protection, The Environmental Law Institute, Clark Boardman Co., Ltd., New York, 1987.

German

Hoppe, W., Umweltschutzrecht, Kurzlehrbuch für Studium und Praxis, München 1987.

Moench, C., Schlarmann, H., Umweltrecht in der betrieblichen Praxis (Reihe „Aktueller Betrieb"), München, 1987.

Mohr, P.C., Umweltberatung durch Privatpersonen und Behörden, ein Beitrag zu den Rechtsgrundlagen der Umweltberatung für die privaten Haushalte, Natur und Recht, Erscheinungsjahr 1988, genauer Zeitpunkt noch ungewiß.

Storm, P., Umweltrecht: Einführung in ein neues Rechtsgebiet, Berlin 1980.
Vogl, J., Heigl, A., Schäfer, K., Handbuch des Umweltschutzes, Loseblattsammlung, München (div. Jahrgänge).

Organisations

American

Government Institutes, Inc., 966 Hungerford Drive, # 24, Rockville, MD 20850, tel. (301)251-9250.

Natural Resources Defense Council, 122 E. 42nd Street, New York, NY 10168, tel. (212)949-0049.

Public Citizen Litigation Group, 2000 P Street, NW, Washington, DC 20036, tel. (202)293-9142.

Sierra Club Legal Defense Fund, Inc., 2044 Fillmore Street, San Francisco, CA 94115, tel. (415)567-6100.

German

Institut für Umweltpolitik und -recht e.V. (IVR), Wunderburgstr. 17, 2900 Oldenburg/Ol., Tel.: 0441/15538.

18. INSURANCE

Publications

International

AIDA (Association Internationale du Droit des Assurances) Working Group on Pollution and Insurance. AIDA World Congress, 1986.

Insuring Environmental Risks, presented to Ambrose Kelly in the 7th AIDA World Congress, 1986.

British

A short guide to the Employers' Liability (Compulsory Insurance) Act, 1969. The Health and Safety Executive, Baynard's House, 1–13 Chepstow Place, London, W2 4TF, tel. 01-229-3456.

German

Ministerium für Ernährung, Landwirtschaft, Umwelt und Forsten Baden-Württemberg, Leitfaden Nr. 15: Umgang mit leicht flüchtigen chlorierten und aromatischen Kohlenwasserstoffen, Stuttgart Dezember 1984; Bezugsquelle: Landesanstalt für Umweltschutz, Baden-Württemberg, Griesbachstraße 3, 7500 Karlsruhe 21.

Münchener Rückversicherungsgesellschaft, Umweltschäden und Haftpflichtversicherung, München, 1984.

Teichler, M., Neue Umweltpolice, Handelsblatt vom 5.11.1987, S. 31; Bezugsquelle: Joost & Preuss, Rödingsmarkt 14, 2000 Hamburg 11.

Verband der Chemischen Industrie, Innerbetrieblicher Umgang mit leicht flüchtigen chlorierten Kohlenwasserstoffen; ein Informationsblatt mit konkreten Handlungsanweisungen. Stand: Dezember 1985; Bezugsquelle: Verband der Chemischen Industrie e.V. (VCI), Postfach 11 19 43, 6000 Frankfurt 11.

Zur EG-Richtlinie 85/374/EWG vom 25.7.1985 über die „Angleichung der Rechts- und Verwaltungsvorschriften der Mitgliedsstaaten über die Haftung für fehlerhafte Produkte", die neben anderen Verschärfungen eine Verschuldensunabhängigkeit der Haftung vorsieht, vgl. L. Wicke, die Ökologischen Milliarden, München 1986, Seite 194 f.

Organisations

International

International Association For Insurance Law (AIDA). A secretariat general is constituted only in preparation of each general assembly. Study group on pollution and insurance. Secretary: Prof. Dr. Carl Martin Roos, Faculty of Law, University of Stockholm, S-10691 Stockholm, tel. (08)16 20 00.

British

Association of British Insurers, Aldermary House, Queen Street, London, EC4N 1TT, tel. 01-248-4477.

American

Public Citizen, 2000 P Street, NW, Washington, DC 20036, tel. (202)293-9142.

Putnam, Hayes and Bartlett, Inc., 124 Mt. Auburn St., Cambridge, MA 02138, tel. (617)492-6900.

German

Bundesdeutscher Arbeitskreis für umweltbewußtes Management e.V. (B.A.U.M.), Christian-Förster-Str. 19, 2000 Hamburg 20, Tel.: 040/40 77 21, 040/491 18 14.

Verband der Haftpflichtversicherer, Unfallversicherer, Autoversicherer und Rechtsschutzversicherer (HUK-Verband), Glockengießerwall 1, 2000 Hamburg 1, Tel.: 040/32 10 70.

Verband der Lebensversicherungsunternehmen e.V., Eduard-Pflüger-Straße 55, 5300 Bonn 1, Tel.: 02 28/23 90 51.

Verband der Sachversicherer e.V., Riehlerstraße 36, 5000 Köln 1, Tel.: 02 21/7 76 60.

19. INTERNATIONAL BUSINESS RELATIONS

Databases

International

Enviroline, (from 1971 to present on all environmental subjects. International Register of Potentially Toxic Chemicals, legislation and hazards of toxic chemicals and recommended disposal methods). UNEP, DOE Library, 2 Marsham Street, London, SW1P 3EB, Compiled by EIC Intelligence Inc.

ENVIROLINE File 40, EIC/Intelligence, Inc., New York.

INFOTERRA (environmental information for UN Member States), UNEP, Infoterra, UK National Focal Point, Departments of the Environment and Transport Library, Room P3/1008C, 2 Marsham Street, London, SW1P 3EB, tel. 01-212-5270.

Publications

International

Commission of the European Communities, The State of the Environment in the European Community 1986 (produced under the direction of Gunter Schneider and Michael-Henri Cornaert), Luxembourg 1987. Available from: HM Stationery Office, HMSO Publications Centre, 51 Nine Elms Lane, London SW8 5DR, tel. 01-211-5656. Sub-agent: Alan Armstrong & Associates Ltd, 72 Park Road, London NW1 4SH, tel. 01-723-3902. European Community Information Service, 2100 M Street, NW, Suite 707, Washington, DC 20037, tel. (202)862-9500.

European Environment Review, The Journal of European Community and International Environmental Policy and Law, Graham & Trotman Ltd., Sterling House, 66 Wilton Road, London SW1V 1DE, tel. 01-821-1123.

The European Environmental Yearbook, DocTer International UK Ltd, 27 Kensington Court, London W8, UK, tel. 01-937-3660.

Government Institutes, Inc., International Environmental Business Requirements. Available from: Government Institutes, Inc., 966 Hungerford Drive, # 24, Rockville, MD 20850, tel. (301)251-9250.

International Chamber of Commerce (ICC), Environmental Guidelines for World Industry 1986, ICC publication No. 435. Available from ICC United Kingdom, Centre Point, 103 New Oxford Street, London WC1A 1QB, tel. 2405558, or: ICC Publishing Inc., 156 Fifth Avenue, New York N.Y. 10010, tel. (212)206-1150.

International Chamber of Commerce (ICC), The Spirit of Versailles: The Business of Environmental Management, report on the World Industry Conference on Environmental Management (WICEM) 1984, Paris 1986, ICC publication No. 425.

International Federation of Pharmaceutical Manufacturers' Associations (IFPMA). Marketing Code of 1981 with supplement, March 1982. Available from Association of the British Pharmaceutical Industry, 12 Whitehall, London, SW1A 2DY, tel. 01-839-3961.

Joyce, Frank E., and Gunter Schneider (eds.), Environment and Economic Development in the Regions of the European Community, Avebury, Gower Publishing Company Limited, Gower House, Croff Road, Aldershot, Hants Gull 3 HR, England 1988.

Leonard, Richard, "After Bhopal: Multinationals and the Management of Hazardous Products and Processes", Multinational Business, No. 2, 1986, pp. 1–9.

Speth, James Gustave, "An Environmental Agenda for World Business" Across the Board, The Conference Board Magazine, Vol. XXIV No. 3, March 1987.

United Nations, Center on Transnational Corporations, Environmental Aspects of the Activities of Transnational Corporations: A Survey, 1985.

World Resources Institute, Publications, P.O. Box 620, Holmes, PA 19043, tel. (202)393-4055

Organisations

International

Part F of this book contains an overview of international governmental organisations and international industry-based non-governmental organisations dealing with environmentalist business management.

Institut für Europäische Umweltpolitik, Aloys-Schulte-Str. 6, D-5300 Bonn 1, Tel. 0228/21 38 10.

International Institute for Environment & Development – North, America; A Center of World Resources Institute, 17 Massachusetts Avenue, NW, Washington, DC 20036, tel. (202)462-0900

United Nations Environment Programme (UNEP), Industry and Environment Office, Tour Mirabeau, 39–43 quai André Citroen, Cedex 15, 75739 Paris, France, tel. 33 1 45 78 33 33.

American

The Center for Environmental Management, Tufts University, Medford, MA 02155, tel. (617)628-5000.

Rocky Mountain Institute, 1739 Snowmass Creek Road, Old Snowmass, CO 81654-9199, tel. (303)744-8665, (303)927-3851.

German

Institut für Europäische Umweltpolitik, Aloys-Schulte-Straße 6, D-5300 Bonn 1, Tel. 0228/21 38 10.

Verband der Chemischen Industrie e.V. (VCI), Leitlinien der Chemischen Industrie vom 10. Juli 1986; Bezugsquelle: Verband der Chemischen Industrie e.V. (VCI), Postfach 11 19 43, D-6000 Frankfurt/Main 11.

Verband der Chemischen Industrie e.V. (VCI), Verhaltenskodex für die Ausfuhr von gefährlichen Chemikalien vom 11. März 1986.

20. PUBLIC RELATIONS WORK

Publications

British

Elkington, John, Tom Burke and Julia Hailes, Green Pages, The Business of Saving the World, Routledge, 11 New Fetter Lane, London EC4P 4EE, 1988.
Haywood, Roger, All about PR, McGraw Hill Marketing Series, Shoppenhangers Road, Maidenhead, Berks, tel. 0628-23431, 1984.

American

Environmental Concerns Force Global Change In the Market, Chemical Week, Vol. 42 # 18, McGraw-Hill, Inc., New York, May 14, 1988, p. 22–39.
Industry and the Environment, Public Relations Review, Winter, 1983.

German

Apitz, K., Konflikte, Krisen, Katastrophen, Präventivmaßnahmen gegen Imageverlust, Frankfurt/M., Wiesbaden 1987.
Liese, H.J., Markt und Umwelt (Ökologie und Ökonomie im Kompromiß aus Kommerz und Vernunft), München 1986; (siehe besonders S. 92ff).
Meffert, H., Bruhn, M., Schubert, F., Walter, Th., Marketing und Ökologie, in: Der Betriebswirt 46, 1986, S. 140 ff.
Schreiber, R.L., Ökologie und Marketing (Ökologische Herausforderungen und wirtschaftliche Problemlösungen), Band 9 der Arbeitspapiere zur Schriftenreihe Schwerpunkt Marketing, herausgegeben von Prof. Dr. Paul W. Meyer und dem Forschungsteam Marketing an der Universität Augsburg, Augsburg 1985; zu beziehen bei der Fördergesellschaft Marketing an der Universität Augsburg, Memminger Str. 14, 8900 Augsburg, Tel. 0821/598270.
Schultheis, H., Der Umweltschutz in der Öffentlichkeitsarbeit der Unternehmen, in: Handbuch des Umweltschutzes (Loseblattsammlung), herausgegeben von J. Vogl, A. Heigl, K. Schäfer, Band 5, München 1977.

Organisations

American

Environmental Communication Research Program, State University of New Jersey Rutgers, Cook College, 122 Ryders Lane, New Brunswick, NJ 08903, tel. (201)932-8795.

Franklin Research & Development Corporation, The Franklin Companies, 711 Atlantic Avenue, Boston, MA 02111, tel. (617) 423-6655.

Media Syndicate/Newsmakers, 15 W. 44 Street, Suite 303, New York, NY 10036, tel. 1-800-533-2324.

German

Bundesdeutscher Arbeitskreis für umweltbewußtes Management e.V. (B.A.U.M.), Christian-Förster-Str. 19, 2000 Hamburg 20, Tel. 040/40 77 21, 040/491 18 14.

Appendix II

Systematic List of Authors

Conceptual planning and overall responsibility	G. Winter
Final revision of the checklists	H.J. Ewers
Preface	G. Winter
Note on the English edition	G. Winter
A. The need for environmentalist business management	
I. The financial losses in Europe resulting from environmental destruction	L. Wicke
II. A challenge for Europe's business community	G. Winter
III. The response: environmentalist business management	G. Winter
B. Practical aspects of environmentalist business management	G. Winter
C. List of arguments for environmentalist business management	G. Winter
D. Checklists	
I. Overview checklist	G. Winter
II. Priority rating checklist	G. Winter
III. Sectoral checklists	
1. Management motivation	G. Winter
2. Corporate aims and strategies	J. Hensman H. Meffert G. Winter
3. Marketing	J. Hensmann H. Meffert
4. In-house environmental protection arrangements	M. Gege
5. Staff motivation and training	G. Winter

6. Working conditions	R. Hackstein F.J. Heeg
7. Canteen food	M. Gege
8. Environmental counselling in employees' households	M. Gege
9. Economising on energy and water	W.G. Jocher
10. Product development	F. Blom
11. Materials management	F. Blom
12. Production technology	H.J. Ewers C. Maas
13. Disposal and recycling	F. Blom
14. Company vehicles	M. Gege
15. Building	H. Jung
16. Finance	M. Gege V. Hoffmann
17. Law	P.C. Mohr
18. Insurance	Joost & Preuss
19. International business relations	G. Winter
20. Public relations work	C.M. Andreas
IV. Pinpointing cost-reducing measures	G. Winter
E. The significance for Europe of environmentalist business management	G. Winter
F. International Organisations dealing with environmental management	N. Blackburn C. Gelderloos
Epilogue	G. Winter
Appendix I	
British resource lists	ERL
American resource lists	INFORM
German resource lists	Authors of individual checklists

The authors

Andreas, C.M., Dipl.-Kfm.
Förderkreis Umwelt „future“ e.V., Lengerich, Director of the Ecology Committee of the Association of Young German Businessmen (to 31.12.1986)

Blackburn, N.
Director at the International Chamber of Commerce

Blom, F., Dipl.-Kfm.
Lecturer in ecological materials and production management at the Nuremberg University Business School

Ewers, H.-J., Prof.
Economics Institute, Technical University of Berlin, Institut für Stadtforschung und Strukturpolitik GmbH, Berlin

Gege, M., Dr.
Director responsible for corporate planning and environment, Manager at Ernst Winter & Sohn (GmbH & Co), Hamburg, and Ernst Winter & Sohn Norderstedt GmbH & Co, Schleswig-Holstein, Member of the Ecology Committee of the Association of Young German Businessmen

Gelderloos, C.
International Chamber of Commerce

Hackstein, R., Prof.
Director of the Work Studies Institute and Director of the Rationalisation Research Institute at the Technical University of Aachen

Heeg, F.J., Prof.
Senior Engineer at the Work Studies Institute at the Technical University of Aachen

Hensmann, J., Prof.
Professor for Marketing at the University of Münster

Hoffmann, V., Dipl.-Kfm.
Senior civil servant at the Federal German Ministry of the Environment, Nature Conservation and Reactor Safety

Jocher, W.G., Dr.
Managing Director, Deutsches Maschinenbau-Institut GmbH, Frankfurt/Main.

Jung, H., Dipl.-Ing.
Freelance architect, biological building expert and environmental counsellor

Maas, C., Dipl.-Volksw.
Economics Institute, Technical University of Berlin

Meffert, H., Prof.
Director of the Marketing and Management Insitute at the University of Münster

Mohr, P.C., Dr.
Attorney at law, Hamburg

Wicke, L., Prof.
Scientific Director at the Federal German Environmental Agency, Berlin

Winter, G., Dr.
Member of the Board of Directors of the Winter-Group – Hamburg, Norderstedt (West-Germany), Enfield (Great Britain), New York, Travelers Rest (United States) etc., producing diamond tools, a member of the Ecology Committees of the Federation of German Chambers of Industry and Commerce (DIHT) and of the German Association of Machinery and Plant Manufacturers (VDMA).

ERL
Environmental Resources Limited, 106 Gloucester Place, London W1H 3DB, tel. 01-486 1211

INFORM
381 Park Avenue South, New York, N.Y. 10016, tel. (212)689-4040

Joost & Preuss
Dr. J. Blankenburg, Managing Director of Joost & Preuss, Hamburg, Dr. M. Teichler, Environment Department